SAVING
AMERICA

SAVING AMERICA

THE WAR WE CAN'T IGNORE

MICHAEL JOLAYEMI

Published by Redemption Press, PO Box 427, Enumclaw, WA 98022.

ISBN 13: 978-1-63232-214-2 (Print)
    978-1-63232-215-9 (ePub)
    978-1-63232-216-6 (Mobi)
Library of Congress Catalog Card Number: 2011931845

GOD BLESS AMERICA

While the storm clouds gather far across the sea,
Let us swear allegiance to a land that's free,
Let us all be grateful for a land so fair,
As we raise our voices in a solemn prayer.

God Bless America,
Land that I love.
Stand beside her, and guide her
Thru the night with a light from above.
From the mountains, to the prairies,
To the oceans, white with foam
God bless America,
My home sweet home.[1]

Pledge of Allegiance

I pledge allegiance to the Flag of the United States of America, and to the Republic for which it stands, one Nation under God, indivisible, with liberty and justice for all.[2]

DEDICATION

To all Christian missionaries past and present; those
who have labored and those that are laboring to make
the world a better place.

And

To my late father, Luke Gbenle Jolayemi: he spent
his life in the services of others that they might know
Christ and lead useful lives.

CONTENTS

ACKNOWLEDGMENTS

WRITING THIS BOOK has been one of the most compelling and challenging projects that I have ever undertaken. However, the success of this work would not have been possible without the priceless contributions of the wonderful people that God put in my way to fulfill His purpose.

I thank Reverend Sunday Banwhort, formal chairman of ECWA USA, who gladly did the first review of the book. I appreciate the hard criticisms of Pastor Linn Black. I am indebted to Kathy Ide, whose editing and criticisms help to shape the work. I thank Minister Simply Arlene, Pastor Kayode Ayeni, and Elder Josiah Osasona for their encouragement and support. I am grateful to many wonderful Christian friends who prayed for me.

Thanks to the various authors from whom I have borrowed materials to further the issues in this book.

I want to thank and recognize my devoted wife, Folarin, for her amazing commitment for proofreading this book, which has added much value to the work. And to my children Femi, Dami and Mayowa: thank you for your prayers.

—**Mike Jolayemi**

INTRODUCTION

Nevertheless, God's solid foundation stands firm, sealed with
this inscription: "The Lord knows those who are his," and,
"Everyone who confesses the name of the Lord must turn
away from wickedness."
—2 Timothy 2:19

THE WORLD IS moving fast into perilous times. There are wars
and rumors of war. Human rights abuses and oppression have become
common. Society is troubled by racial discrimination, child abuse,
assassinations, murders, and suicides. There are corporate and individual
frauds and dishonesty in high and low offices, embezzlements and
corruptions. Family feuds result in fathers, mothers, and children taking
one another to court. Society is overwhelmed with conflict.

No nation is spared. Terrorism and willful human destruction
are happening all over the world, with violence from local gangs and
premeditated killings of innocent people. You would say these things
have always been, but the speed at which these issues are enveloping the
world is alarming, particularly in certain sections of the world like our
country that have had relatively low levels of such problems.

The United States of America has, in the past, been seen as a model
for the rest of the world to imitate because our government maintained

considerably fewer social vices than other countries. However, we too have become enmeshed in the issues common to other, less civilized societies.

This country was founded on freedom, accompanied by a set of responsibilities clearly laid out by godly men. Leaders and citizens alike were aware of their accountability, not only to the delight of man, but to the pleasure of God.

The men who founded America feared God and lived by faith. They sought His leading in their lives so as to better serve their fellow countrymen. The democratic system of government initiated by the early statesmen was successful because it was built on the principles of fairness and equality, the cardinal principles of God's Word.

The founding fathers crafted the Constitution using the Bible as their guide. They knew the only way to have relationships that reflected honesty, transparency, justice, and love was to adhere to the rules delivered to man by God. The Constitution of the United States of America, therefore, emulated and expanded on the Ten Commandments.

Unfortunately, we have allowed the encroachments of other cultures not just to mock the values we inherited but to destroy them. We have become estranged from God, our Creator, through the influences of people who are opposed to a government based on the principles of the Word of God, and who promote a belief in the separation of church and state. They have turned the clause in our constitution protecting the rights of citizens to practice their faith into 'separation of man and God.'

These people do not believe in God and do not want anything related to God in a national system of governance. Over time, this philosophy has undermined a nation founded "under God" and developed a society without the fear of God.

Throughout centuries, deviations from God's laws have always resulted in fractured human relationships. Remove the tenets of the Ten Commandments from any nation's system of government and you have anarchy and futility.

The peaceful society that once flourished in this country has turned violent in recent years. The values that set the course for America no longer exist, and a return to those values seems impossible.

What went wrong with our society? Jeremiah, the prophet of old, sought the answer to this question too. "Is there no balm in Gilead? Is there no physician there? Why then is there no healing for the wound of my people?" (Jeremiah 8:22). Why is our nation perpetually backsliding? Why are we holding fast to deceit instead of repenting?

If we do not take a good look at ourselves, we will become the kind of people the apostle Paul described when he said, "The god of this age has blinded the minds of unbelievers, so that they cannot see the light" (2 Corinthians 4:4).

The War We Can't Ignore traces the genesis of world conflict, how it has entered our society, and the platform on which conflicts can be overcome. This book attempts to disabuse the minds of those who hold the view that life on earth can be lived successfully without God. It will also help Christian believers to understand the importance of their position among their communities and their spreading of the gospel message through their lifestyles and words.

Those who do not believe in salvation through Jesus Christ will not be at fault if no one reaches out to them. "How, then, can they call on the one they have not believed in? And how can they believe in the one of whom they have not heard? And how can they hear without someone preaching to them?" (Romans 10:14).

Satan deceives people into thinking that the knowledge of God is irrelevant in the conduct of our personal lives as well as the management of the society. This book appeals to Christians to approach this deceit of Satan not by being forceful, hostile, or aggressive to those who believe in the lies of the evil one, but by attacking the devil, who has occupied their hearts with falsehoods about God.

The moral ingredient of the Word of God is indispensable for a peaceful and progressive society. Arthur Simon explained this in his book *Christian Faith and Public Policy*. He writes:

> The Bible prescribes no economic policy, foreign policy, or government structure for us, nor does it detail for us the way in which we are to carry out our responsibilities as US citizens in the twentieth century. The Bible gives us a sense of direction, but it leaves the method of traveling to us.... The Bible offers us no economic system, no political blueprint, no proof texts for domestic or foreign policy. But it does give us a solid foundation on which to build.[3]

A reliance on human philosophy and science to the exclusion of God in our social, political, and economic management has aggravated and will continue to blow out the conflicts within our society. The consequences are terrorism, racial segregation, nuclear proliferation, and economic downturns resulting in poverty, hunger, and human suffering.

This book presents a practical approach to winning the war against the devil by rescuing our society from sliding further away from God. The world has no other alternative than a return to our Creator, who understands the source of the conflicts in the world and has the solutions to the problems.

In this book, Christian believers will learn that they hold the road maps to the wellbeing of society as well as the key to required peaceful co-existence in the world. The world looks to us (Christian believers) for refuge in these chaotic and destructive situations. Readers will be equipped with tools available to us to transform our society, so that our nation can sustain our leading role in the world socially, economically, and politically. The book also advises those who think that God is not relevant in our society to stop fooling around.

I have walked with and worked for God since 1974, when I was a leader in Christian fellowship groups in high school and college. I was a resource person for campus students fellowships for about fifteen years. I have also been a teacher and elder in churches and other Christian groups, including Evangelical Churches Winning All (ECWA), other interdenominational soul-winning groups, and Gideon International. I am currently president of the African Christian Fellowship of Los Angeles.

Over the thirty-six years I've been a Christian, I have come to the conclusion that any society that wishes to make significant progress must acknowledge God in its leaders' and citizens' words and actions.

Roy Herron, in his book, *How Can a Christian Be in Politics?*, said:

In 1775, John Adams wrote his wife, Abigail, "Statesmen may plan and speculate for Liberty, but it is Religion and Morality alone which can establish the principles upon which Freedom can securely stand." Adams believed that a patriot must be a religious man.[4]

Godlessness will lead a society into utter darkness. The clarion call of this book is to fight wickedness and maintain uprightness in our land. A spiritual revival is required in this nation, and it is my prayer that this book will ignite the consciousness of the church and its people. I pray for awakening and restoration of citizens to godly living.

I appeal to readers to be passionate about the survival of our society. No one can fight this war for us. The only society that will get better in the current circumstances of the world is that which acknowledges God and teaches the fear of God among the people. Anything short of God's fear anywhere in the world today will be catastrophic.

CHAPTER 1

THE GENESIS OF CONFLICTS

*I see another law at work in me, waging war against the law
of my mind and making me a prisoner of the law of sin at
work within me.*
—Romans 7:23

I FEEL CONCERN about the issues of daily life around the world. It does not appear human life would ever get better. What is really the problem? We continue to witness a high proportion of conflicts within the human race. Conflict is a common issue in the world, ranging from emotional, interpersonal, communal, diplomatic, and national proportions. Conflicts ravage the environment, economics, and religion. And all conflicts center around one common denominator: people.

Every aspect of human endeavor is conflicted, yet we never seem to understand the source of the conflicts in which we find ourselves. Our conflicts appear to defy solutions. Unresolved attempts at resolution can lead to further conflicts and even the ultimate power struggle, war.

Dr. D. L. Moody summed up man's conflicts when he declared, "I have more trouble with D. L. Moody than with any other man I ever met."[5] In other words, "I've never met anyone who has given me so much trouble as myself."

Man's agitated existence dates back to the first family on earth. Since the human disobedience to the instruction of the Creator in the Garden of Eden, man and woman were separated from their God; godlessness has pervaded the world and it has been catastrophic. For example, the first siblings from Adam and Eve, Cain and Abel, were engulfed in fierce competition in their interactions with each other and with God, resulting in the death of the younger brother. Cain was overcome with jealousy and gave in to his emotions rather than attempting to resolve their conflicts and he recorded the unfortunate first in murder on earth.

Irrational and even murderous acts are the norm in the world today. People are bereft of answers when they ponder what motives have driven society to such fierce and extreme actions.

What is the origin of these conflicts? The main source is the heart of mankind. The state of an individual's mind often determines his or her actions. We do not do anything outside of what goes on in our inner feelings. The heart is the engine that drives all our actions, the center of the total human personality leading to our emotions. Through conflicts that occupy our psyche, we are led to hurt ourselves or society and sometimes fight with other people in the world. Prior to the disobedience, man and woman were in close interaction with God and their hearts were occupied with the character of their Creator. The absence of God is doing incalculable damage to our existence.

Fighting! Fighting! Fighting!

Everywhere in the world, we are in some kind of competitions that have taken control of our behavior or thoughts and we have engaged ourselves often in hostile encounters with opposing forces or individuals...a verbal disagreement...a struggle to achieve a goal or an objective.

We sometimes witness a quarrel or misunderstanding, sometimes involving exchange of fists. It could be a heated, instinctive physiological response to a threatening situation that readies one either to resist forcibly or to run away. We also fight in contention for victory with vigor, fierceness, and determination. It may involve striving to overcome, take over, or destroy a person or thing by blows or weapons. It is an action targeted at a perceived opponent. Whatever form it takes, it is the issue of the human heart.

Ironically, conflicts are not limited to enemies. We often quarrel with our friends and blood relations. The intention may not be to harm, but a situation resulting from disagreement could not be resolved. And not all fighting is physical. Two or more people may be locked in a silent cold war with no apparent aggression. Outsiders may be unaware that there is a fight and therefore do nothing to intervene. Silent war can be more dangerous than physical combat. Participants in a cold war may pretend not to be burdened by the disagreement even as they quietly plot each other's downfall. The parties then destroy not only each other but also victims who could have prevented such altercation if they'd known a problem existed.

And we fight each other globally, which may include embargoes, withdrawal of aid, and severance of communication between nations. Disagreements destroy the good relationship that may have existed between these nations. And some of these disagreements snowball into drums of war and panic in society.

Why Do People Fight?

The conflict is not what anyone wants; an average human desires a life of peace. That was the wish of the Creator, that we could live an abundant life. But this has eluded us. Fighting appears to be part of human development. Even the members of our physical body often hurt each other. For example, the teeth sometimes bite the tongue, resulting in pain for other sections of the body.

Though fighting is not good and no one enjoys it, we often end up in contention.

Dr. Gregory Tucker, in his article "Why People Fight," said, "The more we fight, the more we reinforce the fiction that people are 'warlike.' It is all part of The Human Condition."[6]

Fights occur when people disagree, get hurt or offended, or try to usurp another's rights. Diverse perception of needs, values, and interests, either personal or corporate, often results in separation. The reason for the disagreement may be unimportant or trivial, but if left uncontrolled, it can snowball into serious fighting, the consequence of which is pain for those involved and for innocent bystanders.

Disagreements and misunderstandings occur when neither party is willing to shift position. Husbands and wives with normal differences of opinion on domestic issues (such as management of material possessions) have ended up with irreconcilable differences leading to divorce.

And some persons are involved in conflicts they do not understand. They find themselves fighting but do not know why. Others go into struggles for specific reasons. They fight to gain power or to defend themselves from aggression.

Despite loss, pain, and undesirable consequences, we become embroiled in fighting due to a passion we cannot ignore.

Former US President Ronald Reagan, while governor of California, in a speech on June 15, 1972, attested to the fact that war is not pleasant, and that if it were possible, no one would engage in it. "All of us denounce war; all of us consider it man's greatest stupidity. And yet wars happen and they involve the most passionate lovers of peace because there are still barbarians in the world that set the price for peace at death or enslavement and the price is too high."[7]

In spite of people's desire to conquer the threats of war—not only because of the immense damages and losses wars bring, but also because peace is the indispensable principle of life—fights still ravage the land, leading to sorrow for the people. Elimination of war in society is a serious challenge for human endeavor.

Another former US president, Dwight D. Eisenhower, said in a speech before the American Society of Newspaper Editors on April 16, 1953:

> I hate war, as only a soldier who has lived through it can, only as one who has seen its brutality, its futility, its stupidity....Every gun that is made, every warship launched, every rocket fired, signifies, in the final sense, a theft from those who hunger and are not fed, those who are cold and are not clothed....
>
> The cost of one modern heavy bomber is this: a modern brick school in more than 30 cities....We pay for a single fighter plane with half

a million bushels of wheat. We pay for a single destroyer with new homes that could have housed more than 8,000 people....

War is stupid, cruel and costly. Yet wars have persisted. In the name of self-defense, nations have paid the human price and, spurred on by fear and competition, have continued to accept the burdens of armament, the size and cost of which grow ever more fantastic."[8]

The past world wars were no different in their origin, having emanated from human self-interest as well as political, economic, and/or territorial ambitions. Russia, Britain, France, Germany, Austria-Hungary, and Ottoman Turkey helped other countries attain independence not for the sake of independence alone, but to further their national advantage.

In 1829, Russia, Britain, and France cooperated to secure independence from the Ottoman rule of Greece. They were supposedly motivated by their individual nations' interests and the gain that would accrue to their countries. As soon as they were through with the war on colonization, the Great Powers imposed a foreign dynasty over the new kingdom. Their quest for control and expansion led to threats, resulting in mistrust, a cold war, and eventually full-scale war.

The side on which each nation finds itself in the event of war is often dictated by its leaders' interpretation of which side would best serve their country's interests.

Robin Prior and Trevor Wilson, in their book *The First World War*, wrote:

One thing had better be said at the outset, War occurs because the great mass of human beings is prepared, at least in certain circumstances, to regard the resort to arms as an acceptable proceeding. They may wish to enrich their communities, and so enhance their own self-esteem, by engaging in predatory acts at the expense of their neighbors. Or they may only be prepared to engage in battle to resist what appears to be the aggression and violence of others. Either way, a deliberate choice of war is being made.[9]

In an objective analysis of the actions of the conflicting parties, a common denominator is a deep-seated individual interest (often selfish). The decision whether or not to fight is dictated by an interest that is being protected.

For instance, the alliance of Italy, Germany, and Austria-Hungary in 1882 was predicated on the nations' political and economic interests. Prior and Wilson said:

> Again, we may note the case of Italy. That country had entered into Triple alliance with Germany and Austria-Hungary in 1882 at the time when it possessed territorial ambitions at the expense of France. By the early twentieth century Italy's ambitions lay elsewhere. So when war broke out in 1914 Italy did not take side of its allies. That was not because Italian statesmen acted on different principles from the rulers of other European countries. They acted on the same principles: that alliances controlled action only when they embodied a nation's vital interests. Otherwise they did not.[10]

The same trend preceded the Second World War. Breakdown in communication and abandonment of peace initiatives led to gunfire.

No one embarks on war for the mere sake of war. But war at times becomes the inevitable conclusion in trying to prove a point. Society at large, made up of ego-driven individuals, is no different.

Quoting from A. J. P. Taylor's argument on the origins of the Second World War, Prior and Wilson noted:

> The Second World War broke out not because any nation intended it but because governments were engaged in familiar games of bluff and brinkmanship. Their intention was to secure advantages at the expense of their neighbors without actually generating conflict. On this occasion, however, the process went wrong.[11]

But conflicts started manifesting when people began to identify differences between each other in language and color of skins. Their hearts no longer accepted that all humans are created equal as we entered into race segregation, the genesis of division on earth.

The Birth of Race Segregations

Conflicts were minimal among the early people of the world because there was no language or race barrier.

According to the biblical accounts, the first men and women on earth spoke the same language and were cooperative with one another. The teamwork and understanding among them suggests that there was no such thing as race or color, though Bible history is not specific about this.

In human foolishness and arrogance, they attempted to build a tower to reach the heavens. They did not consider God's power and sovereignty; they apparently did not see the need to seek His consent before embarking on the project. God then divided humans with the creation of many languages, making it impossible for them to communicate. That put an end to the most contemptuous event in history and was the beginning of differences in the human race.

"The Lord came down to see the city and the tower the people were building. The Lord said, 'If as one people speaking the same language they have begun to do this, then nothing they plan to do will be impossible for them. Come, let us go down and confuse their language so they will not understand each other.'

So the Lord scattered them from there over all the earth, and they stopped building the city. That is why it was called Babel—because there the Lord confused the language of the whole world. From there the Lord scattered them over the face of the whole earth" (Genesis 11:5–9).

Prior to this human self-inflicted misfortune, "the whole world had one language and a common speech" (Genesis 11:1).

The confusion of language created separations among the people of the world. This resulted in race segregations, different skin colors, and polarization and discrimination in human activities. The lack of cooperation may also have given rise to colonization, in which the more powerful groups (known as nations) forced their economic and political activities on weaker groups.

When the British colonized the New World, their rule was no better. It too displayed the selfishness of the human heart, resulting in ongoing conflicts. The colonialists set the indigenous people against one another.

This "divide and conquer" approach enabled the colonialists to easily have their way by ruling the divided people. Over time, this division eroded the people's trust in one another, which resulted in their inability to work together or live peacefully side by side. Irreconcilable differences eventually gave way to open warfare, which led to destruction of property and loss of lives, furthering the conflicts on earth.

Rwanda is an example of a victim of imperialism. It was colonized by Belgium in 1916. "Under the treaty of Versailles, the former German colony of Rwanda-Urundi was made a UN protectorate to be governed by Belgium."[12]

The Belgians used the two distinct ethnic groups in that country to further their own interests. First, the division created among the people by the colonialists enabled them to rule the nation longer because the ethnic groups did not agree to rule themselves for lack of trust. Second, trades in the natural resources of the colonies benefited the colonists—an interest that beclouded their sense of judgment. As long as they were able to achieve their objectives, disagreements among the natives didn't concern them.

Fergal Keane, in his book *Season of Blood: A Rwandan Journey*, said, "In 1926, Belgians introduced a system of ethnic identity cards differentiating Hutus from Tutsis, the major ethnic group."[13]

By July 2, 1962, when Rwanda formally declared her independence, neighbors in the tiny country could not trust one another. Animosity between the two groups, which had accelerated over years of occupation and through the divisive actions of the colonists, culminated in barbaric genocide. More than one million lives were lost. A long and torturous rebuilding of the country is still evolving.

Human Selfishness

We humans often do not see anything wrong with our actions, provided our personal interests are met. We have a natural tendency to refuse to take responsibility for the myriad problems that besiege us. Issues are usually blamed on other people or things. Sometimes we even hold God responsible for our travail. We expect Him to use His influence to prevail over occurrences of evil. But we forget that we never consulted Him when our hearts pushed us to do what we do.

Does God have such power? And will He exercise it? The answer is both yes and no. God is absolutely powerful, but while God can and often does intervene when we are faced with evil, we must recognize His sovereignty. God cannot be controlled by the humans He created. He reserves the right to intervene or not. He is not accountable to us; rather, we are accountable to Him.

God created us as free beings who can make choices. These choices dictate the events and circumstances in life and within society. It is therefore irresponsible to lay the blame on God for the calamities that have befallen us.

In all the conflicts that have arisen out of the choices of human beings, God has always intervened, either directly through events or by raising individuals to the rescue. We do not always understand how He does it. Nor can we determine when He does it.

When we make bad choices, God sometimes may use wicked individuals to teach us to avoid the same pitfalls and to teach future generations the consequences suffered by those who choose such ways. Unfortunately, we keep repeating the same mistakes. Today, in most nations of the world there are leaders who have no fear of God and lead people into a state of hopelessness.

But even in the midst of hopelessness, God often remembers mercies and has punished wicked leaders. About eight hundred years before Christ, King Ahab of Israel was disobedient to God. Under the influence of his wife, Jezebel, he oppressed the people. God was angry with him and raised Jehu to wipe out all the generations of Ahab (2 Kings 9). This history should have helped subsequent leaders to fear and honor God. But since then, several kings in Israel have also become vain in their imaginations and done wickedly.

Ironically, some of them started their rule with the fear of God, and all was well with the nation. But they soon went astray, doing evil. Because God does not accept wicked acts, these rulers brought calamities to their society. However, God did not leave the people without intervention. When trouble came, they only needed to accept responsibility for their misdeeds, repent of their iniquities, and ask for God's mercy.

Unknown Motives in the Human Heart

It is often difficult to identify the true motives of an individual's actions because the contents of the heart are known only to the actors and the Creator. This makes it hard for people to understand the nature of conflicts when they occur. It is equally formidable to differentiate individuals acting for the sake of humanity (doing the work of God) from those whose hearts have been taken over by the spirit of Satan. This challenge prevents society from accurately ascertaining whether a fight is for a good cause.

Some warriors fight with the objective of defending the common good. They commit all the resources at their disposal without expecting any personal benefit in return. They fight a purposeful war or crusade as Providence has led them. They are not warmongers, as they are sometimes portrayed, but are genuinely concerned with the situations they seek to resolve, using their God-given talents for the common good of society. They may have no desire for war, but the responsibility to defend their people rests on them. The fight became an issue of necessity. Their place in history is etched by their actions in answering the call. All these are, of course, God's creations.

In the fifth century BC, Mordecai, a Jew from the tribe of Benjamin, found himself leading his people out of impending trouble. The Jews were faced with a threatening situation in which an opponent of the Israeli nation planned a mass murder of their people.

Haman, an Agagite, was influential and highly favored in the king's court under King Xerxes, also known as Ahasuerus (486 to 465 BC). Haman hated the Jews and had perfected a plan to annihilate all the Jewish people in the kingdom. He manipulated the king into signing a decree declaring that all Jews in the nation would be killed on a set date.

When Mordecai got this sad news, he could not ignore the fight or make excuses to avoid it. He went into battle to defend his people and save them from annihilation using his niece, Esther, the queen. Initially, Esther did not understand what her guardian was up to. She bought into the cause when it became clear to her it was good.

The Jews' battle for survival under Mordecai did not involve guns or other weapons. Mordecai was not a soldier. He knew nothing of the art or techniques of war. But he understood where true power lies. He had all the Jews fast, as directed by Esther the queen. Fasting is a way for people to show God they need Him in their situation. It is in effect a demonstrated prayer. As a result of those agonized prayers, God's favor came to Esther as she spoke to the king.

Again, but for God the Jews could have been completely wiped out. Mordecai was a willing instrument of God in a moment of desperate need for the Jews. He rose to the challenge at a time when others might have gone into hiding. He knew what was at stake, and he mobilized all the Jews for the deliverance of the nation of Israel.

Individuals are often part of God's intervention in times of conflict in society.

A young Jewish man, David, tended his father's sheep, but circumstances and destiny drew him into formidable leadership of his people. At the time of his youth, the Jews were at war with the Philistines. Goliath, a Philistine army commander and giant, continually challenged the Jews to fight him. This dismayed and terrified the Israelites.

David, small in stature but large of heart and full of faith in the God of Israel, believed his people needed delivery from the Philistines. He shouted to Goliath: "You come against me with sword and spear and javelin, but I come against you in the name of the Lord Almighty, the God of the armies of Israel, whom you have defied. This day the Lord will deliver you into my hands, and I'll strike you down and cut off your head.

This very day I will give the carcasses of the Philistine army to the birds and the wild animals, and the whole world will know that there is a God in Israel. All those gathered here will know that it is not by sword or spear that the Lord saves; for the battle is the Lord's, and he will give all of you into our hands" (1 Samuel 17:45–47).

David faced Goliath with a strategy born out of a vision from God. He was unschooled in the art of war and military practices. He wasn't even large enough in stature to wear armor. To the amazement of both the Philistines and the Israelites, David slew Goliath, answering the call to save his people from the oppression of their foes. His passion, commitment, and dedication demonstrated the intervention of the God of Israel. The war reached a decisive end not by soldier and sword, but by boy and slingshot.

The world has witnessed spirited leaders whose main focus was to resolve conflicts. When Abraham Lincoln was faced with criticisms in his handling of the Civil War and slave trade, he said: "If I were to try to read, much less answer, all the attacks made on me, this shop might as well be closed for any other business. I do the very best I know how—the very best I can; and I mean to keep doing so until the end. If the end brings me out all right, what's said against me won't amount to anything. If the end brings me out wrong, ten angels swearing I was right would make no difference."[14]

Lincoln was raised by his Creator for the purpose of freeing the slaves, an evidence of the intervention of God in a time of conflict.

Human Pride

Our egos often give us a false sense of ability. Can men and women control the conflicts within and outside of ourselves without God? Can we actually exist without fighting in the midst of the godlessness that pervades our society?

Jesus spoke to the people of Capernaum on the limits of human ability when it comes to conflicts. He said, "Woe to the world because of the things that cause people to stumble! Such things must come, but woe to the person through whom they come!" (Matthew 18:7). Jesus was saying in effect that we would continue to be in trouble because of the situation of our hearts which does not give room to God and that the dire consequences are there for us.

It is an illusion on our part to think our efforts could resolve all the conflicts around the world. Past failures attest to this. Admittance that we are at fault and helpless in our situations would elicit the mercies of God. But we keep playing gods in our actions, as if the solutions are in our hands, forgetting that we are really the problem.

The lack of recognition of our inadequacy is a serious setback. That is why when we seek peace, we end up in war. We often regret the effects of war and yet still see it as the only answer. Ironically, some people, in trying to resolve conflict, choose death and destruction as a final solution. Several suicides have come as a result of someone's inability to find solutions for conflicts, resulting in the bizarre conclusion that the appropriate response is to take his or her own life. Some people have even taken other people's lives before taking their own.

Do We Learn from the Past?

The challenge of the human race is that we keep doing the same things, even though they lead us into trouble. God created us as body and soul. The soul, also known as the heart, is where the spirit dwells. The spirit controls the mind and is the ultimate driver of our behavior. We dwell in the body, which is physically seen, but a human being is not the physical body; the body is only the shelter for the real person.

God created human beings in His image, and since He is spirit, so are we. The heart is continually faced with a choice of evil or good, resulting from the influence of the two forces battling for control of our minds.

There are two types of behavior in people all over the world: good and evil. Evil behavior is propelled by Satan, while good behavior is of God.

We were not created for evil, but evil pervades the world as a result of the influence of Satan, which began when he craftily led the first created human on earth to disobey God. This deceit brought sin and guilt to the human heart. Ever since then, our hearts have been polluted, hungry and thirsty for wickedness always (see Genesis 1:31 and Genesis 3).

Paul of Tarsus describes the nature of the human heart this way:

> I do not understand what I do. For what I want to do I do not do, but what I hate I do. And if I do what I do not want to do, I agree that the law is good. As it is, it is no longer I myself who do it, but it is sin living in me. For I know that good itself does not dwell in me, that is, in my sinful nature. For I have the desire to do what is good, but I cannot carry it out. For I do not do the good I want to do, but the evil I do not want to do—this I keep on doing. Now if I do what I do not want to do, it is no longer I who do it, but it is sin living in me that does it.
>
> —Romans 7:15–20

The prophet Jeremiah observed, "The heart is deceitful above all things and desperately wicked: Who can know it?" (Jeremiah 17:9 KJV). Jesus Christ, who has a deep understanding of the human heart, said, "For it is from within, out of a person's heart, that evil thoughts come—sexual immorality, theft, murder, adultery, greed, malice, deceit, lewdness, envy, slander, arrogance and folly. All these evils come from inside and defile a person" (Mark 7:20–23).

Speaking with the Pharisees, the custodians of Jewish law in His day, Jesus said, "You brood of vipers, how can you who are evil say anything good? For the mouth speaks what the heart is full of" (Matthew 12:34). In the heart lies the ultimate cause of war.

The apostle James asked these rhetorical questions concerning conflicts:

> What causes fights and quarrels among you? Don't they come from your desires that battle within you? You desire but do not have, so you kill. You covet but you cannot get what you want, so you quarrel and fight. You do not have because you do not ask God. When you ask, you do not receive, because you ask with wrong motives, that you may spend what you get on your pleasures.
> —James 4:1–3

David, the second king in Israel, who reigned between 1010 and 970 BC, summoned the courage to ask God for mercy because he recognized that he was helpless in his behavior and needed a higher power to deliver him from all the troubles he had put on himself. He said:

"Have mercy on me, O God, according to your unfailing love; according to your great compassion blot out my transgressions. Wash away all my iniquity and cleanse me from my sin. For I know my transgressions, and my sin is always before me. Against you, you only, have I sinned and done what is evil in your sight; so you are right in your verdict and justified when you judge. Surely I was sinful at birth, sinful from the time my mother conceived me" (Psalm 51:1–5).

King David asked God for a new heart because that is where all the conflicts that consumed his life dwelled. "Create in me a pure heart, O God, and renew a steadfast spirit within me" (Psalm 51:10). David did not want God to leave him without a heart. He needed his heart, because if the heart is taken away the physical body becomes useless. He therefore requested from God a new heart. He believed that with a regenerated heart, conflict was bound to cease.

What Can We Do About Our Hearts?

We cannot do anything about our heart, but we can get it regenerated. God provided the answer to the conflicts of the human heart through the Lord Jesus Christ. Jesus was born in the small village of Bethlehem in Judea. He was born as a baby to Jewish parents, and his birth was the only miracle of its kind in the history of the world.

The Bible gives us insight into how God made the provision of Jesus Christ for the reconciliation of human beings to God.

Paul captured the revelation of Jesus Christ when he said:

> In the past God spoke to our ancestors through the prophets at many times and in various ways, but in these last days he has spoken to us by his Son, whom he appointed heir of all things, and through whom also he made the universe. The Son is the radiance of God's glory and the exact representation of his being, sustaining all things by his powerful word. After he had provided purification for sins, he sat down at the right hand of the Majesty in heaven.
> —Hebrews 1:1–3

We cannot help the conflicts that came to us through our forebears. But we can accept a regenerated mind through Jesus Christ, who possesses the power to give us new hearts.

Paul testified of this when he said:

> Consequently, just as one trespass resulted in condemnation for all people, so also one righteous act resulted in justification and life for all people. For just as through the disobedience of the one man [Adam] the many were made sinners, so also through the obedience of the one man [Jesus Christ] the many will be made righteous.
> —Romans 5:18–19

The name of Jesus repulses unregenerate humans, as it is considered synonymous with religion. But the conflicts of the human heart require that we humbly submit ourselves to the lordship of Jesus Christ. We cannot run away from Him if we want to be free from our daily troubles. Our past efforts at resolving conflicts have not yielded any positive results; we need to try a different method.

We will forever continue with our struggles unless we accept what Jesus told the Pharisees, who struggled with an attitude of unbelief. To them he said, "Have you never read in the Scriptures: 'The stone the builders rejected has become the cornerstone; the Lord has done this, and it is marvelous in our eyes'?" (Matthew 21:42). The way to go is to accept the only provision made by God for human freedom from conflicts, Jesus Christ.

And We Can Experience Less War

Our hearts must be changed to avert conflicts, and Jesus is the ultimate heart changer of all time. When Jesus comes into our hearts, our thoughts and our understanding of fighting changes. There is only one common enemy to man and woman; he is Satan. That was the reasoning of Paul the Apostle when he said, "For our struggle is not against flesh and blood, but against the rulers, against the authorities, against the powers of this dark world and against the spiritual forces of evil in the heavenly realms" (Ephesians 6:12). In other words, this is not the war we can use armored mortals or guns to fight but an offensive using the words of God, the Bible and prayers. The Bible says: "The weapons we fight with are not the weapons of the world. On the contrary, they have divine power to demolish strongholds" (2 Corinthians 10:4).

Thoughts

The human situation may appear helpless but the truth is that if our hearts are surrendered to God, we will experience peace and our society will also have less problems. The sinful nature in us does not give us room to do any good, but only evil. But our depraved personality can be changed by the man Jesus, who possesses the power to affect change in the human heart. When the spirit of Jesus Christ enters our hearts, the spirit of Satan departs and we can do only those things God would do. And you know what? God is a good God.

CHAPTER 2

EMERGENT LEADERS IN TIMES OF CONFLICT

> So the Twelve gathered all the disciples together and said,
> "It would not be right for us to neglect the ministry of the
> word of God in order to wait on tables. Brothers and sisters,
> choose seven men from among you who are known to be full
> of the Spirit and wisdom. We will turn this responsibility over
> to them and will give our attention to prayer and the ministry
> of the word."
> —Acts 6:2–4

GOD IS OMNISCIENT; that is, He possesses infinite knowledge. He sees the past, present, and future and makes provision for every challenge in society before it occurs. He also resolves issues in whatever way He chooses. He is not bound by any legal or procedural way. His actions and activities, like the highest court in any nation, become law by precedence. God creates law and procedure for us but no one makes law for Him.

God uses both human and non-human resources to fix problems and accomplish His purposes. Often, we may think the way He chooses to fix a challenge is incorrect or inappropriate. But God always has the best option, and He has never made a mistake in the way He selected.

All our alternatives to fixing problems, other than God's, will fail or result in further calamities.

For instance, when the world was completely overwhelmed with sin and needed a savior, God chose to use His only Son, Jesus Christ, to fix the problem of sin that ravaged the world. We have no understanding of how or why He did this. He chose to use Mary, among all the virgins in Israel and the world, to bring Jesus to earth as a baby; He alone can answer "Why her?" All God's activities are mysteries that only He can explain. But one thing is certain: God addresses every challenge posed by the evil one, and He does so without human input.

Paul said, "Where is the wise person? Where is the teacher of the law? Where is the philosopher of this age? Has not God made foolish the wisdom of the world?" (1 Corinthians 1:20).

A plethora of troubles besets the world. But none of these issues moves or takes God by surprise. Throughout history, He has raised great men and women to intervene and bring about His desired solutions. They championed crusades for the deliverance of their people. The purpose of their engagements became clear when people realized they were fighting for a common good.

God would always use individuals and even things, i.e. non-human to accomplish certain purposes in all human needs. Below are five examples of persons God used to accomplish His will in times of intense conflict. Ironically, we see these people and their service as coincidence.

Moses

Could Moses have been a coincidence in the days when the Jews in Egypt needed someone to deliver them? I doubt this coincidence because it should have occurred years before Moses was born. The circumstances of his birth were a perfect arrangement. A notable leader of the Israelites, I believe he was called by God to lead the nation of Israel out of slavery in Egypt. And Moses obeyed God despite the challenges and foreseeable dangers ahead of him.

In the thirteenth century BC, when Moses was born in Egypt, the Egyptian government issued a decree to kill all Jewish male newborns so the Jews would not become so numerous and strong that they could wage war against the nation. Moses was not killed, because God was ahead of human plans. He had ordained Moses for the task of leading the Jews out of Egypt. Baby Moses was adopted by an Egyptian princess, who found him in the river where his mother had put him to avoid being caught.

Prior to his birth, the nation Israel had left Canaan, their God-given land, for Egypt as a result of famine and draught. Egypt was then blessed in abundance of food and Joseph, (not also any coincidence) the man appointed by Pharaoh, the Egyptian monarch to manage the food resources, was a Jew. Joseph facilitated the temporary relocation of the Israelites to Egypt.

But the Jews became slaves in Egypt when Joseph died and a new king, who did not know Joseph, arose. The new monarch acted spitefully against the fast-growing Israelite community. Joan Comay, in her book *Who's Who in the Bible*, said, "Pharaoh Rameses II (1301–234 BC) may have been the king over Egypt, who did not know Joseph (Exod. 1:8), who started to use the Israelites as forced labor for building the store-cities of Pithom and Rameses."[15]

The Jews were regarded as the greatest builders in Egyptian history. But the labor became so unbearable for the Jews that they called on God for deliverance. Israel remained in slavery for 438 years. But when God's timing was right, Providence beckoned Moses to save his people from bondage. God delivered His people.

While Moses grew up in the royal court of Egypt, he saw the plight of his people and felt their agony. He knew they faced imminent danger of extinction. A desire to fight rose in him, and he could no longer enjoy the comfort of the palace. He engaged in a series of negotiations with Pharaoh for the release of the Jews, insisting that they be allowed to return to the land that had been given to them by God.

The task was not without its challenges. Pharaoh was unwilling to release the Jews because of the free labor they provided. The king forgot history that it was the wisdom of God of Israel in a Jew, Joseph, many centuries past that saved Egypt from the calamities of famine that would have destroyed the nation. He was only interested in the cheap labor the Jews were giving to Egypt. Ten plagues engulfed the land of Egypt before Pharaoh finally agreed to their liberation.

Moses faced a unique problem. He had no idea where their native home was. Neither did anyone among his people, because their fathers who brought them into the land had all passed on. The current generation knew who they were and the history of their migration, but not where they were heading after their freedom was granted. But Moses relied on God, who had called him for this service, to lead them.

Moses was not the most intelligent, knowledgeable, or capable man in Israel. But he willingly took on the responsibility of delivering the people. He was a man of destiny and passion, a defender and deliverer, called to save his people from slavery.

Moses's people had a cold attitude toward him. They did not believe his resolve to get them out of slavery. But he paid no mind to what could befall him in the process of following God's leading.

Moses died on the way to the Promised Land, but not before naming a successor, Joshua, who also believed in the struggle to get the Jews to the Promised Land and to prepare them to possess their homeland. Joshua was a divine provision to complete the assignment given to Moses by God, leading the Jews to freedom. At the ceremony that appointed Joshua as his successor, Moses said:

> I am now a hundred and twenty years old and I am no longer able to lead you. The Lord had said to me, "You shall not cross the Jordan." The Lord your God himself will cross over ahead of you. He will destroy these nations before you, and you will take possession of their land. Joshua also will cross over ahead of you, as the Lord said. And the Lord will do to them what he did to Sihon and Og, the kings of the Amorites, whom he destroyed along with their land. The Lord will deliver them to you, and you must do to them all that I have commanded you. Be strong and courageous. Do not be afraid or terrified because of them, for the Lord your God goes with you; he will never leave you nor forsake you.
>
> —Deuteronomy 31:2–6

Moses summoned Joshua and said to him, "Be strong and courageous, for you must go with this people into the land that the Lord swore to their ancestors to give them, and you must divide it among them as their inheritance. The Lord himself goes before you and will be with you; he will never leave you nor forsake you. Do not be afraid; do not be discouraged" (Deuteronomy 31:7–8).

As a result of the responsible leadership of Moses, the Jews became united through their times of disappointment, discouragement, disillusionment, and despair. When they arrived in Canaan, they had the resolve to take their heritage.

The war was not about Moses and neither was it about Joshua. It was for the people's freedom and their ordained future and destiny. Though Moses did not enter the Promised Land himself, he was an instrument for the attainment of the objective.

Martin Luther King, Jr.

Martin Luther King, Jr. was not a coincidence in the United States of America. This is a fact that a God-fearing person should accept. Who would want to be a coincidence for a slaughter slab just like King did when he laid down his life for his people? Common, that thought cannot be rational.

At a public address on April 4, 1968, the day before he was assassinated, Dr. King said these words:

> I don't know what will happen now; we've got some difficult days ahead. But it really doesn't matter with me now, because I've been to the mountain top. And I don't mind. Like anybody, I would like to live a long life—longevity has its place. But I'm not concerned about that now. I just want to do God's will. And He's allowed me to go up to the mountain. And I've looked over; I've seen the Promised Land. I may not get there with you. But I want you to know tonight, that we, as a people, will get to the Promised Land. And I'm happy tonight. I'm not worried about anything. I'm not fearing any man. Mine eyes have seen the glory of the coming of the Lord.[16]

His commitment to the equality of mankind, particularly in the United States of America, was unique.

Dr. Martin Luther King, Jr. was born on January 15, 1929, to a devoted Christian family. He grew up in an atmosphere of repression, racism, and lack of freedom. Like his father, grandfather, and great-grandfather, he preached the gospel. However, his call went beyond being an eloquent Baptist minister; Providence placed in his lap a task that would make him celebrated by a nation. He became a freedom fighter.

Dr. King had a vision of how life should be. He developed an objective and committed his life to the execution of that goal: the liberation of his people. He obeyed this calling despite the dangers and threats to his life. He traveled all over America, promoting his war against oppression and degrading treatment.

His struggle began because segregation had filled the United States of America. A white man could not sit at the same table with a black man. Blacks did not have the same seating section on the public bus as whites. Black men were underpaid for doing jobs no white man would do. The black man could not vote or be voted for. These situations generated fights, culminating in nationwide tension.

King undertook sensitization of the world for equality of men, which included identifying with countries in Africa that were still dominated by colonial rule. At the ceremony marking Ghana's independence in 1957, Dr. King was overwhelmed with joy at seeing people freed from the jaws of colonialism. He said, "Before I knew it, I started weeping. I was crying for joy. And I knew about all the struggles, all of the pain, and all of the agony that these people had gone through for this moment....I could hear people shouting all over that vast audience, Freedom! Freedom! Freedom!"[17]

King organized mass protests against racism and oppression, yet preached nonviolence.

Some people are called to pay the supreme price for the survival and well-being of their people. Dr. Martin Luther King, Jr. is one example of a man who voluntarily accepted the call of God on his life. In an address at Bishop Charles J. Mason Temple in Memphis, Tennessee, on April 3, 1968, he said: "If you want to say that I was a drum major, say that I was a drum major for justice. Say that I was a drum major for peace. I was a drum major for righteousness. And all of the other shallow things will not matter. I won't have the fine luxurious things of life to leave behind. But I just want to leave a committed life behind."[18]

King would not compromise his convictions for anything. In March 1965, in response to governmental authorities' threats against a proposed protest march by the civil rights movement, Dr. King said, "I say to you this afternoon that I would rather die on the highways of Alabama than make a butchery of my conscience."[19]

Dr. King lived the words of the Lord Jesus Christ, who said, "Whoever wants to save their life will lose it, but whoever loses their life for me will find it. What good will it be for someone to gain the whole world, yet forfeit their soul? Or what can anyone give in exchange for their soul?" (Matthew 16:25–26). Dr. King accepted the call to lead the people to freedom.

All that mattered for this civil rights leader was the freedom of his people, even though he knew the war could cost him his life. His actions have enabled him to live on in our hearts and minds, and he has a place in heaven with other saints.

Dr. King could say at the end of his life the words of Paul the apostle: "I have fought the good fight, I have finished the race, I have kept the faith" (2 Timothy 4:7).

Dr. King was not an accident of history but the perfect plan of God in a time of racial segregation and conflict in the United States of America.

Dr. Nelson Mandela

Another bogus thought is to take the advent of Nelson Mandela in South Africa as a coincidence. The people of South Africa who passed through years of the ordeal of inequality in the land of their birth would definitely not regard Mandela as coincidence. And I am sure Mandela knows he was never an accident. The first democratically elected president of the Republic of South Africa was surely a design of the Creator. He was born in Mvezo, a small town in South Africa, on July 18, 1918. For many years, his people had been subjected to hardship by white settlers.

Mandela grew up in relative comfort. He attended the only black university in existence at the time: the South African Native College at Fort Hare. Its student body was aristocratic and meritocratic, with both royal and missionary backgrounds. He had earlier attended a prestigious mission school, Clarkeburry, founded by his great-grandfather. He did not need to get involved with the struggle for liberation. But like Martin Luther King, Jr., Mandela had a destiny to accomplish.

In Johannesburg, Mandela met Walter Sisulu, who became a good friend. Sisulu, knowing that Mandela was interested in the law profession, introduced him to Lazar Sidelsky. Mr. Sidelsky was a successful lawyer who had his own law firm. He warned Mandela not to get involved with politics. However, Mandela was determined to accomplish his mission to free his people from the tyranny of oppression and domination.

As an aristocrat, he had come up against the frustrations and humiliations of living in a white man's city where he was the only black man among millions. In spite of the glaring obstacles in his path, he knew Providence had placed on him the task of fighting racism and liberating the people of South Africa.

Mandela brought pressure against the apartheid regime by drawing the attention of the international community to the plight of the South African people. He also led a mass revolt against the racist government, which finally succumbed. But he paid a heavy price.

In August 1962, Mandela was jailed for life. He remained committed to the struggle even in prison and would not negotiate in the struggle for freedom. Throughout the twenty-seven years and six months he spent in prison, he was an effective leader in the war to free his people.

At one of the court proceedings after the government of South Africa convicted him of treason, he said:

> During my lifetime I have dedicated myself to this struggle of the African people. I have fought against white domination, and I have fought against black domination. I have cherished the ideal of a democratic and free society in which all persons live together in harmony and with equal opportunities. It is an ideal which I hope to live for and to achieve. But if needs be, it is an ideal for which I am prepared to die.[20]

In the heat of the struggle for freedom, Mandela encouraged other freedom fighters even as he was being hassled by the government. He said, "The time comes in the life of any nation when there remains only two choices—submit or fight. That time has now come to South Africa.

We shall not submit and we have no choice but to hit back by all means in our power in defense of our people."[21]

Mr. Mandela walked out of the prison gates on February 11, 1990. Four years later, in May 1994, he was sworn in as the first black president of the Republic of South Africa. He served only one term of office, as he believed he had accomplished his mission by laying a solid foundation for democracy in his country. He fought the evil of apartheid with doggedness and won.

Ronald Reagan

The naïve individuals with godless hearts would also take the presidency of Ronald Reagan, at the time it was, as mere coincidence. But the God-fearing people in America and those of the Soviet Union who had longed and prayed for freedom from communists' wickedness would certainly thank God for answered prayers.

After the end of the Second World War, a cold war began between the West and the East. The main actors were the United States of America and the former Soviet Union. Both sides struggled to persuade the rest of the world to accept their principles of governance. Capitalism was based on God, while communism was an ideology focused on man as the ultimate source of wisdom.

Naturally, conflicts arose, not by the will of God but by human choices. God watched while evils were perpetrated against human beings. But at His appointed time, He raised someone to dismantle communism.

Ronald Reagan was born on the sixth of February, 1911. He became the fortieth American president on January 21, 1981.

Mr. Reagan never hid his distaste for communism, which he referred to as evil. At every opportunity, even when he was governor of California, he spoke out against the destructive nature of communism.

When Reagan became president of the United States, the world was gripped with fear of imminent war between the two most powerful nations of the world. In diplomatic discussions, the ideological differences between the East and the West were so huge that the Soviet Union and the United States were opposed to each other on all issues. It was a bitter relationship.

On May 2, 1974, during his tenure as governor of California, Reagan addressed a group of students in California on the issues between the Soviet communists and America's market economy. He said:

> I have had students sometimes ask me if there is really such a great difference between our two systems. They say they have read the Soviet constitution and their laws, and found frequent use of the words freedom and justice. The right of free speech, which we often take for granted, is mentioned too. But there is a difference between our two constitutions. The difference is so subtle we often do overlook it, but it is so great it tells the entire story. Their constitution says government grants these rights. Our constitution says we, the people, are born with these rights and no government can take them from us.[22]

Mr. Reagan, from his early life, saw the communist system as a worldwide political plague that had to be confronted headlong. This was one reason he chose to venture into politics: he knew if there was a nation strong enough to challenge communism, it would be the United States of America.

Reagan was specially prepared for this task. The war that could have been fought with mortals was unbelievably won without firing any shot. Reagan fought communism from the perspective of his faith in Jesus Christ; the faith he got from his godly mother, Nelle Reagan.

Paul Kengor testified to the Christian values imparted to Reagan by his mother, which ultimately prepared him for the call of God on his life. In his book *God and Ronald Reagan,* Kengor said, "Nelle Reagan had a heart for God, and she did her best to impart that faith to her son Ronald. It was her aspiration that he should one day take that faith to the world."[23] This knowledge of God accounted for the destruction of communist teachings without pulling a trigger.

According to Paul Kengor, Ronald Reagan believed the war against communism was a war of faith, ordained by God Himself. Reagan knew that God had bestowed on him the opportunity to act as His instrument of power to bring down the tower of darkness.

Kengor goes on to say, "In Reagan's view, the American Revolution was anchored in Judeo-Christian values; the Bolshevik Revolution was deliberately established upon an antithetical premise. The founders of Soviet communism divorced their 'faith' from Christianity."[24]

Reagan predicted the end of communism not by the might of the military but by spiritual might when he said, "Let us pray for the salvation of all those who live in that totalitarian darkness—pray they will discover the joy of knowing God. But until they do, let us be aware that while they preach the supremacy of the state, declare its omnipotence over individual man, and predict its eventual domination of all peoples on the earth, they are the focus of evil in the modern world."[25]

Other leaders of the world were skeptical of victory over communism, and back home, the press in America vilified the president for "spiritualizing" the issue of grave foreign policy. But Reagan stood on his faith in God that the war against communism would be won. He said:

> I believe we shall rise to the challenge. I believe that communism is another sad, bizarre chapter in human history whose last pages even now are being written. I believe this because the source of our strength in the quest for human freedom is not material, but spiritual. And because it knows no limitation, it must terrify and ultimately triumph over those who would enslave their fellow man. For in the words of Isaiah: He gives power to the faint; and to them that have no might he increases strength....But they that wait upon the Lord shall renew their strength; they shall mount up with wings as eagles; they shall run and not be weary."[26]

Reagan also realized that the main cause of conflict in society is not the system of government, but the absence of God in the heart of the people. According to Paul Kengor, Reagan said, "In many countries, people aren't even allowed to read the Bible. It is up to us to make sure the message of hope and salvation gets through."[27]

In an end-of-the-year letter (December 1984) to Mother Teresa, Reagan cited Scripture in expressing a desire to help those suffering abroad, noting that Christ spoke of the need to bind the brokenhearted and to proclaim liberty to the captives.

Reagan carried a spiritual message to the atheistic nation of China. In 1984 he traveled to Beijing. Standing beside Chinese leaders on April 27, he declared that "America was founded by people who sought freedom to worship God and trust in Him to guide them in their daily lives."[28]

Addressing Chinese students on April 30, Reagan emphasized the need for young people to take their fate in their own hands as future leaders. Kengor writes:

> Halfway through the speech, he recited his treasured lines from the declaration of independence "that all men are created equal, that they are endowed by their Creator with certain unalienable rights." As he closed, he added that there was "one other part of our national character I wish to speak of. Religion and faith are very important to us."

> He noted that America was a nation of many religions. "But most Americans derive their religious beliefs from the Bible of Moses, who delivered a people from slavery, the Bible of Jesus Christ, who told us to love thy neighbor as thyself."[29]

Mr. Reagan depended on God and the prayers of American Christians to win the war against communism. At his inauguration on January 20, 1981, he said:

> I'm told that tens of thousands of prayer meetings are being held on this day, and for that I'm deeply grateful. We are a nation under God, and I believe God intended for us to be free. It would be fitting and good, I think, if on each Inaugural Day in future years it should be declared a day of prayer.[30]

Prayer was important because the communists were prepared, within the limits of international law and civilized society, to negotiate. Yet they were an opponent to deal with cautiously. They had unpredictable moves. They were open to dialogue to avoid war but ready to fight if words failed.

Reagan played his part, and the world marked the collapse of communism. Though it appeared that communism had not died completely, it would not be the same again. What we require is follow-up to the spiritual work Reagan started among the communists. Reeducation of the people, and giving them a new focus in the knowledge of God, would consolidate the job Reagan started for generations to come.

Reagan's exploit in the fight against the evil of communism was acknowledged by both Americans and non-Americans. At his funeral in June 2004, Dick Cheney, vice president of the United States of America, said of him, "He was a providential man who came along just when our Nation and the world most needed him."[31]

According to Paul Kengor, Ronald Reagan said in a 1968 interview with *Christian Life* magazine, "I'm not able to explain how my election happened or why I'm here, apart from believing it is a part of God's plan for me."[32]

Reagan's presidency was a planned act of God in a time of international conflict.

George W. Bush

I know that many Americans would not agree with me that George Bush Jr. was a messiah that America and the rest of the world needed in 2001, but nothing can be further from the truth. Born on July 6, 1946, he became the forty-third president of the United States in January 2001. Mr. Bush did not come into office seeking reasons to go to war. However, as president, he took a solemn oath to defend and protect America and Americans.

George W. Bush became president at a time when the world was faced with increased threats of terrorism. He did not create the situation, but he had the duty to identify the enemies and checkmate them. God brought him in at the nick of time, when terrorists could have taken over the world.

After America was attacked on September 11, 2001, every American looked to a leader who would reassure them of their safety and protection. President Bush immediately rose to the challenge. He traveled to the World Trade Center, where rescue and recovery efforts had begun. The president told the people who gathered in agony at the Trade Center in New York, "I heard you." He made a profound promise to the nation that the perpetrators of the dastardly act would be fished out, no matter where they were in the world.

On September 20, 2001, the president disclosed to Congress and the nation his determination to fight all acts of terrorism anywhere in the world to protect Americans. He said, "Our war on terror begins with al Qaeda, but it does not end there. It will not end until every terrorist group of global reach has been found, stopped and defeated."[33]

Intelligence reports linked al Qaeda, a group known to sponsor acts of terrorism, with this heinous crime.

By November 2001, Mr. Bush made good on his promise by going after the al Qaeda regime in Afghanistan to dislodge a government that was known to breed, train, and harbor terrorists. Since then and throughout his presidency, he never looked back from fighting known terrorists.

The president, in his lecture at the University of Kansas on January 23, 2006, asserted that no American ever believed that America could be that easily attacked by enemies on our soil. The myth was suddenly removed; terrorists were in America without being detected. It was therefore imperative to take the enemy seriously.

President Bush said, "Right after they attacked us, I laid out a doctrine, and it said, if you harbor terrorists, you're equally as guilty as the terrorists. The reason I said that is because I understand that a terrorist network can sometimes burrow in society and can sometimes find safe haven from which to plot and plan." He added, "The decision I made right off the bat is, we will find them, and we will hunt them down and we will bring them to justice before they hurt America again."[34]

America has always lent her voice to the war against terror, but it became personal and urgent in the wake of September 11. The world needed a like-Moses to lead them in facing this challenge, and George W. Bush rose to rescue his people.

The president, at the University of Kansas lecture, said, "Today's war on terror is like the Cold War. It is an ideological struggle with an enemy that despises freedom and pursues totalitarian aims....I vowed then that I would use all assets of our power of Shock and Awe to win the war on terror. And so I said we are going to stay on the offensive two ways: one, hunt down the enemy and bring them to justice, and take threats seriously; and two, spread freedom."[35]

Mr. Bush took the fight to the adversary's doorstep, asserting that since the enemy had boldly attacked America on its own soil, staying here to defend the home front was insufficient. He effectively checked the activities of violent radicals who could have done more harm to America's interests around the world.

In his war on terrorism, the president kept an eye on all enemies of America. One of them was Saddam Hussein of Iraq, whose government sponsored and harbored terrorist groups and leaders of al Qaeda. Hussein posed a danger to the peace of the world because of his territorial ambition. Bush knew that to win the war on terrorism, Saddam must be disarmed.

Saddam Hussein, the strong man of Iraq, did not hide his hatred for America. His actions, utterances, and support of terrorist acts all over the world were a serious concern, not only for America and Europe but also the Middle East.

In an effort to discredit his God-given mission, some critics alleged that President Bush targeted Iraq for personal business interests. They insinuated that Bush had his eyes on Iraq before the September 11 attacks. But the president refused to be persuaded by critics that something was wrong with his mission in Iraq. He told a journalist at a press conference that our children would not be safe if we lost that war.

At the beginning, most Americans supported Bush, as demonstrated by the overwhelming support of Congress and American citizens for the war on terror. In general, the people acknowledged that we needed to defend ourselves from the aggression of the terrorists who had picked us as their main target. However, the war in Iraq became unpopular as a result of the many casualties. The high cost of executing the war and the extended time it took added to the discouragement of the American people.

George W. Bush could not have ignored this war. Anyone who overlooks terrorist threats does so to his peril and that of his people. And besides that was the mission in times like this. Hence, Mr. Bush would not pacify the enemy, wait for more attacks, or give up to fate. He acted decisively. At the Kansas State University lecture, he said:

> When you make decisions, you've got to stand on principle. If you're
> going to make decisions, you've got to know what you believe.... The

threat to the United States is forefront in my mind. I knew people would say, you know, it may be an isolated incident; let's just don't worry about it. Well for me it's not an isolated incident, I understand there is still an enemy which lurks out there....And the other group of course is the al Qaeda types, Mr. Zarqawi who wants us to leave Iraq. They want us to get out of Iraq so Iraq can be a safe haven for them.[36]

President Bush's decisive response to 9/11 put the terrorists in check; it destabilized their organization, put some of the suspected disciples of Osama bin Laden in jail, and put pressure on bin Laden himself.

Mr. Bush is not a warmonger but someone who took pains to fulfill his mission to his country and his people. In an article on CBC News Online dated November 19, 2004, titled "Indepth: George W. Bush, 43rd President of the United States," Gail Sheehy said, "George W. Bush never makes anyone feel less intelligent than he is. He's just a good old guy trying to do the right thing."[37]

Though President Bush did not win completely before his term as president ended, he nevertheless accomplished the goal set for him by God. He will go down in history as a man who was focused and undaunted in his fight against terrorism. No one can imagine the situation in the world today if the terrorists had been left to move about in the world unchecked.

The God of Response in Times of Conflicts

God is therefore not a God of coincidence but a compassionate Creator who acts when it matters. It is wrong to believe that nothing was sacrosanct about the emergence of Moses, Dr. King, Reagan, or Bush at the time these men appeared on the scene. Nothing happens in the world without the knowledge of God. Coincidence is a human word not in the language of God.

These individuals are just a few examples of those whom God has used to fix the troubles on earth. And there was no doubt they were brought in at the nick of time. He is a God who knows today from yesterday. Tomorrow and the future are before His face. As the Lord said to Jeremiah, "Before I formed you in the womb I knew you, before you were born I set you apart; I appointed you as a prophet to the nations" (Jeremiah 1:5).

We need to appreciate that God is not weak or helpless; He is ahead of every conflict the heart of man could generate, and He has prepared persons and non-human instruments to accomplish the task of resolving conflict. God's intervention is His way of assuring us that despite our disobedience, He loves us and will always take care of all that concerns us. Conflicts are created by the devil, but God is always on time to destroy the works of Satan.

Thoughts

God created us individually for a unique purpose. The world and society will benefit from our lives if we accept the call of Providence on us. The talents God gave to us are to be channeled towards achieving the objective of God for creating us. It does not matter the level we are at socially or economically. Not all of us would be president; neither would all of us be doctors. Some are called to be engineers, some teachers, and some others, chefs, etc. God places importance on the contributions we make in fixing the conflicts in the world.

The Bible says, "There are different kinds of gifts, but the same Spirit distributes them. There are different kinds of service, but the same Lord. There are different kinds of working, but in all of them and in everyone it is the same God at work. Now to each one the manifestation of the Spirit is given for the common good" (1 Corinthians 12: 5-7). And mind you, we shall give account of how we have used the tools that the Creator gave to us for the benefit of our society. Paul said, "So then, each of us will give an account of ourselves to God" (Romans 14:12).

CHAPTER 3

EFFECTS OF CONFLICT ON HUMANITY

Woe to the earth and the sea, because the devil has
gone down to you!
He is filled with fury, because he knows that his time is short.
—Revelation 12:12

THE GODLESSNESS IN our societies has become more pronounced today, and the human heart with the absence of God is generating more and more conflicts, giving humanity no peace. On the contrary, the effects of conflict have been devastating. These include hunger, poverty, and poor health, resulting in premature death. People are depressed, tired of their lives, and often end up committing suicide. In some cases, these individuals terminate the lives of other innocent persons before taking their own.

Peace has been overtaken by violence and destruction. The human race has lost control. Life is full of anxieties. No one is spared from the effects of conflict. Those who create the conflicts and the innocent victims all pay a high price. When we appreciate the damages conflicts have continued to do to our world, we will rise as a nation to confront the dissensions with a view to resolving them and give ourselves reprieve.

Because conflict is an issue of the heart, we require a change of heart to achieve a permanent solution. The only plausible way is to seek the intervention of the Creator of the human heart. Not any efforts of man will change our conflicted situations. The transformation of the human heart will resolve our relationship problems, help us to have a good understanding of one another, and work together with less suspicion. We therefore cannot alienate ourselves or the people from God and expect any change for good in our society.

So long as we continue to hold God in contempt, and believe in our arrogance that we can resolve these conflicts on our own, we will not cease to go through the accompanying hardships.

And we do not have reasons to continue to pass through these struggles. It is also not the will of God for us. Jesus said, "Come to me, all you who are weary and burdened, and I will give you rest" (Matthew 11:28). Here are some of the costs a nation would pay for the ravaging conflicts.

Loss of Human Life

Conflicts destroy human lives, either permanently in death or by preventing individuals from achieving their full potential. Many intelligent, hardworking people, who could have contributed to the well-being of society, have died in avoidable battles.

Wars within nations and between different countries have cost numerous human lives. World Wars I and II resulted in many casualties, both soldiers and civilians.

Zaryab Iqbal, in her book *War and the Health of Nations*, said, "The World Health Organization's (WHO) 2002 World Report on Violence and Health revealed that 1.6 million people die each year due to violence, including collective violence such as conflicts within or between states, and a large number of people who lose their lives due to militarized conflict are noncombatants."[38]

Iqbal stated further, "The 25 largest instances of conflict in the twentieth century led to the deaths of approximately 191 million people, and 60 percent of those fatalities occurred among people who were not engaged in fighting. (World Health Organization 2002a)."[39]

On August 6, 1945, during the height of World War II, Colonel Paul W. Tibbets dropped the first atomic weapon on Japanese soil. "Sixty percent of Hiroshima was destroyed and more than 150,000 people perished in the blast.[40]

In 2011, the United States Census Bureau recorded a loss of about 4,000 military personnel through hostile actions (war and terrorism) between 2003 and 2009.[41]

The consequences of war often override its objectives. J. M. Winter, author of *The Experience of World War I*, said:

> The aftermath of the war was a time of reckoning and a time of mourning for millions of people throughout the world. This indeed is another way of seeing the conflict as a "people's war." They paid the price. The casualty lists which grew and grew as the war continued preclude any conclusion other than that the war was one of the most miserable chapters in human history. The fact that much bravery and some good came out of it is beside the point; the war was an abomination.[42]

And there are others who did not go to battle as soldiers but at war within themselves have committed suicide. Personal suicides have claimed not a few lives within our society. The personal termination of life often occurs as a result of depression of the heart due to political, social, or economic problems. For example, Tori Richards, an AOL news contributor, reported from Costa Mesa, California on March 18, 2011, how "a municipal employee leaped to his death off City Hall here after getting laid off from his job along with hundreds of colleagues in a cost-cutting move."[43] The 29 year-old maintenance worker Huy Pham committed suicide and died Thursday, March 18, 2011 as a result of job loss. Pham was not the only one who had fought himself to death.

Some commit suicide but do not terminate their personal life alone. They kill others in the process. In most terrorist acts, the victims often have nothing to do with the grievances of the assailant. But they become sacrificial lambs for the terrorists to make their point.

Psychological Damage

The pain does not stop with the loss of human lives. Many soldiers who survive war nurse the guilt of their involvement in killing others the rest of their lives. Lt. Col. Dave Grossman evidenced this in his book *On Killing: The Psychological Cost of Learning to Kill in War and Society*.

He said, "With very few exceptions, everyone associated with killing in combat reaps a bitter harvest of guilt."[44]

Grossman recorded the following words from soldiers who had been involved in killing in the war front:

> "Killing is the worst thing that one man can do to another man.... It's the last thing that should happen anywhere." – Israeli lieutenant.

> "I reproached myself as a destroyer. An indescribable uneasiness came over me. I felt almost like a criminal." – Napoleonic-era British soldier.

> "This was the first time I had killed anybody and when things quieted down I went and looked at a German I knew I had shot. I remember thinking that he looked old enough to have a family and I felt very sorry." – British World War I veteran after his first kill.[45]

Furthermore, the deaths of war victims are accompanied by pain and hardship for the family members, friends, and communities who mourn them. Wives become widows. Children become orphans. Some kids lose their bearings in life after the loss of their parents. Without proper guidance growing up, they do not attain their full potential.

Destruction of Property and Nations' Infrastructures

Destruction of property resulting from war takes a toll on communities as they struggle to rebuild. Some reconstructions may not be accomplished in the lifetime of the generation who witnessed the war. Most people are displaced, losing all valuables and property.

The nation of Sudan has gone through two civil wars, 1955 to 1972 and 1983 to 2005. The conflict that has ravaged that country for these decades has destroyed families and homes and is splitting the nation into two, the North and the South. It has been a torturous situation that will affect many generations to come.

Also, Liberia has experienced two civil wars: the first from 1989 to 1996, the second from 1999 to 2003. These wars claimed many lives, displaced hundreds of thousands of people, and destroyed the country's infrastructure and economy. Several Liberians who lost their homes are still struggling to rebuild.

Effect on Social life and Health Facilities

Years of conflict have had devastating consequences for the humanitarian situation in Liberia, which is currently ranked 174 out of 175 counties by the UN World Human Development Index, which measures health and living conditions. The Liberian civil war had horrific consequences on the Liberian people. The fourteen-year civil conflict left more than 100,000 people dead. Mostly innocent civilians were murdered, and hundreds of thousands became refugees or were displaced throughout the region.

One of the tragic consequences of the Liberian civil war was the use of children as soldiers. An estimated 15,000 children fought in Liberia's civil war. Most of them are now vulnerable and are suffering from drug addiction and post-traumatic stress syndrome. Women and girls were reported to have suffered the most: they were raped and murdered with impunity by all the fighting groups.[46]

Zaryab Iqbal wrote:

In September 2003, the WHO reported that only 32 percent of the population had access to latrines, and there had been no regular garbage collection in Monrovia [Liberia's capital] since 1996. The SKD Stadium, the largest camp for internally displaced people in Monrovia, housed about 45,000 people who "cook and sleep in any sheltered spot they can find, in hallways and in tiny slots under the stadium seats" with six nurses in the health center for 400 daily patients (World Health Organization 2003). After the civil war, life expectancy in Liberia remains 41 years.[47]

Refugees

In times of war, many individuals are displaced from their homes; they become refugees in another land.

Neighbors of warring nations suffer economic and political trouble when they take on refugees from other countries. People who have been deprived of their homes by war are usually a menace to the countries that accommodate them because they are additional population that no one planned for in the provision of the nation's social services. Even the United Nations' High Commissioner for Refugees whose responsibility is for such international emergencies could not do much to resolve the pain that accompanied the surge in refugees as a result of war. The organization was often overwhelmed with the unexpected number of displaced persons in the world.

Light, water, and sanitation services in refugee camps are unable to cope with the sudden rise in the number of people, resulting in unhealthy environments and social problems. International relief organizations and volunteer non-governmental organizations cannot handle all the needs. Both refugees and citizens of the accommodating country are subjected to human degradation and appalling living conditions.

Most refugees also have their careers retarded, if not shattered. Some children's early education is terminated. Those in college who were pursuing a career are cut off from their dreams.

In refugee camps, the officers responsible for protecting the people often take advantage of the situation. Girls are molested and sometimes become pregnant by someone who is not willing to parent the child. Many illegitimate children resulting from war grow up with single parents.

War stops or slows down productive ventures such as farming and manufacturing as the land is overtaken by soldiers. By the time the war is over and the refugees return to their homeland, they have lost their skills, either as a result of disabilities or through extended times of idleness. They are forced to start life all over.

Fractured Relationships

One reason world leaders have been unable to work together for world peace is the mutual suspicion resulting from past experiences. The absence of trust does not allow them to feel comfortable opening up to one another. No matter how hard diplomats work to mend fences after a war, they still find it difficult to maintain transparent associations.

In many organized forums, particularly under the umbrella of the United Nations the nations' heads of governments have met to dialogue on how to avoid the catastrophe of deadly confrontation. These diplomatic meetings often result in a temporary understanding, but soon after, all agreements evaporate. Negotiations end on the table of discussion. The political leaders return to their countries to further the secret development of atomic bombs and other weapons of mass destruction.

Since 2006, six resolutions have been passed by the United Nations Security Council to stop Iran's development of nuclear weapons.[48] But to date, the world does not believe Iran has given up the idea of nuclear weapons. The Nuclear Non-Proliferation Treaty was signed by 189 nations on March 5, 1970. Iran was a signatory. Similarly, the world is not comfortable with North Korea, which is also believed to be developing nuclear arms.

In the 2011 Year Book of the Stockholm International Peace Research Institute (SIPRI), Dr. Susan T. Jackson, head of the Arms Production Project of the SIPRI Military Expenditure and Arms Production Programme, states, "The world is likely to face a difficult period of growing uncertainty and fragility and a diffusion of risks and threats."[49] The human heart is preoccupied with devising ways of wiping itself out of existence.

Dr. Jackson adds, "Despite the financial crisis of 2008 and the ensuing global economic recession, arms producers and military services companies continued their upward trend in arms sales."[50] The fact that arms sales are still going up is evidence that we do not trust one another for peace. We are secretly getting ourselves prepared for the eventual war when it comes.

Fractured relationships occur in all forms of human conflict. For example, slavery was abolished in United States several decades ago. Though most of our current generation does not know when or how slavery started and ended except through written history, conflicts resulting from past slavery experiences still manifest in our nation and some people continue to hate the descendants of that battle.

Blacks and whites in our present day struggle with the perceptions of the past. The actions and inactions of individuals and groups of different races are seen in light of issues that occurred many decades ago, leaving our society highly polarized.

On July 16, 2009, Harvard professor Henry Louis Gates, Jr., one of the nation's pre-eminent African-American scholars, was in his home

Cambridge Police (mainly whites) visited his house to interrogate and/or arrest him. They were investigating reports of unlawful house break-in.

According to the reporter, "The incident raised concerns among some Harvard faculty that Gates was a victim of racial profiling. Police arrived at Gates's Ware Street home near Harvard Square at 12:44 p.m. to question him. Gates, director of the W.E.B. Du Bois Institute for African and African American Research at Harvard, had trouble unlocking his door after it became jammed.

He was booked for disorderly conduct after "exhibiting loud and tumultuous behavior," according to a police report. Gates accused the investigating officer of being a racist and told him he had "no idea who he was messing with," the report said.

Gates told the officer that he was being targeted because "I'm a black man in America."[51]

It took the interventions of President Barack Obama to douse the racial issues resulting from Gates's encounter with police. This happened because of mutual suspicions between the blacks and the whites in our nation based on the events of history.

The reporter quoted a colleague of Professor Gates thus: "He and I both raised the question of if he had been a white professor, whether this kind of thing would have happened to him, that they arrested him without any corroborating evidence," said S. Allen Counter, a Harvard Medical School professor who spoke with Gates about the incident Friday. "I am deeply concerned about the way he was treated, and called him to express my deepest sadness and sympathy."[52]

Emotional Stress

Conflicts cause emotional stress. For example, ever since the terrorist attack on 9/11, traveling has been more worrisome. People are concerned about their safety when they fly, either for pleasure or for business.

We have good reason to remain on our guard, because we never know when we might be the victim of another attack. For instance, a Nigerian suspected terrorist, 23-year-old Umar Farouk Abdulmutallab, ignited an explosive device Friday, December 25, 2009 shortly before a Northwest (KLM) flight from Amsterdam, Netherlands, made its landing in Detroit, Michigan. It was by the providence of God that 278 travelers aboard KLM Flight #253 escaped unhurt.

According to Anahad O'Connor and Eric Schmitt of the *New York Times,* "A Nigerian man tried to ignite an explosive device aboard a trans-Atlantic Northwest Airlines flight as the plane prepared to land in Detroit on Friday, in an incident the United States believes was 'an attempted act of terrorism,' according to a White House official who declined to be identified."[53]

The uncertainties both on the road and in the air have led government to take security resolutions that are not too pleasant to the people. Security measures at our nation's airports add to people's stress. Travelers spend significantly more time at airports because they have to get there earlier than they'd like. They are subjected to body scans, which operators sometimes misuse to inconvenience people.

Also, the fear of safe locations in the world to go to do business or for holiday pleasure is all over the people. On September 20, 2008, a dump truck filled with explosives detonated in front of the Marriott Hotel in Islamabad, the Pakistani capital, killing fifty-four persons and leaving 266 others injured. Five foreign nationals who were in the city were killed and others were injured.[54]

Local Acts of Terrorism

We are losing control of our younger generation through absence of the influence of God's Word in their lives. When kids grow up in communities that do not value the knowledge of God, they often end up in violent gangs and become involved in other social vices.

Locally bred radicals can do more damage than international terrorists. These kids are armed with weapons. They maim and kill people in response to whatever resentments they have generated in their hearts.

On April 20, 1999, two students massacred thirteen of their classmates at Columbine High School in Colorado. "Eric Harris and Dylan Klebold, who went on a shooting rampage and killed 12 of their classmates and a teacher, injured 23 others and then turned their guns on themselves."[55]

On April 16, 2007, a student at the Virginia Polytechnic Institute, Seung-Hui Cho, killed thirty-two people and wounded many others before committing suicide. The shooter was described as a depressed and deeply disturbed young man. One news reporter called this shooting "the deadliest rampage in American history."[56]

Later that year, a nineteen-year-old, Robert A. Hawkins in Omaha, went on a shooting spree at the West Roads Mall, killing eight people. He left a note stating, "I am going out in style," and "I'm going to be famous."

These incidents represent the high price we pay for the conflicts within our society. The sanctity of life is no longer respected. Human lives are terminated because one angry individual is prepared to submit to death as long as his mission to kill innocent people is achieved.

Deadly Habits in Society

As we sink deeper into troubles, we can feel overwhelmed by our afflictions. We then develop habits that are injurious to our living conditions. Though we have no explanation as to why we engaged in them in the first place, the disorders they cause are not bad enough to convince us to drop them.

Cigarette smoking is one such deadly habit. According to the Centers for Disease Control and Prevention, "Smoking harms nearly every organ of the body. Smoking causes many diseases and reduces the health of smokers in general."[57]

Despite the warnings, tobacco manufacturers thrive because people are addicted to smoking. Many people want to quit, but they can't, evidence that they have lost control of themselves despite the negative effects of this habit.

CDC's website says:

- The adverse health effects from cigarette smoking account for an estimated 443,000 deaths, or nearly one of every five deaths, each year in the United States.
- More deaths are caused each year by tobacco use than by all deaths from human immunodeficiency virus (HIV), illegal drug use, alcohol use, motor vehicle injuries, suicides, and murders combined.

- Smoking causes 90% of all lung cancer deaths in men and 80% of all lung cancer deaths in women.
- An estimated 90% of all deaths from chronic obstructive lung disease are caused by smoking.[58]

Cigarettes manufactured in the US have the following caption on their packaging: "Surgeon General Warning: Smoking by pregnant women may result in fetal injury, premature birth and low birth weight." Certain people who are addicted do not consider seriously such warning. They eventually have babies with deformations. Our nation and others across the globe have a growing concern for children born with disabilities resulting from effects of addictions of parents at pregnancy.

Drug addiction is another common but deadly habit in this country.

Marijuana is a crude drug that contains ingredients that alter the human mind. According to the Missouri Department of Mental Health, Division of Alcohol and Drug Abuse, "Studies of marijuana's mental effects show that the drug can impair or reduce short-term memory, alter sense of time, and reduce ability to do things which require concentration, swift reactions, and coordination, such as driving a car or operating machinery."[59]

Young people who take marijuana or other hard drugs lose out on a proper education, because their thinking, comprehension, and learning skills are affected. They are eventually addicted to dangerous drugs and are involved in violent crimes in the nation causing unimaginable damages to their victims. This is why governments all over the world take actions to control such drugs.

Ironically, the state of California accepts marijuana as a cure for certain ailments; hence, the legalization of marijuana for medical purposes. The legal sale of marijuana also generates added revenue for the state. In the *Daily Breeze*, a newspaper in California's South Bay, September 27, 2010, Marcus Wohlsen stated:

California has a long history of defying conventional wisdom on the issue of marijuana, including its embrace of the drug in the 1960s and its landmark medical pot law 14 years ago. So it may not be all that surprising that a November ballot measure to legalize the drug has created some odd alliances and scenarios….

Proponents say this measure is a way for the struggling state and its cities to raise badly needed funds. A legal pot industry, they say, would create jobs while undercutting violent criminals who profit off the illegal trade in the drug.[60]

However, the voice of reason prevailed on November 2, 2010, when Proposition 19, which would have legalized the personal growth, use, and distribution of marijuana, failed to pass on the California mid-election ballot.

It is unbelievable that with all the effects caused by these bad human choices, our hearts still get persuaded to continue in such deadly habits. This is the reason why we should agree that something is amiss in the human heart and it requires our attention to properly address the issue of the heart; otherwise we will end in destruction.

I approached a few friends who smoke to persuade them to drop the habit, but the common response I have had from them is that 'they wish they could, but have not succeeded'. Psychologists and other people call this helpless situation addiction but the Word of God, the Bible, calls it 'power of spirit'. We are so controlled by forces of addiction that our life does not matter anymore to us so long as such deadly habits are satisfied.

Paul tried the same way to drop bad habits but was unsuccessful before he found Jesus Christ, who changed his heart completely. Paul said, "What a terrible failure I am! Who will save me from this sin that brings death to my body? I give thanks to God. He will do it through Jesus Christ our Lord" (Romans 7:24-25a).

The only requirement for deliverance is to accept our helpless state that we cannot manage ourselves from these deadly habits, and also to take freely the offer of God through Jesus Christ to deliver us from the issues. The problem with my friends who have accepted that they are not in control of their wrong habits is that they have also not taken the right step of surrendering their situation to God.

Poor Leadership

One of the serious problems of society is the growth of bad leadership resulting from prolonged conflicts. Leadership is an important issue in a nation. The greatest threat to society is bad leadership. The growth and development of the nation is retarded under an ungodly leader. The purpose of civil authority in any community is to check evil and bring about sustainable relationships among the people. But when the leaders are not God-fearing, they constitute further obstacles to the peace of the nation.

Paul, in the book of Romans 13:4, said, "The ruler doesn't carry a sword for no reason at all. He serves God. And God is carrying out his anger through him. The ruler punishes anyone who does wrong." Leaders are tools to put society on the path of sanity.

But because the knowledge of God is now lacking within our society, for decades, we have produced leaders who are bereft, lacking the wisdom of God because their heart are not right with God. This has resulted in the promotion of selfish interests, corruption, and fraud at all levels of service. The resulting poor management and waste of public resources have done damages to the nation's economy, leading to unemployment and unacceptable standards of living for the people.

The nation of Zimbabwe in Africa has been devastated by the leadership's poor choices. Since 2000, the situations in this country have been desperate, with an unemployment rate of about 94%. People are lacking food and other basic life necessities. The country is in a total mess. My friend and his family who lived for a few years in Zimbabwe on missionary efforts had to relocate to Ghana because life completely ground to a halt. They could not move around for lack of gas. Food is not available for purchase if you have the money to do so. Zimbabwe was one of the strong economies in Africa before this sorry state resulting from bad leadership.

The point is that Zimbabwe's experience must not be seen as an isolation; dictatorship can emerge anywhere in the world. And when dictators get hold of power, they do not always use it in the interest of the people.

Economic Effects

The economies of many nations of the word today are under severe stress resulting from conflicts of war, hatred for one another, selfish living, and greediness in our societies. In times of war, resources that would otherwise be used to develop the nation's infrastructures and to feed and educate the people, are diverted to prosecuting the war. It is difficult to estimate the monetary cost of a war until it is over. Therefore, budgets for administering such conflicts are never correct. Such miscalculations affect other plans of the nation. When the needs to prosecute the war suddenly arise, the funds marked for other social services may often be diverted. Conflicts take tolls on resource management at the expense of other equally important needs of the people.

Also in times of war human and material resources that could have been deployed to the production of goods and services are instead engaged in battle. This situation diminishes the required goods and commodities and also the buying power of a country.

The war on terrorism championed by United States of America has been a significant factor in our current economic trouble.

In 2008, Joseph E. Stiglitz, a recipient of the Nobel Memorial Prize in Economic Sciences (2001), and Linda J. Bilmes, in their book *The Trillion Dollar War*, estimated that the Iraqi war would cost the United States about three trillion dollars in military spending, overheads, borrowing, and financing of debt.[61]

The US national debt as of June 11, 2011 was about $14.35 trillion Analysts said national debt has continued to increase an average of $3.95 billion per day since September 2007.[62]

The burden of debt was aggravated by the prosecution of wars in Iraq and Afghanistan. The president of the United States of America, Mr. Barack Obama, on June 22, 2011 announced his decision to reduce the number of soldiers serving in Afghanistan because of its effect on the nation's economy.

Laura Rozen, on Yahoo News of June 22, 2011, quoted the president thus: "'We are a nation whose strength abroad has been anchored in opportunity for our citizens at home,' Obama said in the brief twelve minute speech from the White House East Room. 'Over the last decade, we have spent a trillion dollars on war, at a time of rising debt and hard economic times. Now, we must invest in America's greatest resource — our people.'"[63] About one hundred thousand Americans are in Afghanistan fighting against the terrorists who once took over that country.

The War Resisters League argued that money spent on military personnel, operations, procurements, and intelligence services has doubled since 2003 from about 18% to 36%.[64] This is in addition to aids given in the past six years by the United States Government to allied countries such as Pakistan on the war against terrorists.

Another factor in America and other nations' financial concerns is the macroeconomic effects of rising prices. The current war on terrorism has affected the oil-producing nations of the world, particularly countries in the Middle East, where most of the terrorists hide under the cover of religion. Production of oil in Iraq slowed down as a result of the war on terrorism. The escalating cost of oil has resulted in rising costs of production of goods and services and has led to inflation, which means higher prices for goods and services. The high cost of living impacts negatively on the real economy: savings of people dropped, borrowers could not meet up with obligations to creditors, and lenders also are weary of continuing to lend. This is why since 2009, it appears the economy has been stagnant in the United States and unemployment is not getting better.

The global economy is connected. Most nations' trade activities are linked, and many are dependent on America. Manufacturers in China, Japan, Italy, and South Korea lost their market of manufactured goods and raw materials, particularly farm produce, during the economic downturn in America between 2003 and 2008. When sales dropped, the manufacturing industries had trouble meeting the immediate and long-term costs of doing business.

Social Problems

Also, failure in a nation's economy, resulting in unemployment and inflation, has serious consequences on the life of the people. According to the Bureau of Labor Statistics, United States Department of Labor, unemployment has moved up from 5.7% in December 2001 to 9.4% in December 2010. As of May 2011, the rate only dropped to 9.1%.[65]

In an article published by Bloomberg Online on February 3, 2009, Kathleen M. Howley said, "A record 19 million U.S. homes stood empty at the end of 2008 and homeownership fell to an eight-year low as banks seized homes faster than they could sell them."[66]

Unemployment has led to an increase in crimes such as identity theft and burglary. Many people have been pressured into corrupt activities in order to survive. These criminal activities have created pains for the nation and the victims; some individuals have been led to a premature death as a result of loss suffered, either by committing suicide or through health issues arising from the shocks.

Natural Disasters

The world has continued to witness unprecedented natural disasters. Before Adam and Eve disobeyed God, there was no record of sickness, such as cancer, or natural disaster, like an earthquake. But today, many sicknesses and disasters devastate the world.

The first tsunami on earth occurred when God was angry about the wickedness of man, and He decided to destroy the world with a flood. The Bible says:

> The Lord saw how great the wickedness of the human race had become on the earth, and that every inclination of the thoughts of the human heart was only evil all the time. The Lord regretted that he had made human beings on the earth, and his heart was deeply troubled. So the Lord said, "I will wipe from the face of the earth the human race I have created—and with them the animals, the birds and the creatures that move along the ground—for I regret that I have made them."
>
> —Genesis 6:5–7

Since the great flood, we have had to live with disasters in climate and other natural occurrences such as earthquakes. These are part of the Bible's predictions for the end of the earth. The world will end because sin has destroyed its foundation and God intends to bring a new world that will continue to meet His plan, where His creatures will live without pain.

The Bible confirms this in Revelation 21:1-4. "Then I saw a new heaven and a new earth, for the first heaven and the first earth had passed away, and there was no longer any sea. I saw the Holy City, the New Jerusalem, coming down out of heaven from God, prepared as a bride beautifully dressed for her husband. And I heard a loud voice from the throne saying, 'Look! God's dwelling place is now among the people, and he will dwell with them. They will be his people, and God himself will be with them and be their God. "He will wipe every tear from their eyes. There will be no more death" or mourning or crying or pain, for the old order of things has passed away.'"

When Jesus' disciples asked Him when the end of the world would be, He answered:

"Watch out that no one deceives you. For many will come in my name, claiming, 'I am the Messiah,' and will deceive many. You will hear of wars and rumors of wars, but see to it that you are not alarmed. Such things must happen, but the end is still to come. Nation will rise against nation, and kingdom against kingdom. There will be famines and earthquakes in various places" (Matthew 24:4–7).

What Jesus was telling His disciples, including today's Christian believers, is that the pressure of conflicts would become severe in this end time. Satan, the owner and source of conflicts, knows that his end will soon come but wants to exert pressure on those who trust in God to drop their faith in the Creator. Satan is furthering his ultimate objective to destroy humans when he cunningly led us to disobey God in the Garden of Eden by his current onslaughts of leading the human race completely away from the knowledge of God.

Analysts described the Japan earthquakes in 2011, and the tsunami that ensued as a result, as the greatest tragedy recorded in that nation. But we have not seen anything yet. The Bible says, "All these [bad events occurring in the world today] are the beginning of birth pains" (Matthew 24:8).

It is therefore instructive that Christians be true to their faith in words and conducts. Our godly lives and words would help our communities and nations to overcome the last day's conflicts that are now plaguing the world.

The Final Human End and the Judgment of God

The greatest human tragedy resulting from our conflicted world is death. The Bible says, "The one who sins is the one who will die" (Ezekiel 18:20). Our troubles are linked to the state of sinfulness on earth. We received the generational curse of death when the first family, Adam and Eve, disobeyed God in the Garden of Eden. God had explicitly told them that the consequence of disobedience was death.

The Lord God commanded the man, "You are free to eat from any tree in the garden; but you must not eat from the tree of the knowledge of good and evil, for when you eat from it you will certainly die" (Genesis 2:16–17).

The apostle Paul said, "The wages of sin is death, but the gift of God is eternal life in Christ Jesus our Lord" (Romans 6:23). James says we can blame no one else for the tragedy of death because it is our own making. He said, "Each person is tempted when they are dragged away by their own evil desire and enticed. Then, after desire has conceived, it gives birth to sin; and sin, when it is full-grown, gives birth to death" (James 1:14–15). The physical death is however not the only consequence. The big issue is that after death we will all face the throne of God for His righteous judgment. We cannot hide from the Judge what we did while on earth. No matter our influence, power, or wealth, the Bible says people are destined to die once, and after that to face judgment (Hebrews 9:27).

The good news is that we shall be free from the wrath of God if we accept the gift of salvation, which God made available to all through the Lord Jesus Christ. Paul said, "Christ was sacrificed once to take away the sins of many; and he will appear a second time, not to bear sin, but to bring salvation to those who are waiting for him" (Hebrews 9:28).

Peaceful life and human co-existence are possible but cannot be achieved by only the diplomatic efforts of politicians. The human drive for peace must be accompanied with the true knowledge of God. A peaceful society is of God's making. Jesus said, "I leave my peace with you. I give my peace to you. I do not give it to you as the world does. Do not let your hearts be troubled. And do not be afraid" (John 14:27). The people of the world offers temporary relief but God gives lasting peace.

The way of salvation is to accept Jesus Christ into our hearts and get ourselves acquainted with the words of God through the Bible. The knowledge of God's Word is able to change human hearts and eliminate all conflicts.

Those who already believe in God should not be terrified at the conflicts around us because our lives are in the good hands of the Lord. Paul's advice to us (Christians) through the church at Philippi is, "Do not be anxious about anything, but in every situation, by prayer and petition, with thanksgiving, present your requests to God. And the peace of God, which transcends all understanding, will guard your hearts and your minds in Christ Jesus" (Philippians 4:6-7).

And the point here is that we are not meant to come into this world and pass through these issues without reprieve. Most people often live their sojourn here as if in hell. The reason for this is because the people are lacking the knowledge of God and His word as a result of policies hampering the free flow of the word of God. So long as we continue to despise the knowledge of God, which is the ultimate plan of Satan for the people of the world, we will continue to experience devastating blows in all our endeavors. The Lord spoke through Hosea the prophet:

> My people are destroyed from lack of knowledge. "Because you have rejected knowledge, I also reject you as my priests; because you have ignored the law of your God, I also will ignore your children…They will eat but not have enough; they will engage in prostitution but not flourish, because they have deserted the LORD to give themselves to prostitution; old wine and new wine take away their understanding."
> —Hosea 4: 6, 10-11

Thoughts

Are we ever going to get out of these messes? Certainly, we shall. The just shall live by faith. The political, economic and social upheavals will not cease because the understanding about the God who created us is being taken away from us and replaced continually with the knowledge of Satan. Though we are not pleased with the repercussions of conflicts in the world and in our society, and the effects of conflicts on our individual lives are also huge, we are captives of the knowledge of Satan, which leads to destruction.

The issues of life sometimes drive us crazy and we seem not to have peace for a large portion of our living on earth. This was not the plan of the Creator but the growing godlessness in the world. The solution is therefore to embrace the knowledge of God our Creator, who is the gate to peace. He said: "Peace I leave with you; my peace I give you. I do not give to you as the world gives. Do not let your hearts be troubled and do not be afraid" (John 14:27). Isaiah the prophet said of God: "You will keep in perfect peace those whose minds are steadfast, because they trust in you" (Isaiah 26:3). It is only in the Lord Jesus Christ that the world will have peace.

CHAPTER 4

CONFLICTS BASED ON RELIGIOUS DOMINANCE

The Lord had said to Abram…"I will make you into a great nation, and I will bless you; I will make your name great, and you will be a blessing. I will bless those who bless you, and whoever curses you I will curse; and all peoples on earth will be blessed through you."
—Genesis 12:1–3

The Human Nature and God

HUMAN BEINGS ARE created in the image of God (Genesis 1:27), and He designed us to have constant physical access to Him. God says, "Here I am! I stand at the door and knock. If any of you hears my voice and opens the door, I will come in and eat with you. And you will eat with me" (Revelation 3:20). Thus, we should be able to meet with God at will.

God visited Adam and Eve in the cool of the day. The Bible says, "Then the man and his wife heard the sound of the LORD God as he was walking in the garden in the cool of the day, and they hid from the LORD God among the trees of the garden. But the LORD God called to the man, 'Where are you?'" (Genesis 3:8-9).

David, a former Israelite king, attested to the desire of the Lord for humans in his praises to God. He said, "What is mankind that you [God] are mindful of them, human beings that you care for them? You have made them a little lower than the angels and crowned them with glory and honor. You made them rulers over the works of your hands; you put everything under their feet" (Psalm 8:4–6).

The first family on earth, Adam and Eve, had the privilege of daily fellowship with God. They were residents in the Garden of Eden, where God visited them on a regular basis. But when they disobeyed God, they were driven out of the garden and were separated from God (Genesis 3:23-24).

Ever since then, it has been the yearning of the human heart to be reunited to our Creator. We are constantly preoccupied with efforts to reach God.

God sent some prophets to the world in response to man's persistent desire to re-unite with the Creator. The prophets spoke the mind of God to the people. Some of the old prophets recorded in history, particularly in the land of Israel, included Isaiah, Jeremiah, Ezekiel, Elijah, and Elisha. They spoke against the backdrop of conflicts in their society and the provision of God's reconciliation and resolutions to the problems. They prophesied about the vehicle, Jesus Christ, with which the Lord was going to restore to Himself the human race.

God's Providence

God, in His infinite power, authority, and love for humankind, fulfilled His promise of restoration of man and woman through His Son, who came to the world by the lineage of a man named Abraham. Abraham was of Middle Eastern origin but was called out of his home and given a land known as Canaan for an inheritance. Because of the continuous wickedness in the human heart, this land has also become a source of conflict today.

I need to stress here that the provision of God to reconcile man to Himself through His Son Jesus Christ was an issue for the devil. It was terrifying for Satan because it was going to deliver man and woman, who were and are under the devil's bondage. He had fought this plan from the beginning. Satan had continued to make life difficult for the lineage of Abraham as he did to their father, the father of faith. Satan turned Canaan, the land of promise, to a source of conflicts of no lesser magnitude to date. But Christ came to the world, fulfilled His purpose, and has gone back to heaven preparing for the time He will come for His followers while Satan keeps the offensive on the world, making it a difficult place to live.

Religious Views in the World

The human efforts to reach God led to the creation of different religious views in the world, including the worship of creations like man, the constellations, and even animals. But of all the religions in the world, Islam and Christianity have been prominent. And Satan has exploited the differences between the two religious views to create instabilities in the world.

As of 2000, Christianity and Islam account for fifty-nine percent of the world population, with Christianity having thirty-four percent and Islam twenty-five. Christians are in large numbers in Europe and America, accounting for about eighty percent of the population, as a result of the efforts of the early apostles of Jesus Christ. The apostles also impacted the continent of Africa, the reason why the two religious views, Christianity and Islam, have almost equal proportions in Africa. But in Asian and Middle Eastern countries, Islam faithfuls are in the majority.[67]

The dominant religions have affected, and sometimes dictated, events around the world because of the position the adherents occupy in the economic, social and political sectors of nations. The religion shapes the political, economic and social culture of the people where it holds sway. For example, Christianity shaped education in Europe and America. The 'western education' has made good progress because it translated into science and technology, which have revolutionized the world systems. The democratic system of governance in Europe and America could also be traced to their Christian values.

The Middle East, where Islam has dominance, is blessed with abundance of natural resources of oil and gas. The world has depended on oil and gas to power its technological growth. In the Arab world and Asia, the Islamic religion is the source of political power. Only leaders who pay allegiance to this power would survive their rule.

The Friction Between Both Religions

Christianity and Islam both originated in the same geographical region, the Middle East, and their adherents share roots in history. But there have been decades of conflicts between the followers of both religions.

Abraham was the father of the Jews and through him the nation of Israel came into existence. He was noted for his faith in God and was called the father of the faithful. He did whatever God told him to do, even in the face of difficulties (Hebrews 11:8-12). Abraham's wife, Sarah, for many years was without a child, though God had promised them a son through whom a great nation would be born.

The travail of the family led Abraham, under pressure from his wife Sarah, to have a sexual relationship with his wife's house help, Hagar. Hagar bore a son for Abraham, named Ishmael. About fourteen years later, the Lord fulfilled His promise for a son through Sarah. His name was Isaac.

But before the birth of Ishmael, his mother, Hagar, held her master's wife, Sarah, in contempt and had to run away from Abraham's home as a result of the hostility between her and Sarah. (See Genesis 16:1–16.) The angel of the Lord met her along the way with a message of continued hostility between the baby and his brothers. The angel said to Hagar:

> You are now pregnant and you will give birth to a son. You shall name him Ishmael, for the Lord has heard of your misery. He will be a wild donkey of a man; his hand will be against everyone and everyone's hand against him, and he will live in hostility toward all his brothers.
>
> —Genesis 16:11–12

Over the centuries, hatred developed between the descendants of Isaac and the descendants of Ishmael. This animosity is the underlying cause of the violence centered on these two religions today.

Joan Comay, author of *Who's Who in the Bible*, said, "By Jewish and Moslem tradition Ishmael came to be regarded as the ancestor of the nomad desert tribes, particularly those inhabiting the area from the Sinai desert across the Negev to southern Jordan. The Hebrews considered themselves superior to these primitive (and usually hostile) desert kinsmen, descended from the common forefather Abraham. The Arabs on their part venerate Ishmael as their forefather, and there is a Moslem legend that he and his mother Hagar are buried in the sacred Ka'aba at Mecca. It is interesting that in some Arab tribes male children are circumcised at the age of thirteen, as Ishmael was in the Bible story. [Gen. 16, 17, 25, 36:3; 1 Chr. 1:28-31]."[68]

Birth of the Christian Religion

The founder of the Christian faith, Jesus Christ, was born of a Jewish virgin named Mary. Mary was engaged to be married to Joseph, who was of the lineage of Abraham. The Bible records, "… and Jacob the father of Joseph, the husband of Mary, and Mary was the mother of Jesus who is called the Messiah. Thus there were fourteen generations in all from Abraham to David, fourteen from David to the exile to Babylon, and fourteen from the exile to the Messiah [i.e., Christ]" (Matthew 1:16–17).

Mary conceived Jesus without the natural sexual contact with her husband. And the husband contemplated divorcing her secretly, but God stopped him. The Bible records further, "But after he had considered this, an angel of the Lord appeared to him in a dream and said, 'Joseph son of David, do not be afraid to take Mary home as your wife, because what is conceived in her is from the Holy Spirit. She will give birth to a son, and you are to give him the name Jesus, because he will save his people from their sins'" (Matthew 1: 20-21).

The Christian religion began after the death and resurrection of Jesus. The name *Christian* was given to the disciples of Jesus who lived as He did when He was physically on earth. They were called Christians, meaning "Christ-like people."

"Barnabas went to Tarsus to look for Saul [both were disciples of Christ], and when he found him, he brought him to Antioch. So for a whole year Barnabas and Saul met with the church and taught great numbers of people. The disciples were called Christians first at Antioch" (Acts 11:25–26).

But the church was already in existence before then. The church was made known by Jesus Christ in a discussion with His disciples. He asked them who the people thought Him to be. Most were expecting a Messiah in line with the prophecies, but did not believe that Jesus was the Messiah.

"When Jesus came to the region of Caesarea Philippi, he asked his disciples, 'Who do people say the Son of Man is?'

They replied, 'Some say John the Baptist; others say Elijah; and still others, Jeremiah or one of the prophets.'

'But what about you?' he asked. 'Who do you say I am?'

Simon Peter answered, 'You are the Messiah, the Son of the living God.'

Jesus replied, 'Blessed are you, Simon son of Jonah, for this was not revealed to you by flesh and blood, but by my Father in heaven. And I tell you that you are Peter, and on this rock I will build my church, and the gates of Hades will not overcome it. I will give you the keys of the kingdom of heaven; whatever you bind on earth will be bound in heaven, and whatever you loose on earth will be loosed in heaven'" (Matthew 16:13–19).

At that time Jesus announced Himself as the Savior of mankind. He also proclaimed the people who continued His work after He left to be His "church." The church is God's instrument for the evangelization of the world and the reconciling agency between God and man.

Jesus Christ, shortly before His ascension to heaven, commissioned His disciples to go to proclaim the good news of salvation to the world. He had just completed the task of redeeming man and woman from sin by His death and resurrection.

Jesus said, "All authority in heaven and on earth has been given to me. Therefore go and make disciples of all nations, baptizing them in the name of the Father and of the Son and of the Holy Spirit, and teaching them to obey everything I have commanded you. And surely I am with you always, to the very end of the age" (Matthew 28:18–20).

The disciples went as they were commanded. The job continues today for those who believe in the teachings of Jesus Christ, spreading the message of salvation among people.

The Founder of Islam

Islam was started by Muhammad, a prophet who claimed to have received divine inspiration during an encounter with the angel Gabriel while in a trance.

Robert Goldston, in his book *The Sword of the Prophet: A History of the Arab World from the Time of Mohammed to the Present Day*, said, "In the year 610, Mohammed, forty years old, was believed to have grown more inclined to solitude and meditation." Robert Goldston: The Sword of the Prophet, The Dial Press New York, 1979. Page 25. According to Goldston:

> On one of these solitary vigils in the hills (it was in the month of Ramadan in the year 610), while sleeping in a cave on Mount Hira, Mohammed was visited by the Archangel Gabriel. "He came to me while I was asleep, with a coverlet of brocade, on which was some writing," Mohammed later declared. Four times Gabriel embraced him tightly and cried, "Read" and each time Mohammed answered, "What shall I read?" Then the Archangel replied:
>
> > Recite thou, in the name of the Lord who created;
> > Created man from Clots of Blood:
> > Recite thou! For thy Lord is most Beneficent,
> > Who hath taught the use of the pen?
> > Hath taught Man that which he knoweth not.[69]

Muhammad lived in Mecca, in the midst of the Arab people. He wanted to be in close touch with God, his Creator, but not through the idol worship that was prominent among the Arab generations of his time.

Tanya Gulevich, in her book *Understanding Islam and Muslim Traditions*, said:

> At the time of Muhammad's birth Arabia was already brimming with religious ideas. Many Arabians were polytheists; that is, they believed in a variety of gods and goddesses. People often prayed and made offerings to local deities worshipped only by their own tribe. Other gods and goddesses gained a following that transcended tribal boundaries...

Some people also worshipped a god they called Allah, not as the only God but rather as a high god among many. Nevertheless, their devotion to Allah may have contained the seeds of monotheism—the belief in one all-powerful God. In Arabic, the word "Allah" is not a personal name, but rather means "God" (literally "the God").[70]

The prophet Muhammad preached against the worship of idols, urging people to worship the one true God. He faced persecution as a result, because the people thought he was out to destroy their gods and goddesses.

Fred James Hill and Nicholas Awde, in their book *A History of the Islamic World,* said this about the place where Muhammad started his prophetic mission:

Mecca itself, though an extremely busy marketplace controlled by the Quraysh, had long been a major pilgrim center for a variety of traditional faiths. It was home to a shrine known as the Ka'aba (from the Arab meaning "cube"), a windowless stone cubic structure which, reflecting the region's Biblical heritage, was traditionally held to have been built by Adam and then rebuilt by Abraham. Set in one of its corners is the Black Stone (Hajar); a piece of rock (possibly a meteorite) said to have been given to Abraham by the Archangel Gabriel.[71]

The prophet Muhammad fled Mecca and was warmly received in Medina, where he settled with his followers. Robert Goldston, in his book, said:

Prophet Mohammed faced persecution by the Arabs who had held on to their idols which the prophet had spoken against. The persecution drove the prophet and his disciples away from Mecca and he lived in Medina until his death June 8, 632. On his death bed, he was quoted to have said, "O Lord, I beseech thee. Assist me in the agonies of death!" Then his voice sinking to a whisper, he prayed, "Lord, grant me pardon. Eternity in paradise. Pardon." And he died.[72]

Successors to Muhammad continued his work. But various ideas and interpretations of what needed to be done evolved over time. Caliph

Abu Bakr succeeded Mohammed in the leadership of the Muslim world. When he died on August 22, 634, he was succeeded by Caliph Omar. Under Omar, who was a warrior, the Islamic empire expanded at a high rate, but became militant, conquering the Persian Empire and part of the Roman Empire. Caliph Omar persecuted Christians and created fear among the Christian believers.

Mistrust Between Christianity and Islam

There has been no love lost between the adherents of Christianity and Islam over the decades, resulting from Islamic militancy. The message of both religions is peace, but most of the followers do not live by the tenets of their faith because of the condition of their hearts. They talk about God but do not honor Him. Closeness to God is not an issue of religion, but a matter of a prepared heart ready to obey the instructions of God. It should be a complete transformation of character and behavior of a man or a woman in every situation of life.

But religious deception is now prevalent on earth. And deception is not new. Jesus Christ, in an encounter with the religious men and women of His day, told them, "Isaiah was right when he prophesied about you hypocrites; as it is written: 'these people honor me with their lips, but their hearts are far from me'" (Mark 7:6).

Since the days of Omar, Islamic intolerance was evident in the teachings of most Islamic clerics. They followed the dictates of their hearts to perpetrate evil in the name of God. They engaged in *jihad*, the holy war of Islam, killing individuals who did not share their faith. The religious intolerance has added significantly to the level of conflicts in the world. Also the Muslim states came under totalitarian rule, with no accommodation for any other faith. In most nations where Islam is declared a state religion, Bibles and other Christian literature are forbidden. Those who defer from Islamic views are forced to go underground to practice their religion. Some decided for voluntary exile in order to escape persecution and death. The word *jihad* has been targeted at opponents of faith but the original intention of jihad, which was aimed at self-cleansing of individual heart from sins and wickedness, was not followed.

In their book *The Pillars of Islam: An Introduction to the Islamic Faith,* authors Frances Gumley and Brian Redhead quote Jabal Buaben, a Muslim from Ghana:

> Jihad, he says, is a very sensitive technical term in Islam. It consists of two branches—the lesser jihad and the greater jihad. The greater jihad is the jihad of one's own self, the jihad of the soul. The Qur'an says that man was created primarily for worship of God. People therefore must strive to achieve this. Striving or struggle, in Arabic, is jihad. Struggling to worship God—to live a monotheistic life according to the moral principles in the scriptures—is in itself a greater jihad.
>
> The lesser jihad, which involves use of arms or other forms of struggle, is justified, according to the Qur'an, to fight oppression. So, wherever there is oppression, it is incumbent on Muslims to do whatever they can to remove it. Jihad is primarily to remove evil and to instill good. How it is done is the problem.[73]

Islamic clerics have cited verses from the Koran to force "infidels" to obey Islamic injunctions. One such verse is, "Fight those who have not faith in God, nor in the hereafter, and who forbid not what God and His Prophet have forbidden and who are not committed to the religion of truth, of those who have been brought the Book, until they pay tribute by hand, and they are the low" (Koran 9:29).

According to Reuven Firestone, author of *Jihad: The Origin of Holy War in Islam*:

> Jihad is a verbal noun of the third Arabic form of the root *jahada*, which is defined classically as exerting one's utmost power, efforts, endeavors, or ability in contending with an object of disapprobation. Such an object is often categorized in the literature as deriving from one of three sources: a visible enemy, the devil, and aspects of one's own self. There are, therefore, many kinds of jihad, and most have nothing to do with warfare. Jihad of the heart, for example, denotes struggle against one's own sinful inclinations.[74]

Ironically, at no time in his life did Mohammed attack people, but rather he focused his aggressions against the idols that people were worshipping. He strove to make peace with those who were opposed to him, and he never fought those who persecuted him. That changed after his death, when his successors were determined to make everyone in the world a Muslim. They are prepared to see dead those who do not buy into their faith.

Difference between Christian and Islamic Teachings

The central truth in the Christian faith is love. "For God so loved the world that he gave his one and only Son, that whoever believes in him shall not perish but have eternal life. For God did not send his Son into the world to condemn the world, but to save the world through him" (John 3:16–17).

A Pharisee once asked Jesus to identify the greatest commandment. Jesus replied, "'Love the Lord your God with all your heart and with all your soul and with all your mind.' This is the first and greatest commandment. And the second is like it: 'Love your neighbor as yourself.' All the Law and the Prophets hang on these two commandments" (Matthew 22:37–40).

Love is the test of the identity of a true Christian believer; it is the basis on which we can demonstrate that we have God in us. The apostle John said, "Whoever does not love does not know God, because God is love" (1 John 4:8). And love is the character trait that promotes peace and neighborliness. The absence of love is hate, which is the source of all evil in society. Love cannot be legislated; it flows freely from a pure heart. It is not enough to say with the mouth we love; we can only be true to it when our neighbor wrongs us or by how we respond to our known adversaries.

Jesus taught His disciples to follow not laws, but love. He told them:

> You have heard that it was said, "Eye for eye, and tooth for tooth."
> But I tell you, do not resist an evil person. If anyone slaps you on the
> right cheek, turn to them the other cheek also. And if anyone wants
> to sue you and take your shirt, hand over your coat as well. If anyone
> forces you to go one mile, go with them two miles. Give to the one

who asks you, and do not turn away from the one who wants to borrow from you.

—Matthew 5:38–42

Jesus also told His followers they were to love their enemies.

"You have heard that it was said, 'Love your neighbor and hate your enemy.' But I tell you, love your enemies and pray for those who persecute you, that you may be children of your Father in heaven. He causes his sun to rise on the evil and the good, and sends rain on the righteous and the unrighteous. If you love those who love you, what reward will you get? Are not even the tax collectors doing that? And if you greet only your own people, what are you doing more than others? Do not even pagans do that? Be perfect, therefore, as your heavenly Father is perfect" (Matthew 5:43-48). Perfection is the art of unfailing love.

Jesus Christ demonstrated love to His disciples in various ways. For example, when He was traveling with His disciples through Samaria, they requested His permission to command fire from heaven to consume the people who had wronged them. But Jesus rebuked His disciples, saying, "You do not know what manner of spirit you are of. For the Son of Man did not come to destroy men's lives but to save them" (Luke 9:55–56 NKJV). God is not interested in the destruction of people; rather, He desires that they have life.

On another occasion, Jesus was confronted by the Jewish leaders of the law. They had caught a young woman in the act of adultery and brought her to Jesus to pronounce judgment on her. According to the law, she was to be stoned to death. But Jesus had compassion on the sinful woman because His nature is love. He ordered that only those who were not guilty of any sin should be involved in stoning her. No one could raise a hand because all were guilty of one offense or another. Jesus thereafter set the woman free to "go and sin no more" (John 8:11 NKJV). Jesus knew that no human has the capacity to condemn sinners, and He (God) who possesses the power to condemn would not always do so because of His love for mankind.

When Jesus was arrested by Roman soldiers, one of His disciples, Peter, took his sword and struck the servant of the high priest, cutting off his ear. Jesus rebuked Peter. "Put your sword back in its place…for all who draw the sword will die by the sword. Do you think I cannot call on my Father, and he will at once put at my disposal more than twelve legions of angels?" (Matthew 26:52–53). The only reason for the condemnation of Peter was because of the love nature in Jesus Christ.

On the cross when Jesus was crucified and was about to die, He prayed for his assailants: "Father, forgive them, for they do not know what they are doing" (Luke 23:34). It is an amazing love that cannot be found anywhere but in Jesus only.

This is the pattern of life that Jesus expects His disciples to live. Peter the apostle, in his epistle to other disciples of Jesus, said, "To this you were called, because Christ suffered for you, leaving you an example, that you should follow in his steps" (1 Peter 2:21). True love comes from a heart that is transformed.

The Christian religion teaches its followers to be prepared to lay down their lives for others, just as Jesus Christ laid down His life for the salvation of the world. The principle on which Christ died and lives is that of giving to others in personal service and sacrifice, even at the cost of one's life and liberty. Apostle John puts it this way: "This is how we know what love is: Jesus Christ laid down his life for us. And we ought to lay down our lives for our brothers and sisters" (1 John 3:16).

Christians cannot wage war as other people do. Paul the apostle said, "For though we live in the world, we do not wage war as the world does. The weapons we fight with are not weapons of the world. On the contrary, they have divine power to demolish strongholds. We demolish arguments and every pretension that sets itself up against the knowledge of God" (2 Corinthians 10:3–5).

Love gives freedom to others, even if they do not agree with us. It says that despite our differences, we can live together in peace. The teachings of Christianity demand that efforts at persuading people of other views must be done in love. Christian witnessing is sharing Christ through the power of the Holy Spirit and leaving the results to God. Acts of force are foreign to true Christian worship and practice.

However, this is lacking in other faiths and religions, in particular Islam, where people of differing faith are not to be seen or heard. Individual rights are denied based on different views held on religion. Such religions are not founded on the principles of tolerance. This is why several terrorist acts have been linked to religious war and Islam. The perpetrators resort to terrorism because they could not tolerate others and they do not possess the capacity or power to overrun these nations that are predominantly Christian.

Intolerance

One of the major problems in the world today is therefore religious intolerance. The rate of intolerance among the Muslims is high. Most people who profess the faith are found to be demonizing the religion. In countries where Islam dominates, no other religion has the right to speak. And in the societies where they are in minority, they hold others prisoner by resorting to violence to 'defend' their faith. But Christians and Muslims can live together in harmony if only the people of Islamic faith would show a little more restraint. We cannot do for God what he did not commission us to do. God has not commissioned any pastor or cleric to take life for whatever reason.

Heaven or hell is a personal choice of individuals and no one should force another to go to either of the two. We should be free to profess and witness our faith without hurting anyone. This has not been so with propagation of Islam by those who wish to convert the world to Islam. The jihadists want to force everyone in the world into Islamic faith and they believe that those who do not accept should be eliminated, killed.

Islam as represented by the majority of Muslims in the world is practiced in totalitarianism. In Iran, people of other religious views are crammed into jail while others have been killed. Yousef Nadarkhani, an Iranian house church pastor was hounded into the Iranian court on charges of 'apostasy'. He was convicted and sentenced to death. His sin of apostasy is that the 32-year-old pastor born to Muslim parents converted to Christianity at the age of nineteen. Apostasy by the definition of the Iranian prosecutor included having Muslim parents or ancestors but not embracing the Islamic faith. The Iranian Supreme Court overturned the judgment but asked the accused pastor to denounce his Christian faith. Not many faithful born-again Christians would renounce their faith in Christ. Pastor Nadarkhani has remained in prison since October 2009, constantly under the fear of death.

Amnesty International, in its public statement of August 31, 2011 said: "Members of some Iran's religious minorities also remain held as prisoners of conscience, such as seven Baha'i leaders serving 20-year prison sentences imposed for alleged "espionage", which they deny, and Pastor Yousef Nadarkhani, a Christian whose death sentence for "apostasy" was overturned, but who remains in prison awaiting a review of his case, which could see the death sentence re-imposed."[75]

And this is the trend in most Muslim dominated nations of the world. Christian Solidarity Worldwide, a Christian organization working for religious freedom through advocacy and human rights, in the pursuit of justice, makes press releases on the violence against innocents mostly in Islamic and Communist countries. According to its chief executive officer, Mervyn Thomas, notable countries among focus of the organization are Turkey, Cuba, Bulgaria, Algeria, Egypt, Iran, Nigeria, Pakistan, China, North Korea, and Indonesia.[76]

Most people particularly in America who are not Muslims but argue for Islam simply do not understand the issue. The argument has always been that Islam is peaceful, and that the problem is with the fundamentalists among people of Islamic faith. But today, it is difficult to know the difference between the fundamentalist and the peaceful Muslim. And it is not the fault of the people who find it difficult to separate them, because the Muslims who do not follow the peaceful doctrine are in the majority. The peaceful minority are also sympathetic to the violent majority not necessarily because they believe in them but for their personal safety and survival.

We all therefore are in coercion, and an effort to separate between fundamentalist and peace-loving Muslim may be at the peril of the victim. No doubt, there are peace-loving Muslims in Pakistan, Afghanistan, Iran, or Iraq. The peace-loving Muslims do not speak against the acts of violence perpetrated in the name of Islam because doing so will be considered an act of disloyalty and could be met with death. The violent fundamentalists are powerful within the Muslim societies and whatever they do in the name of the religion must be accepted.

Also, the political leaders in the Islamic nations have embraced religious fundamentalism to keep their hold on power even when they have nothing to offer their people. The despots in most Islamic nations of the world care less about the economy or welfare of the people but hide under the cover of religion for the sympathy of the populace. They maintain their rule over the majority by foisting their religious beliefs on the people, indoctrinating them and making them subservient to their own self-interests. The 2011 uprising and revolts against some of the Islamic leaders of the world is evidence that these leaders are without the fear of God. They were merely engaged in political religion while godlessness was visible in their governance.

These leaders are often not in obedience to the teachings of Islam but force same on the people for political interest. In Nigeria, during the regime of a former governor of a state in the north of the country, a citizen's hand was ordered amputated by Sharia (Islamic law) because he was found guilty of stealing a goat. The governor using religion for political interest believed he was demonstrating in his governance the principles of Islamic law. The same governor after his tenure, was found wanting in various cases of corruption, and outright stealing of government's fund. He evaded sharia justice, an outright double standard. God is a God of justice and is no respecter of any person.

What to do about the Fundamentalists?

God commanded Christians to love all people, including the Islamic fundamentalists. We should however condemn acts of violence and intolerance. Christians are also advised to be prepared for the challenges posed by acts of intolerance while we pray for the people to change. Jesus told His disciples to be wise as serpents but gentle in their dealings as doves (Matthew 6:10). The prophetic utterance about the birth of Ishmael is very instructive for Christians. The angel told Hagar, his mother, that there would be no peace between the child and his brothers and other people.

The people who argue that the current Islamic fundamentalists are isolated cases are lacking in knowledge. The path of hostility that the Islamic fundamentalists are following today is not different from the prophecy of old on Ishmael. Hostility by the Muslims cannot be resolved by ordinary human intellect. The appropriate solution can only be from God. Godlessness in our society will only continue to aggravate the situation. No society that neglects God will prosper. An antidote to the menace is closeness to God in words, prayers, and deeds so that such agents of violence will always be exposed before they do damage to the society.

As a matter of fact, no area of our lives, Islamic fundamentalist issue inclusive, can be successfully handled without the intervention of God. And those who have reduced the issues of Islamic religious extremism to politics should be careful because political power cannot handle religious fundamentalists where they exist. Those who also think appeasing the Islamic extremists would stop them from wrecking havoc on society as they do now had better rethink. Our human ideas and methods to solve these problems have not helped; rather we are daily witnessing an intense situation all over the world. Taking God away from our governance is therefore exposing us to more troubles.

We require leaders who embrace the wisdom and knowledge of God in their governance, which would help to restore peace to our nation. We may engage Muslim fundamentalists but our engagement must be purposeful, accompanied with the fear of God to change their hearts and possibly get them to buy into the principles of peace and love laid down by the life of our Lord Jesus Christ. The current style of engagement with Islamic fundamentalists without considering the spiritual aspects of the situation makes our people vulnerable to their violent acts. The point is that while we show love by accommodating all people, we cannot leave our doors wide open for someone who is showing signs of violence for whatever reason.

Thoughts

Ironically, religion should be a unifying factor in the world because it is seeking after God. But Satan is always quick to turn every good cause to destroy the peace of the world. He has used issues of religion to cause disharmony among the creations of God. Religious fundamentalism is evil and should be fought by all godly individuals on earth. The Creator of the earth, who should be the primary focus of religion, says: "Do I take any pleasure in the death of the wicked…

Rather; am I not pleased when they turn from their ways and live?" (Ezekiel 18:23).

There is something fundamentally wrong with religious views that destroy human lives that God created.

CHAPTER 5

THE WEST, ISRAEL, AND THE ARAB NATIONS

Blessed is the nation whose God is the Lord,
the people he chose for his inheritance.
—Psalm 33:12

IN MAY 2010, Faisal Shahzad, a thirty-one-year-old Pakistani immigrant, built a propane-and-gasoline bomb. On a busy Saturday night, he drove it in an SUV to Times Square in New York, with the intention of detonating the bomb to kill Americans. By providence, security agents discovered the plan before he could hatch it and he was arrested by the FBI.

Shahzad was taken to court in New York on October 5, 2010, and found guilty as charged. He was sentenced to life in prison. The judge, US District Judge Miriam Goldman Cedarbaum, told Shahzad to spend some of his time in prison thinking about whether the Koran directed him to kill lots of people.

In his response to the court verdict, Shahzad said:

Brace yourselves, because the war with Muslims has just begun, consider me the first droplet of the blood that will follow. We are only Muslims trying to defend our religion, people, homes and land, but if you call us terrorists, then we are proud terrorists and we will keep on terrorizing you until you leave our lands and people at peace.[77]

Usually when terrorism is challenged, the terrorist gives the impression that the battle against terrorism is a fight against the Islamic faith. Young people like Faisal grow up convinced that the issue at stake is that of religion and that of defense of land. The challenge for world leaders is to clear the misunderstanding among the new generation that has put the world in jeopardy. And this is why we require godly leaders who depend on God for wisdom to face the challenges.

The Western nations have traditionally been perceived as having a good relationship with Israel, and being against the Arabs, based on religious views. But America, Britain, France, and other European countries do not support Israel based on their mutual religious views. After all, not all Jews are Christians, and some Arabs are Christians. Past decisions among countries of the world have been made based on political and economic interests rather than religion, but the perception persists in some parts of the world and in particular among the new generations of Muslim Arabs that the powers in the West support the Jews against them.

After the September 11, 2001 terrorist attack against America, President Bush said that the war against terrorism was neither against the Arabs nor the Muslims. His opinion was supported by other politicians of the West. But the terrorist leaders continued to draw religion into their actions because that was the easiest way to gain the sympathy of the people. They appear to have achieved their goal because most terrorists are protected in countries like Pakistan and Afghanistan due to a sense of loyalty among people and their religions.

Effects of Past Foreign Relations

The foreign-affairs relations of Western nations give credence to the perception people have about us, even if the assertion is not true. Events in history tend to support their wrong perception.

Bernard Lewis, in his book *The Crisis of Islam*, wrote about the events of 1918. He said:

In 1918, the Ottoman sultanate, the last of the great Muslim empires, was finally defeated—its capital, Constantinople occupied, its sovereign held captive, and much of its territory partitioned between the victorious British and French Empires. The Arab-speaking former Ottoman provinces of the Fertile Crescent were divided into three new entities, with new names and frontiers. Two of them, Iraq and Palestine, were under British Mandate; the third, under the name Syria, was given to the French. Later, the French subdivided their mandate into two, calling one part Lebanon and retaining the name Syria for the rest.[78]

Palestine, Syria, and Lebanon, the West Bank, Jordan, and Israel are at the center of the crisis in the Middle East. Early colonization, followed by the struggle between the West and the East, the cold war of capitalism and communism, tend to build up the misunderstandings and conflicts around the world and in the Middle East. It also resulted in the level of terrorism that has enveloped the world.

The perception appears difficult to change because the environment has been taken over by diverse interests, including the religious politicians. The conflict in the Middle East, which has defied any solution, has stressed nations beyond limits, and because of lack of the knowledge of God in the handling of the issues, no one seems to be able to control the unimaginable destruction.

Israel in World Affairs

The father of the Jews was a man named Jacob [the son of Isaac, the son of Abraham]. God changed his name to Israel when Jacob wrestled with Him in a trance. God was pleased with Jacob because he stood by his faith to receive blessings from the Lord. The name Israel means "one who overcomes."

The Bible says:

Then the man said, "Let me go, for it is daybreak." But Jacob replied, "I will not let you go unless you bless me." The man asked him, "What is your name?" "Jacob," he answered. Then the man said, "Your name will no longer be Jacob, but Israel, because you have struggled with God and with humans and have overcome."

—Genesis 32:27–28

The change of Jacob's name was a great moment in the history of the world. The Jews as they are known today came into world focus. Israel, a nation with rich history, can therefore not be mentioned without the mention of the name of God. The Jews' yesterday, today, and their future have much to do with God and their fortune has always been tied to their relationship with the God of Israel.

It is an irony therefore to see the new generations of Jewish leaders handling their issues, political or economic, without considering the importance of God, the reason for failure in all the efforts to resolve the crisis in their land.

Israelis' Return to the Promised Land

The Jews have been through many turbulent times as a nation. Their disobedience to God has usually led them to defeat, making them captives and often forcing them into exile. They were slaves in Egypt until they were led by Moses, and later Joshua, to the Promised Land. They fought several nations, mostly Arab countries that occupied their homeland while they were exiled. They incurred the wrath of many groups, particularly those who sympathized with the Palestinians who were forced out of Israeli land (Canaan) by the Jews when they returned from exile.

It is the opinion of some that the Israelis could no longer lay claim to the land of their possession because of their long absence resulting from many exiles. Again, these are arguments not properly researched, or which are based on the usual godlessness in society. Those who subscribe to this idea may have not read history, or they consider such history as mere religion. This ignorance can only aggravate the bad situation.

God made an unbreakable covenant with Abraham, the patriarch of the Jews. The Lord said to him, "Lift up your eyes from where you are and look north and south, east and west. All the land that you see I will give to you and your offspring forever" (Genesis 13:14–15). This is the land that is being disputed today in the Middle East. The problem is that we treat God as if He does not exist and we have not been able to explain Him away.

Israeli Nation: Implication of US Recognition

In 1947, the United Nations General Assembly drafted Resolution 181, terminating the British mandate to partition the territory of Palestine into two states, Jewish and Arab. The resolution enabled the Jews to return to the Promised Land.

On November 29, the resolution was adopted by thirty-three countries (fifty-nine percent), mostly Eastern Europe and the United States. Thirteen countries (twenty-three percent) were opposed, mostly in the Middle East and Asia. Ten countries, including China and Great Britain, did not vote, and one country, Thailand, was not present.

In May of 1948, President Truman declared recognition of the State of Israel, making the United States of America the first country in the world to do so. This declaration met with severe opposition from US citizens. Some feared that supporting the Jewish state would harm relations with the Muslim world. Because oil and gas, the main sources of energy in the world, are in great supply in the Muslim countries of Saudi Arabia, Libya, and others, they feared such declaration would jeopardize American relationship with these countries and limit access to Middle Eastern oil.

The prompt recognition of Israel as a nation in 1948 by the United States of America, the most powerful country of the world, was a major boost for a new independent state but not to the pleasure of the Arab world. However, the position of America in the community of nations could not be easily ignored by all, including those not favorably disposed to it.

Was Truman's decision based on religion? The president was simply a godly man. Godliness surpasses religion. Though he alone knows why he took such a step, I believe his decision was on a good reason. Besides the fact that it was a fact of history that Canaan was the land given by God, the Landlord of the world, to the Jews, the president must have been mindful of the covenant of God with the Jews. He was careful not to regard God's words as mere religion. Only those who know God's word would act to escape His wrath. Here is the dilemma of the president, who was knowledgeable in the words of God:

God told Abraham, "I will bless those who bless you and whoever curses you I will curse: and all people on earth will be blessed through you" (Genesis 12:3).

President Harry S. Truman, a man who feared God, must have weighed the options between the benefits of oil and gas and obeying the will of God. It appeared he acted to protect America and the people from the curse and fierce anger of God in line with the oath he swore to. This is one of the reasons America is blessed.

Unfortunately, before the resolution to settle the two states (Jewish and Arab) could be implemented, war broke out. While the Jews declared their independence on May 14, 1948, five Arab states—Egypt, Iraq, Jordan, Lebanon, and Syria—attacked Israel. The crisis and its effects have remained in the world until today.

Foreign Policy Design

Foreign policy is usually designed to promote cooperation between nations of the world for mutual political and economic benefits. The policies are framed to consider the national interests of all countries. In theory, at least, interaction among the nations is evaluated and monitored to maximize benefits of multilateral cooperation.

No nation can be self-sufficient; one reason why a nation would further its interests through peaceful cooperation with other countries. When a foreign policy is good, the relationship can blossom because everyone is happy and value is added to the lives of the citizens. But this is not always the case; diverse situations often occur in relationships between different nations because of the unique backgrounds of the people. The makers of foreign policies, therefore, should consider those peculiarities in order to make positive changes for the well-being of all the people.

Nations that have suffered deprivations in the past as a result of slow development require assurance from developed nations. Even when there appears to have been mistakes in the past, the leading nations of the world should allay the fear of the less developed nations that such disadvantages will not be allowed to occur again. The engagement of these poor nations by the developed countries should not only be transparent but must be seen as such by the people. The suspicions resulting from past relationships will, however, always be a problem until an honest engagement over time is sustained. With such reassurance, the aggrieved nations of the world may be convinced that this new engagement is for mutual benefits.

However, the condition of man's sinful heart militates against the attainment of this objective of achieving mutual trust among nations of the world. The planners of foreign policies usually do not consider the important issue of common interest; rather, the interests of the planning nation are considered as priority. In addition, the individuals responsible for formulating the guidelines try to weave their individual interests into the planning document. The result is an arrangement that does not protect the interests of all but rather the selfish interests of a few.

Self-serving foreign policies do not promote understanding, because other nations feel exploited. For example, America is the leading advocate of democracy in the world. But the democratic nation's engagement of some world dictators and leaders, like Hosni Mubarak of Egypt, former president of Pakistan Pervez Musharraf, and others, gave the impression to the world that there is no sincerity in the fight for democracy. It appears it is an issue of play when it suits.

The revolt in the Middle Eastern countries of Syria and Egypt, and also some African countries by their citizens against their leaders at the turn of this decade has exposed the insincerity of such foreign policies. The people see democratic nations as hypocrites who only preach democracy but are willing to deal with dictators so long as their interests are served.

As long as international relationships are predicated on only what we can get from others, such efforts will end in bitterness and war.

Ideological Differences

The West and the East have engaged in many serious conflicts in their competition to have the greatest political and economic impact on other nations of the world, especially in Africa, the Middle East, and Asia. The goal has been to spread their ideological views and style of government across the world. The West wanted to ensure democracy; the East, socialism and communism. In doing so, it is believed they will also have good access to trade and economic benefits.

The struggle for influence in world affairs has therefore resulted in these powerful nations backstabbing each other in their quest to gain access and control in various parts of the world. The decades of cold war between the West and the East, particularly the Soviet Union and the United States of America, was not only an issue of ideological differences but also the level of influence each was able to have in the nations of the world. The Cold War and the way it was handled over the years aggravated the suspicions most Arab nations had about the super powers of the West and the East in domination of world affairs.

This perception was created from wrong information that both the West and the East sent out about themselves in each one's attempt to present the other in a bad light in order to have an upper hand politically and economically.

Osama Bin Laden

Osama bin Laden, the official arrowhead of world terrorism, bought into suspicion early in his life that the developed nations of the world only care for their national/nations' interest. He had lost his father in 1967 at the age of ten, and was thereafter sent to Broumanna High School in Beirut, Lebanon by his family to continue his education.

Before he completed his schooling, war broke out in Lebanon. Forced to leave the country he loved due to the fighting that devastated the nation, he returned to Saudi Arabia a sad man. The suspicion in bin Laden grew as he understood that the war that broke out in Lebanon was the handiwork of the West in an attempt to promote the interest of the Jews in the Middle East and also to destroy the Islamic religion.

In 1975 bin Laden returned to Saudi Arabia with the belief that the super powers were responsible for the destruction of his beloved home country, Lebanon. The seed of discord was promoted by the super powers themselves, who thought they were outdoing each other but unknowingly created monsters that would be very difficult to control.

In Saudi Arabia, bin Laden embraced Dr. Sheikh Abdullah Yusuf Azzam, an Islamic scholar and teacher at King Abdul Aziz University in Jeddah. Dr. Azzam was an influential Palestinian Sunni Islamic scholar and theologian who preached in favor of defensive jihad by Muslims to help the Afghan *mujahedeen* against the Soviet Union. He influenced bin Laden and motivated him to fight any "heathen" nation of "infidels" who would invade and occupy a Muslim country.

The invasion of Afghanistan by the Soviet Union in 1978 was therefore a turning point for the young bin Laden. He saw the Soviet

Union's actions as an affront against Islam and determined to defend his religion. He recruited persons of like mind and waged war to resist the Soviet army. His leadership was hailed among the Islamic world. Bin Laden easily mobilized people to resist the Soviets. All over the world, particularly in the Arab nations and Africa, young men enlisted in the war. Recruitment and training camps were full and active.

Adam Robinson captures this scenario in his book *Bin Laden: Behind the Mask of the Terrorist*. Robinson wrote, "Outrage of the soviet invasion immediately attracted hundreds of Arabs and Muslims from around the world, vowing to protect Islamic land."[79]

According to Robinson, in February 1980, the Afghan *mujahedeen* group, who were in the forefront of the resistance against the Soviets, printed propagandas meant to sensitize the people of Afghanistan on the war against Soviets who occupied a Muslim land and to attract more support for the war. The leaflets contained the following wording:

Do not accept the orders of the infidels, wage jihad against them.... The Muslim people and the mujahideen of Afghanistan, with the sublime cry of "Allah o Akbar" ["God is great"], will bring down their iron fist on the brainless head of the infidel and Communist government....

Mujahideen Muslims, remember that our weapons are the weapons of faith. These are the strongest and most effective weapons in the world. Even the most modern weapons will be unable to resist ours. That is why, if we resist Soviet imperialism's infidel government we will be victorious, and it will suffer a crushing defeat....

The only path to happiness is faith in the jihad and martyrdom.[80]

Osama bin Laden appeared to be an intelligent man who could have been an asset to society. Instead, he spent the better part of his life in deserts and trenches, with no freedom. His potential was wasted. Most of the world wishes he had not been born. Bin Laden had been on the wanted lists of the United States since the 9/11 attack on America. He was believed to be behind most terrorist attacks on Americans and American interests. He was killed on Sunday, May 1, 2011 by the Navy SEALs of the United States Military "in a compound in Abbottabad, Pakistan."[81]

Afghanistan's Soviet Invasion and the Mistake of the West

The contributions of the Western world, particularly the United States, towards the build-up of getting the Soviets out of Afghanistan was done without considering its ripple effect on the world. The West condemned the Soviet invasion. Their condemnation further strained the tenuous relationship that had existed between the Soviet Union and America. But not only that, actions taken in furtherance of getting Soviets out of Afghanistan become a source of security breaches.

The Western nations subsidized a volunteer army to fight the Soviet Union. Their aid included recruitment of troops and training for the soldiers. Schools and camps were operated in centers throughout the West. Little did these democratic nations know that among those they were training were members of a group of Islamic fundamentalists who called themselves Mekhtab al Khadamat (MAK). MAK later became al Qaeda, the world's most dreaded terrorist group.

In 1991, when the Soviet Union withdrew troops from Afghanistan, the graduates of these schools and camps had no other jobs to occupy them. They toppled the governments of many African countries, using state resources to further terrorist operations. Trained terrorists are now scattered all over the world, and the West has become the victim of the terrorism they helped fund.

The fight the West had against communism cannot compare to the acts of international terrorism under the guise of Islamic jihad. The communist-capitalist Cold War was well defined, the players were known, and the war was fought within the confines of law. Leaders often found themselves at negotiating tables. But terrorism has no definition, no visible players, no rules, and no negotiations.

Middle East Resolution

The way the world has always treated God as if He does not exist in the handling of issues is also the bane of the problem today as we grapple with the crisis in the Middle East. Since the Arab-Israeli war in 1948, the Middle East has remained a hot spot in international diplomacy. This conflict has dominated world affairs more than any other. It has been exploited by individuals to justify terrorist attacks all over the world.

Many pragmatic steps have been initiated by world leaders and organizations, such as the United Nations, to find a solution to the Arab-Israeli conflict. Several American presidents, Jimmy Carter, Bill Clinton, and George W. Bush, etc., have brought Israeli and Arab leaders to the negotiation table. But none of the efforts have considered the relevance of God, and have therefore not succeeded.

President Jimmy Carter in particular had a genuine passion for peace in the Middle East. He made numerous visits to the Jewish nation and to the Palestinians, the main opponents of the Jews. He wrote books on practical solutions to the Middle East crisis. During his time as president of the United States, he rallied leaders in the Middle East, including the president of Egypt and the king of Jordan, to broker peace between the Jews and their Arab neighbors.

In September 1978, Jimmy Carter initiated thirteen days of secret negotiations between Israeli Prime Minister Menachem Begin and Egyptian President Anwar El Sadat. The agreement which was signed on March 26, 1979 with all hopes to end the Arab/Israeli conflicts did not make much impact. Mr. Sadat was assassinated on October 7, 1981, two years after the agreement by members of Islamist nationalists associated with the Muslim Brotherhood under the name of Islamic jihad.

It appears, however, that Carter's and other past leaders' zeal for peace, though genuine, was not fruitful because it did not consider the history and the importance of the interventions of God in this issue that has defied all known human solutions. A serious consideration of the history of the Jews, as recorded in the Bible, perhaps could have given proper understanding as to the limitations of man and woman to broker peace between Israel and her neighbors. But that has not been the case.

President Carter expressed in his book *We Can Have Peace in the Holy Land: A Plan that Will Work*:

> Although President Gerald Ford was known as a friend of Israel, neither he nor his predecessors had considered a strong move toward a comprehensive peace agreement. Instead of the gradualist approach

being pursued by him and Secretary of State Kissinger, I argued during the general election campaign that a "limited settlement, as we have seen in the past, still leaves unresolved the underlying threat to Israel. A common comprehensive settlement is needed—one that will end the conflict between Israel and its neighbors once and for all."[82]

Decades after Mr. Carter left office, the world is still far from restoring peace in the Middle East. Rather, the issue has become more complicated.

Presidents Bill Clinton and George W. Bush also played a role in the Middle East crisis with a view to finding an enduring solution to the problem. Their efforts have been continued by the current American president, Barack Obama. But no visible progress has been achieved. Rather, the world continues having trouble from the Middle East.

The fact that peace meetings and initiatives have not achieved much is an indication that something is missing in all the negotiations, and that is 'God'. The understanding of the history of the Jews and the relevance of God is fundamental to the resolution of the Middle East crisis.

Peace can be achieved in Israel and the Middle East, but not on human terms. It can only be on the terms of God. God holds the key to the determination of the crisis. It will continue to be fruitless if in our efforts we think we can make peace in this circumstance without the interventions of God. And unfortunately, the leaders appear not to believe that God does exist, and when they have some convictions of His existence, they do not want to be seen mentioning God for political reasons because God is associated with religion, which politicians want to avoid.

The issue is too complex for the human methods being used. Many issues involved are too hot to handle. There is the contentious issue of the city of Jerusalem, the eternal capital of Israel; Also many other historical cities, like Bethlehem, where Jesus was born. To ask the Jews to give up these places is like asking Israel to lose her identity. But it is the rationalizing of some individuals that Israel should give up the land if the action would bring peace in the Middle East. Good as these opinions are, the decision of God overrides any human idea.

The solution to the problems of Israel and her neighbors does not therefore lie in the White House or with the United Nations. The answer to the Middle East crisis is with God. I, however, have two suggestions: first, what world leaders and peace brokers can do, which is temporary; second, what only God can do, which is ultimate.

The Temporary Human Solution

Israel and the land of Canaan came into being by the word and promise of God. The land in dispute in the Middle East was therefore the creation of God.

> When Abram was ninety-nine years old, the Lord appeared to him and said, "I am God Almighty walk before me faithfully and be blameless. Then I will make my covenant between me and you and will greatly increase your numbers."

> Abram fell facedown, and God said to him, "As for me, this is my covenant with you: You will be the father of many nations. No longer will you be called Abram; your name will be Abraham, for I have made you a father of many nations. "I will make you very fruitful; I will make nations of you, and kings will come from you. I will establish my covenant as an everlasting covenant between me and you and your descendants after you for the generations to come, to be your God and the God of your descendants after you. The whole land of Canaan, where you now reside as a foreigner, I will give as an everlasting possession to you and your descendants after you; and I will be their God."
>
> —Genesis 17:1–8

This covenant of God with Abraham cannot be broken by man. And there is no evidence in history that God has changed His mind. We therefore need to take God seriously. We seldom remember that God is a higher Being whose words are law and none of us can disobey His words without serious consequences. We are ordinary clay that has temporary existence on earth, but God and His words last forever. The Bible says, "All people are like grass, and all their glory is like the flowers of the field; the grass withers and the flowers fall, but the word of the Lord endures forever" (1 Peter 1:24).

God is supreme and He does not defer to us on any issues unless He chooses to. David reminds us that "the earth is the LORD's, and everything in it, the world, and all who live in it" (Psalm 24:1). When God speaks, we should reverence His words and take him seriously.

All parties to the conflict in the Middle East should therefore appreciate the importance of God and His covenant in regards to these issues. Suffice to say, God is above all leaders and kings in the world; America, Israel, and the Arabs should defer to Him on all decisions affecting the land. The resolution of God cannot be faulted.

The world, including the Arabs, should accept Israel as a nation and a fact of history which cannot be broken. That appreciation would enable Israelis and Arabs to tolerate one another, bearing in mind that God has the ultimate power. Both parties could live together in peace if they humbly accepted the facts and respected them. The hearts of the people in Israel and Palestine should eschew the bitterness of the past and respect human life and peaceful coexistence.

Also, the current and past Jewish leaders have not helped the crisis because of their failure to recognize and put in proper perspectives the God of Israel. That God remains relevant today, tomorrow, and forever in the affairs of Israel and the Middle East as well as in the entire world. Peace will be an illusion until the Jews find leaders who will take them back to the God of Israel.

As in the past, so also now, the situation in Israel is dependent on the people's relationship with God. When they disobeyed Him in the past, they were punished. Sin accounted for most of the afflictions and forced exiles their forefathers went through. But when they repented, God had mercy on them and delivered them. He will do the same today.

The current travail of the Jews is not new. Attempts to destroy or exterminate them date back to the time of David and Goliath. But the Jewish leaders of old did not depend on negotiation with enemies and on mere arms and ammunitions. They relied on the power of the Almighty. They received instructions from God through the prophets who were raised from among them. These prophets gave the nation's leaders divine direction, and it worked. The God of Israel never failed them.

For example, during the reign of King Jehoshaphat between 870 and 48 BC, a great army of Ammonites and Moabites tried to destroy the Jewish nation. When Jehoshaphat received the security report, he feared. The king and a panic-stricken people turned to God and prayed for divine help. They knew that He alone could deliver them. They sought God's help, and God sent His prophet Jahaziel to assure the army of Israel that they would be victorious.

"Then the Spirit of the Lord came on Jahaziel son of Zechariah, the son of Benaiah, the son of Jeiel, the son of Mattaniah, a Levite and descendant of Asaph, as he stood in the assembly. He said: 'Listen, King Jehoshaphat and all who live in Judah and Jerusalem! This is what the Lord says to you: do not be afraid or discouraged because of this vast army. For the battle is not yours, but God's'" (2 Chronicles 20:14–15).

The invading armies fought each other, and Israel won without any physical combat. Thereafter, "for most of Jehoshaphat's long reign, Judah was at peace with its neighbors and enjoyed rising prosperity" (2 Chronicles 20:30).

The nation of Israel requires a leader who will call the people to reconcile with the God of Abraham, Isaac, and Jacob. If such a leader arose, there would be a monumental change in their political and economic fortune. The only hope for a new beginning for the nation Israel is for them to seek after God's heart. His compassion and love is always available to them. When Israel makes peace with God, her enemies will be at peace with her. The Bible says, "When the Lord takes pleasure in anyone's way, he causes their enemies to make peace with them" (Proverbs 16:7).

All believers in the Lord Jesus Christ are encouraged to pray for peace for the nation of Israel. The Lord commands it. "Pray for the peace of Jerusalem: may those who love you be secure'" (Psalm 122:6).

The Permanent Divine Solution

Besides the important issue of the covenant of God with Abraham, the founder of the Jewish nation, there are also subsequent documented prophecies in the Bible which outline what God intends to do with Israel and those who fight against them. These prophetic events will happen alongside the activities to end this current world. God has a definite program for the end of the world. Israel and her current travails is one of the central issues in the program for the end of the world.

The challenge here is that no one knows when the world will end; it is the exclusive prerogative of God. So we should make efforts to palliate the issues as the Lord gives us wisdom to do. This is the relevance of prayers, constantly asking God for directions in the management of the situation in the Middle East. Again, we can see the importance of godly leaders who would not disparage God, but reverence and depend on God for solutions. The permanent resolution is that of God.

Thoughts

Godlessness in society will continue to be a serious challenge towards the maintenance of the relationships of nations all over the world. Satan's job is to continuously get people into conflicts with one another. Conflicts are created through Satan's influence on people's hearts, resulting in human carnage and creation of fear. The roadmap to peace is to approach local and foreign relations with the fear of God. According to Paul Kengor, author of *God and Ronald Reagan*, Reagan approached American foreign policy with the understanding that only God, who made America great, could remove evil from other parts of the world.

Apostle Paul encouraged Christian believers to seek for peace always. He said, "Make every effort to live in peace with everyone and to be holy; without holiness no one will see the Lord" (Hebrews 12:14). We also have this hope that we will attain everlasting peace when the Lord Jesus Christ returns. When He comes, all conflicts will be gone. For now, we need to improve our relationships with our neighbors to reduce the level of suspicion in the world and to restore confidence in people so we can live a life of relative peace with one another. And we require God's presence in our interactions and relationships to be able to deal fairly with each other.

The world needs the presence of God to resolve conflicts.

CHAPTER 6

EDUCATION: A PINNACLE FOR RESOLVING CONFLICTS

This book of the law shall not depart from your mouth,
but you shall meditate therein day and night, that you may
observe to do according to all that is written in it; for then
you shall make your way prosperous and then you shall have
good success.
—Joshua 1:8

THROUGHOUT HISTORY, EDUCATION has been the key to the success of human development. The acquisition of knowledge helps to stimulate and develop the mental and moral growth of a society. Education points to what a man is, what he is not, and what he is likely to become. It is a method of discovering self and the true meaning of life. Any society's character and culture is a direct product of the kind of education it is exposed to. Most governments in the world consider education as an important instrument of change.

Manu Goel, in his article "The Importance of Education," said, "Education has an immense impact on the human society. One can safely assume that a person is not in the proper sense till he is educated. In other words, man becomes a rational animal when he is educated."[83]

Education is meant to stimulate the mental and moral growth of a person. It should draw out the potential in an individual, which in turn enhances the well-being of society. Education gives people the correct direction in life. And our choice of education is important to the acquisition of God's knowledge and also reduces the godlessness in society.

We struggle daily with adulterated education, where truth is mixed with half-truths and falsehoods. This bastardized knowledge, rather than proffering solutions, adds to the conflicts on earth, because any knowledge that does not acknowledge God, rather than helping society, will add to the world's problem.

What Manner of Education

At the beginning of creation, God commended education to the first family on earth, Adam and Eve, by giving them instructions on what they should do and what they must not do. That knowledge guided their relationship with each other and with God, and it kept them out of trouble. But Satan visited them and cunningly attacked the knowledge God had imparted to them. The perversion of that knowledge led the world's first couple to disobey God. As a result of that disobedience, the human race lost its direct connection with the Creator. Man and woman were no longer guided by the pure knowledge that is from God which is able to sustain the society.

A proper education develops the total person—soul, body, and moral values. It also reflects the importance of the person's relationship to his neighbor, the society, and ultimately with God, his Creator.

The aim of early education often from childhood was to instill discipline and morals for the good of the people. There was no difference between education and morality. The resolution of conflicts, personal or corporate, within a society was predicated on the level of education its people had acquired. When the Lord Jesus walked the earth, He was known to be a great teacher not only in words but in actions. At one of his teachings, it was recorded how people were amazed. The Bible says, "When Jesus had finished saying these things, the crowds were amazed at his teaching, because he taught as one who had authority, and not as their teachers of the law" (Matthew 7:28-29).

The anchor for good education is the fear of God. "Now all has been heard; here is the conclusion of the matter: Fear God and keep his commandment, for this is the duty of all mankind" (Ecclesiastes 12:13).

Human attempts to forge understandings in the face of conflict have not succeeded because they were not accompanied by the fear of God. "There is a way that appears to be right, but in the end it leads to death" (Proverbs 14:12). Education is the source of support for human relationships with one another and with God.

Former US president Dwight D. Eisenhower corroborated this thought when he was chancellor of Columbia University in New York. He disagreed with Columbia University scholars who believed that the sign of a good education was mere scholarship. Eisenhower believed that scholarship without human virtue makes no sense.

Stephen E. Ambrose, in his book *Eisenhower: Soldier and President,* captured Eisenhower's encounter with university scholars thus:

> Columbia was an outstanding university with a brilliant faculty composed of highly sophisticated specialists who were dedicated to their research. They regarded Eisenhower as hopelessly naïve. When one scholar told Eisenhower that "we have some of America's most exceptional physicists, mathematics, chemists and engineers," Eisenhower asked if they were also exceptional Americans. The scholar, confused, mumbled that Eisenhower did not understand—they were research scholars. "Dammit," Eisenhower shot back, "What good are exceptional physicists...exceptional anything, unless they are exceptional Americans?" He added that every student who came to Columbia must leave it first a better citizen and only secondarily a better scholar.[84]

Education is the Way to Truth

Knowledge is the practical understanding of issues, the whole body of truth and facts, connoting comprehensiveness and profundity. No man can achieve success beyond the level of knowledge he possesses. He is limited by how much education he has acquired. God supports man's search for knowledge, as He said in the Bible, "My people are destroyed for lack of knowledge" (Hosea 4:6).

In the search for knowledge, we find the truth. It is written, "Then you will know the truth, and the truth will set you free" (John 8:32). The truth sets the human soul, heart, and mind at liberty from the conflicts that endanger humankind. Solomon opined that knowledge has the advantage of preserving the life of its possessor (Ecclesiastes 7:2). But some people do not understand what freedom entails. True freedom is not doing what you want to do but doing what you ought to do. And this kind of freedom can only be attained with the acquisition of the knowledge of God.

Knowledge without the fear of God often adds to human problems on earth. The medical profession was initiated to protect human lives, yet some of its members have terminated lives in the name of legal abortion. Why? The plausible reason is that the moral ingredients that make such knowledge useful have been removed.

Accountants, who have the social responsibility of keeping accurate books of financial records, have sometimes criminally altered and falsified records and have added to the economic problems of society because they acquired intellect and not education.

Albert Mohler, president of Southern Baptist Theological Seminary said, "Martin Luther once warned Christians with these words: 'I greatly fear that schools for higher learning are wide gates to hell if they do not diligently teach the Holy Scripture and impress them on the young folk.' The great Reformer knew of the importance of Christian education and the development of Christian thinkers, but his great fear of schools as potential "wide gates to hell" is all too justified."[85]

A society can only work properly and achieve its purposes when its intellectuals acknowledge God and operate in the fear of God. Education is way into the truth only to the extent in which it mixes with the fear of God. Education without God is adulterated and it brings calamities such as stealing, bribery, corruption, and other wrongdoings, commonly referred to as white-collar crimes, perpetrated by people with impure knowledge.

Violent crime is a great distress to any society. No economy can survive in an atmosphere of shameful acts. The downturn in the world economy today has its root in the wickedness of society. Resources that could have been employed to enhance the social and economic lives of the people are channeled to fight this menace. We have the added trouble of those who are saddled with the responsibilities to fight the evils but also lack the moral education to do a good job. They therefore often lose the war because they are equally guilty of similar crimes. This accounts for why the world is not getting any better.

America's Great Education Experience

The United States of America has one of the best educational systems in the world. It was built on the Word of God. America did not become powerful and prosperous because of its size or population alone but by its good beginning of men who cherished the instruction of their Creator. China and the former Soviet Union are also blessed with size and population, but America towers above them all. The American nation has been distinct in its achievements over many decades because it is a society whose education was built on the knowledge of the Most High God.

Former President Ronald Reagan said, "We've come a long way since those first settlers reached these shores, asking nothing more than the freedom to worship God. They asked that He would work His will in our daily lives, so America would be a land of fairness, morality, justice, and compassion."[86]

The early settlers of America considered not only their mental and physical development but also the knowledge of God. They believed that education without moral principles is ineffective in raising any society. This was proved in the actions of the Pilgrims and the Puritans, the early educators in America.

The Pilgrims and Puritans labored to impart a powerful education that would liberate the mind and soul of the nation. They knew how critical the knowledge of God was to the hearts and minds of the people. They recognized that the only way to build a good country was to instill the fear of God in the hearts of its people. Hence the Bible was a high priority in their curriculum. They believed the Word of God to be indispensable to the success and effectiveness of education.

Edmund S. Morgan, in his book *The Puritan Family*, said about the Puritans: "They wrote hundreds of books explaining the exact conduct demanded by God in every human situation. They had, in fact, complete blueprints for a smooth, honest, civil life in family, church, and state, and they were willing to live in wilderness in order to build a society according to those blueprints…In other words, the Puritans came to New England not merely to save their souls but to establish a 'visible' kingdom of God, a society where outward conduct would be according to God's laws, a society where a smooth, honest, civil life would prevail in family, church and state."[87]

The Pilgrims' spirit was similar to the early apostles of Jesus Christ, who were committed to a life of consecration to the ministry of Jesus. In their obedience to the Word of God, the Pilgrims sought to perform their civic duties to their country and society. Whatever they did was done as unto the Lord, ensuring that their lives of witness for Christ were not destroyed.

For example, the first colony and first English democracy was created in the northern parts of Virginia in September 1620. The pact called the "Mayflower Compact" was signed, creating the colony. The following are in the signed compact: "In the name of God, Amen. We whose names are underwritten, the loyal subjects of our dread sovereign Lord King James, by the Grace of God of Great Britain, France, and Ireland King, Defender of the Faith, etc. Having undertaken, for the Glory of God and advancement of the Christian Faith and Honor of our King and Country, a Voyage to plant the First Colony in the Northern Parts of Virginia, do by these presents solemnly and mutually in the presence of God and of one another, Covenant and Combine ourselves together into a Civil Body politic, for our better ordering and preservation…."[88]

These two groups worked together to pass on basic moral knowledge to their children from the time they were born. They knew that every human is born with a sin nature, a condition of the human heart that does not regard God, and that this was the source of conflict in society. They therefore tried to give the child a foundation that would earn him or her a regenerated heart, which is a means of life sustenance.

Gordon S. Wood, professor of history at Brown University, wrote:

> The Puritans felt sure that children were born without a fear of God—indeed with an original sinfulness and an obstinate pride that resisted God. They and their stubborn wills, declared John Robinson,

the Pilgrims' minister, must "be broken and beaten down; so that the foundation of their education being laid in humility and tractableness," they could be taught a proper awareness of God by parents, clergy, and others.

The seventeenth-century Puritans were obsessed with their children, but they did not sentimentalize them. A severe regimen to arm them against the lures of the Devil included family prayers twice a day, daily Scripture readings, and repeated explanations of church sacraments. Most important was catechizing—a personal process of questions and answers that formed for colonial children the most constant and ever-present means of instruction in the faith.[89]

Importance of the Bible in Education

No other book on earth has been so fought and yet has remained relevant to society. The Bible was the ultimate resource book for the Pilgrims and the Puritans in the development of a solid foundation for education.

The book of books, the Bible, was the end and means of education for early Americans. Children learned letters and moral lessons from vivid tales and proverbs and absorbed the cadences of psalms and prayers. The epochal King James Version, new in 1611, remained the religious and cultural keystone in families like that of the Reverend John Atwood, nineteenth century Baptist minister and treasurer of New Hampshire.[90]

The issue of early education was so compelling for the Puritans that they promoted strict punishment for children's behavior resulting from a lack of moral discipline. Gordon S. Wood wrote:

"In the 1640s the government of Massachusetts Bay, realizing 'the great neglects in many parents and masters in training up their children in learning and labor,' empowered the local officials 'to take accompt from time to time of their parents and masters......concerning their calling and implement of their children...and to impose fines upon all those who refuse to render such accompt......'"

Virginia passed a similar law. In addition, Puritan Massachusetts declared parents and masters responsible for children's ability to read and understand the principles of religion and the capital laws of the country."[91]

Amy L. Matzat, in her article "Massachusetts Education Laws of 1642 and 1647," wrote:

"We see that it was during this period in Massachusetts that religious concerns (e.g., learning to read in order to read the Bible) laid the groundwork for modern education. Although it was a response to an ecclesiastical quest in the new world, it was adequately catalyzed and necessity eventually turned itself into education being conceptually pursued in and of itself in America. The early immigrants were paving the way toward a better educational system, one brick at a time."[92]

The early teachers and educators of this country were mainly clerics and priests who taught their students the importance of their personal existence, the existence of God, and the value of life.

Kay Kiser, a Ph.D research student at the University of Notre Dame–Indiana, wrote:

The Puritans formed the first formal school in 1635, called Roxbury Latin School, before the establishment of the first college in America, Harvard in Cambridge. Religion provided a stimulus and prelude for scientific thought. Of those Americans who were admitted into the scientific "Royal Society of London," the vast majority were New England Puritans.[93]

Kiser added:

The large number of people who ascribed to the life-style of the Puritans did much to firmly establish a presence on American soil. Bound together, they established a community that maintained a healthy economy, established a school system, and focused on an efficient eye on political concerns. The moral character of England and America were shaped in part by the words and actions of this strong group of Christian believers called the Puritans.[94]

Harvard University, the oldest college in the United States, was established sixteen years after the arrival of the Pilgrims at Plymouth. In the early days of the college, courses and curriculum were developed based on the English university model but consistent with the Puritan philosophy of the first colonists. Many of its graduates became ministers in Puritan congregations throughout New England. Harvard is regarded today as a citadel of knowledge. It has produced many great American leaders, including some presidents of the United States; namely, John Quincy Adams, John Adams, Theodore Roosevelt, Franklin Delano Roosevelt, Rutherford B. Hayes, John Fitzgerald Kennedy, and George W. Bush, Jr.

In Great Britain, the Church of England was responsible for most of the early schools up to the end of the nineteenth century, when free and compulsory education was introduced. The church therefore had the opportunity to instill education with the knowledge and fear of God. Britain became a world power that was able to colonize other nations through strong leadership knowledge.

One of the issues the Pilgrims had with Great Britain was the observance of Christian practices to the extreme, whereby anyone not practicing appropriately was punished by law. The Pilgrims considered good practice to be desirable, but acts of force were a violation of the people's rights to practice their religion.

Christianity as the official religion in Great Britain positively shaped the lives of the people. Intellectual leaders, such as Winston Churchill, passed through that great system and acquired knowledge with the fear of God, and this paved the path to greatness for their nations.

They affected other countries as well, particularly the developing nations. Their societies produced great men and women who went out as missionaries, inculcating moral values that successfully stamped out many demonic, ungodly, and primitive practices in those countries. They worked in rural communities, established schools, built hospitals and health centers, and created a society with high moral values. The peace that prevails in some parts of the world today can be traced to the work of early missionaries.

In some African nations, before the advent of Christian education, the birth of twin babies was regarded as evil. If a woman gave birth to twins, both babies were killed. When a king died, his servants were buried with him because the people believed that the deceased king would require the services of his aides in the afterlife. These evil practices were stopped when missionaries brought education to the people.

God Intended Education for Human Relationship

God armed Moses, His servant and leader of the Jewish exodus, with the code of conduct known as the Ten Commandments. This moral instruction would guide the Jews on their journey to the Promised Land and in their daily lives after they arrived there.

God called Moses to Mount Sinai, where He gave him the Ten Commandments (Exodus 19–20). The Ten Commandments were transcribed onto scrolls, which Moses instructed the people to memorize and meditate on daily. These commandments have since become the foundation for all good laws and governments all over the world. The American Constitution mirrors the Ten Commandments.

Toward the end of his life, Moses handed the baton of leadership to Joshua with strong advice on the importance of education. He said, "This book of the law shall not depart from your mouth; meditate on it day and night so that you may be careful to do everything in it. Then you will be prosperous and successful" (Joshua 1:8).

The Collapse of Education

Our society has continued to witness the killing and maiming of innocent persons because we have removed God from our education system. The social vices previously known only in irreverent societies are now common with us because of the liberal culture brought into our educational system by those whose hearts are occupied with the spirit of Satan.

Separation of church and state has been abused. You can separate religion from government, but you cannot separate people from their value systems. It is wrong to forbid people to practice their faith in public places simply because some do not agree with their beliefs. Government infringes on its citizens' liberty when it tells people they cannot pray, read the Bible, or practice their faith in a public domain. Wherever God is removed, all forms of wickedness are usually used to replace Him.

The misinterpretation of the "separation of church and state" has resulted in the destruction of the value system that the early settlers labored hard for. We are now mixing the knowledge passed on to us by our forefathers with ungodly culture. This has resulted in Americans living in fear at schools, on the streets, and even in their own homes.

Darrell Scott, who lost his daughter in the shooting spree at Columbine High School in Colorado on April 20, 1999, gave his testimony on May 27, 1999, before the House Judiciary Subcommittee. He said:

> Columbine was not just a tragedy—it was a spiritual event that should be forcing us to look at where the real blame lies. Much of the blame lies here in this room. Much of the blame lies behind the pointing fingers of the accusers themselves....
>
> I wrote a poem just four nights ago that expresses my feelings best. This was written way before I knew I would be speaking here today:
>
> > Your laws ignore our deepest needs.
> > Your words are empty air.
> > You've stripped away our heritage.
> > You've outlawed simple prayer.
> > Now gunshots fill our classrooms
> > And precious children die.
> > You seek for answers everywhere
> > And ask the question "Why?"
> > You regulate restrictive laws
> > Through legislative creed.
> > And yet you fail to understand
> > That God is what we need.[95]

In 2008, the mayor of Los Angeles, California, Antonio Villaraigosa, publicly expressed concern about the activities of gangs in his city. In his state address on April 14, 2008, the mayor signaled his determination to wage war against the breeding centers of gangs. He identified one of the sources as a lack of moral teachings for the children. He focused attention on redirecting the lives of children through proper and functional education early in their schools. He proposed a reform within the schools that would engage students and take them away from gangs.

The mayor addressed six risk factors associated with gang activities:

- Poor parental supervision
- Early childhood aggression
- Delinquent beliefs, including acceptance of antisocial behavior, guilt neutralization, and disengagement
- Negative life events
- Having peers or friends involved in delinquent and deviant behavior
- Commitment to street-oriented peers

The mayor did a great job identifying the risk factors. But the process of finding controls to mitigate the risks was lacking. His comprehensive program included recruiting more policemen on the streets of Los Angeles. But it failed to reeducate or reorient our misguided youth and adult population. Law officers have continued to confront gangs.

The mayor's methodology of school reformation was not sufficient to solve the problems. Regeneration of the heart cannot be accomplished by anything other than the Word of God, the Bible. And children will only recognize the evils in gangs when their hearts are transformed.

The Bible records the admonition of God to His people:

> Fix these words of mine in your hearts and minds; tie them as symbols on your hands and bind them on your foreheads. Teach them to your children, talking about them when you sit at home and when you walk along the road, when you lie down and when you get up. Write them on the doorframes of your houses and on your gates, so that your days and the days of your children may be many in the land the Lord swore to give your ancestors, as many as the days that the heavens are above the earth.
>
> —Deuteronomy 11:18–21

The antidote to society's menace is the return to the old foundations in which the American youths grew up with the words of God written boldly on their hearts. The current situation is pathetic; the psalmist said: "When the foundations are being destroyed, what can the righteous do?" (Psalm 11:3).

Paul warned the Romans about the continuous destruction of the knowledge of God among the generations. If the destruction was not stopped, society was going to become wicked and dead to anything upright. He said:

> For although they knew God, they neither glorified him as God nor gave thanks to him, but their thinking became futile and their foolish hearts were darkened. Although they claimed to be wise, they became fools and exchanged the glory of the immortal God for images made to look like a mortal human being and birds and animals and reptiles.

> Therefore God gave them over in the sinful desires of their hearts to sexual impurity for the degrading of their bodies with one another. They exchanged the truth about God for a lie, and worshiped and served created things rather than the Creator—who is forever praised. Amen.

> Because of this, God gave them over to shameful lusts. Even their women exchanged natural sexual relations for unnatural ones. In the same way the men also abandoned natural relations with women and were inflamed with lust for one another. Men committed shameful acts with other men, and received in themselves the due penalty for their error.

> Furthermore, just as they did not think it worthwhile to retain the knowledge of God, so God gave them over to a depraved mind, so that they do what ought not to be done. They have become filled with every kind of wickedness, evil, greed and depravity. They are full of envy, murder, strife, deceit and malice.

> They are gossips, slanderers, God-haters, insolent, arrogant and boastful; they invent ways of doing evil; they disobey their parents; they have no understanding, no fidelity, no love, no mercy. Although they know God's righteous decree that those who do such things deserve death, they not only continue to do these very things but also approve of those who practice them.
>
> —Romans 1:21–32

It appears our society and most nations of the world have reached this dangerous level of decadence. Our education is controlled with knowledge of sin. Sins have become acceptable in our society and backed with signed laws in the land. Has God given us up to do what we want to do? If this is the case, we are simply waiting for the ultimate judgment and the result cannot be less than destruction.

Hope for the Future

David, former king in Israel, recognized the importance of the Word of God in a person's life. He said, "How can a young person stay on the path of purity? By living according to your word. I seek you with all my heart; do not let me stray from your commands. I have hidden your word in my heart that I might not sin against you" (Psalm 119:9–11).

The only book that has consistently influenced the lives of people in the world in a positive way is the Bible. Former President George W. Bush attested to this when he told some clergymen he'd invited to the White House that the reason he was in the Oval Office was that he had faith in Christ. In his book *The Right Man: The Surprise Presidency of George W. Bush,* author David Frum said:

> In September 2002, Bush invited five religious leaders—three Christians, one Jewish, one Muslim—to meet with him in the Oval Office. He wanted them to know that the war on terror had not ended and that some of its hardest battles still lay ahead. Then he asked them to pray for him.
>
> "You know," he said, "I had a drinking problem. Right now I should be in a bar in Texas, not the Oval Office. There is only one reason that I am in the Oval Office and not in a bar. I found faith. I found God. I am here because of the power of prayer."[96]

Targeting young ones at school is the most effective thing we can do to reform our society and produce better future leaders and citizens who will run our society to stardom in the fear of God. Solomon says, "Train up a child in the way he should go; and when he is old, he will not depart from it" (Proverbs 22:6). Unfortunately, not many parents today are in touch with societal values. The schools, therefore, must teach not only academics but also issues of character and human integrity.

I believe we will return to the standards of our early leaders if we take the following steps:

- Develop a school system that instills discipline in students and provides a constructive, godly education
- Reach out to churches, other religious groups, civil and liberty groups, and other nonprofit organizations for input on school curriculum
- Put moral-building books like the Bible in school libraries

Paul testified to the value of the Bible. He said, "All Scripture is God-breathed and is useful for teaching, rebuking, correcting and training in righteousness, so that the servant of God may be thoroughly equipped for every good work" (2 Timothy 3:16–17).

Children will appreciate the Bible if it is imparted to them early in their lives. This will ensure that what God has done for His people throughout history can be passed on to the generations that follow.

The Christian communities in our nation should fight to restore books of the Bible to our public school library and also give easy access for our children to obtain and read the Bible as they grow up in the schools. Our continued laxity in fighting to get our children to be taught in the fear of God is helping to raise an army of opposition against the knowledge and fear of God in the nation. The children will always be occupied with something; if we do not make efforts to occupy them with the instructions from God's Word, they will be occupied with teachings on godlessness and sinfulness. If we continue to shape our young generations with disobedience to God, and unrighteousness, wickedness will take over our country and we will see no peace again.

Exploits in the old days' warfare was achieved with the use of guns and other deadly weapons of war. The greatest weapon of war Satan and his disciples use to destroy societies and nations today is the destruction of the school system. The system on which the future of the nation is dependent has been hijacked by the devil. A nation without God in its education system will create a society that will destroy itself.

Thoughts

The importance of moral education in the development of nations is high. When God is present in our knowledge, it impacts the growth of the people and society. The powerful people of the world yesterday and today and those that will attain power in the future are people who acknowledge God in their lives. The nations without God will continue to witness calamities, for the knowledge of God is the foundation of all true education. The Bible says: "The fear of the LORD is the beginning of wisdom, and knowledge of the Holy One is understanding" (Proverbs 9:10).

CHAPTER 7

IS GOD AN ENEMY OF THE STATE?

THIS IS WHAT the Lord says:

> "What fault did your ancestors find in me,
>   that they strayed so far from me?
> They followed worthless idols and be-
>   came worthless themselves."
> —Jeremiah 2:5

The rebellion against God has become common in society. Not many want to consider that they have a Creator and are responsible to Him in the conduct of their lives. Ever since Adam and Eve disobeyed God in the Garden of Eden, the human race has continued to rebel against God. A spirit of dissention has overtaken our hearts, and in our arrogance we have denied the existence of a Creator. The psalmist says that pride led us into trouble with God. "In his pride the wicked man does not seek him; in all his thoughts there is no room for God" (Psalm 10:4).

Ironically, pride also set Satan against God, causing him to be cast out of heaven. Soon after, he came to earth and created enmity between the Creator and humanity.

The Bible says this about Satan:

How you have fallen from heaven, morning star, son of the dawn! You have been cast down to the earth, you who once laid low the nations! You said in your heart, "I will ascend to the heavens; I will raise my throne above the stars of God; I will sit enthroned on the mount of assembly, on the utmost heights of Mount Zaphon. I will ascend above the tops of the clouds; I will make myself like the Most High." But you are brought down to the realm of the dead, to the depths of the pit.

—Isaiah 14:12–15

Our rebellion notwithstanding, God cannot be ignored by man. The concept of God is accepted by most people. Some, however, do not subscribe to the existence of a Creator. Many individuals believe that God is all in the imagination of weak-minded folks in response to fear and frustration. These people promote anything that seems to prove that God does not exist.

It is needless to argue with atheists because their minds are made up. As David pointed out, "The fool says in his heart, 'There is no God.' They are corrupt, their deeds are vile; there is no one who does good" (Psalm 14:1). But the truth is that the argument against God has always been weak. There is more convincing evidence that God exists than anything that suggests He does not exist.

God Is Not Weak

Our perverted hearts keep telling us that we can do without God. And most of the time, it appears as if that's true. But the only reason we seem to get away with our sins and wickedness is that God is patient and loving. He told the prophet Ezekiel, "As surely as I live, declares the Sovereign Lord, I take no pleasure in the death of the wicked, but rather that they turn from their ways and live" (Ezekiel 33:11).

In the Old Testament, God became angry with the wickedness of a generation of human beings. He wiped them out with a flood, saving only Noah and his family. He possesses the absolute power to determine what to do with His creations. This is the reason why it is advisable not to play into His anger. The Bible says: "It is a dreadful thing to fall into the hands of the living God" (Hebrews 10:31).

"The Lord saw how great the wickedness of the human race had become on the earth, and that every inclination of the thoughts of the human heart was only evil all the time. The Lord regretted that he had made human beings on the earth, and his heart was deeply troubled. So the Lord said, 'I will wipe from the face of the earth the human race I have created—and with them the animals, the birds and the creatures that move along the ground—for I regret that I have made them.' But Noah found favor in the eyes of the Lord" (Genesis 6:5–8).

The devastations caused by the flood were too much that God promised never to destroy mankind in that way again. He has kept his promise, even though humans have remained evil. The Lord said in his heart, "Never again will I curse the ground because of humans, even though every inclination of the human heart is evil from childhood. And never again will I destroy all living creatures, as I have done" (Genesis 8:21).

The human heart is at variance with the expectations of God. He wants man to be obedient and upright before Him. But the human heart is full of iniquity; therefore, we cannot stand the righteousness of God. This problem has resulted in mankind's continuous attack on the name of God.

Sin Invites God's Anger

Our disbelief in God does not change the truth of His existence, His power, or His nature of mercy and love. But His love does not preclude His anger when we disobey Him or refuse to give Him the honor He deserves. And the anger of God cannot be compared with human anger. Jesus advised His disciples to fear God, who has the unlimited power. "Do not be afraid of those who kill the body but cannot kill the soul. Rather, be afraid of the One who can destroy both soul and body in hell" (Matthew 10:28).

When God so desires, He makes His power known in our disobedience by allowing evil on us so that others may learn to reverence Him. Peter the Apostle said about God, "For if God did not spare angels when they sinned, but sent them to hell, putting them in chains of darkness to be held for judgment; if he did not spare the ancient world when he brought the flood on its ungodly people, but protected Noah, a preacher of righteousness, and seven others, if he condemned the cities of Sodom and Gomorrah by burning them to ashes, and made them an example of what is going to happen to the ungodly" (2 Peter 2:4-7).

We can only escape the wrath of God when He chooses to have mercy on us. His verdict cannot be challenged by anyone. Satan also often deceives man and woman when he makes us to think that we can escape the wrath of God when we sin. Adam and Eve hid somewhere in the Garden of Eden but they were found. When God's anger comes on the land, we cannot escape it. The only way out from the Lord's anger is human repentance from our sins.

How God Showed His Anger To Some People

No one in the world is big before the Almighty God. The human status or the heights an individual has attained in life cannot overshadow God. God possesses the power to bring us down from the pinnacle of our pride. He has done it before when God, showing forth His power, brought ungodly thrones down. God's judgment, no one can overturn.

For example, King Herod Agrippa I, who prided himself before God and man, died a shameful death.

Between AD 37 and 44, Herod Agrippa I was king of Iturea, Gaulanitis, Trachonitis, and also Galilee and Perea.[97] He was an aristocrat, being a descendant of King Herod the Great, the first to be called king of the Jews in the first century. Agrippa was very powerful and persecuted the church. He killed James, an apostle of Christ, and had Peter imprisoned.

Herod became arrogant and forced the people to hail him as god. He put himself in the position of God, and the Lord used him to teach other people that He, God could not be toyed with by any man or woman. At the age of thirty-four, Herod died a horrifying death.

"On the appointed day Herod, wearing his royal robes, sat on his throne and delivered a public address to the people. They shouted, 'This is the voice of a god, not of a man.' Immediately, because Herod did not give praise to God, an angel of the Lord struck him down, and he was eaten by worms and died" (Acts 12:21–23).

Also King Nebuchadnezzar was a great monarch in the Babylonian empire about 587 BC. He was a powerful and energetic ruler.[98] Drunk with power, he put himself in the place of God, saying, "Is not this the great Babylon I have built as the royal residence, by my mighty power and for the glory of my majesty?" (Daniel 4:30).

The Bible says:

> Even as the words were on his lips, a voice came from heaven, "This is what is decreed for you, King Nebuchadnezzar: Your royal authority has been taken from you. You will be driven away from people and will live with the wild animals; you will eat grass like the ox. Seven times will pass by for you until you acknowledge that the Most High is sovereign over all kingdoms on earth and gives them to anyone he wishes."
>
> —Daniel 4:31–32

The king was banished by God from the palace into the bush as he completely lost his mind. He ate and dwelt in the midst of the wild animals until he came back to his senses at the words of the Lord. The king had learned his lessons; when he was restored he said:

"At the end of that time, I, Nebuchadnezzar, raised my eyes toward heaven, and my sanity was restored. Then I praised the Most High; I honored and glorified him who lives forever. His dominion is an eternal dominion; his kingdom endures from generation to generation. All the peoples of the earth are regarded as nothing. He does as he pleases with the powers of heaven and the peoples of the earth. No one can hold back his hand or say to him: 'What have you done?'

At the same time that my sanity was restored, my honor and splendor were returned to me for the glory of my kingdom. My advisers and nobles sought me out, and I was restored to my throne and became even greater than before. Now I, Nebuchadnezzar, praise and exalt and glorify the King of heaven, because everything he does is right and all his ways are just. And those who walk in pride he is able to humble" (Daniel 4:34–37).

The anger of the Lord must not always come because it is serious, but when it comes it is meant to help us appreciate our frailty and feebleness compared to our Creator. But these warnings have still not convinced people who arrogate power to themselves to know that the ultimate power lies with the Almighty. Nonetheless, we also have people in history who desired to have God in all their affairs, and the early American leaders were such.

Early Americans and Their Love for God

The early leaders of America wanted God to be involved in all areas of their lives: economic, social, and political. They believed that the knowledge of God drove every successful endeavor. Those who did not acknowledge God were ineligible for elective positions because the people knew the aspirations of such individuals were bound to fail. The early Americans would not deal with anyone who wanted to rule the nation but did not acknowledge God in his life and actions.

Thomas Jefferson, the third president of the United States, was an erudite and charismatic politician, credited with the crafting of the Declaration of Independence. But his campaign for American presidency was met with stiff opposition because the electorate perceived in him some behaviors inconsistent with Christian conduct.

David Barton, in his book *The Myth of Separation*, stated:

> Jefferson was strongly attacked for his religious beliefs when he ran for President against John Adams in 1800. One of the most powerful attacks came from Rev. Williams Linn, a Dutch Reformed minister in New York City. In the pamphlet, "Serious Considerations on the Election of a President," Linn asked, "Does Jefferson ever go to Church? How does he spend the Lord's Day? Is he known to worship with any denomination of Christians?"

Linn continued, "Let the first magistrate be a professed infidel, and infidels will surround him. Let him spend the Sabbath...never in going to church; and to frequent public worship will become unfashionable....Universal dissoluteness will follow....

> Will you then, my fellow-citizens, with all this evidence...vote for Mr. Jefferson?...As to myself, were Mr. Jefferson connected with me by the nearest ties of blood, and did I owe him a thousand obligations, I would not, and could not vote for him. No; sooner than stretch forth

my hand to place him at the head of the nation…let mine arms fall from my shoulder blade and mine arm be broken from the bone.[99]

The public outcry of the Dutch minister was the stand of the general American populace at that time. In choosing their leaders or electing representatives, the citizens made it clear, in writing and in their law, that only Christians would lead them. And the issue is not just Christian professors but those who live by what they profess the totality of Christian life.

Here are some excerpts from the early American code of governance as captured by David Barton:

1796 Tennessee Constitution, Article VIII, Section II
No person who denies the being of God, or a future state of rewards and punishments, shall hold any office in the civil department of this state.

1776 Maryland Constitution, Article XXXV
No other test or qualification ought to be required…than such oath of support and fidelity to this state…and a declaration of a belief in the Christian religion.

1786 Vermont, Frame of Government, Section 9
Each member (of the legislature), before he takes his seat, shall make and subscribe the following declaration, viz: "I do believe in one God, the Creator and Governor of the universe, the rewarder of the good and punisher of the wicked. And I do acknowledge the scriptures of the Old and New Testament to be given by divine inspiration, and own and profess the (Christian) religion."

Massachusetts Constitution, Chapter VI Article 1
(All persons elected to state office or to the legislature must) make and subscribe the following declaration, viz. "I, _____, do declare that I believe the Christian religion and have firm persuasion of its truth."

North Carolina Constitution, Article XXXII

No person who shall deny the being of God, or the truth of the protestant religion, or the divine authority either of the Old or New Testaments, or who shall hold religious principles incompatible with the freedom and safety of the state, shall be capable of holding any office, or place of trust or profit in the civil department, within this state.

Pennsylvania Constitution, Frame of Government, Section 10
Each member (of the legislature), before he takes his seat, shall make and subscribe the following declaration, viz: "I do believe in one God, the Creator and Governor of the universe, the rewarder of the good and punisher of the wicked. And I do acknowledge the scriptures of the Old and New Testament to be given by Divine Inspiration."

Delaware Constitution, Article 22
Every person who shall be chosen a member of either house, or appointed to any office or place of trust shall make and subscribe the following declaration, to wit: "I, _____, do profess faith in God the Father, and in Jesus Christ His only Son, and in the Holy Ghost, one God, blessed for evermore; and I do acknowledge the holy scriptures of the Old and New Testament to be given by divine interpretation."[100]

These are wonderful Americans who worked to make America great. They attested to the fact that the only means to manage human and material resources of society creditably was to ensure that leaders responsible for the operations and supervisions are those with transformed hearts. No heart that is yet to be transformed by the words, knowledge, and fear of God can make a success of administration of society.

It is a fact that religion and politics are two different things but they are interwoven, and the proper management of both determines how well people can live and work together. Religion is a way of life. It defines who we are and gives us direction, purpose, and meaning. It is the pinnacle on which we judge the behavior of others. Politics, on the other hand, defines the direction and objectives of a society, their goals and aspirations, which are prerequisites to their joy, happiness, and contentment. The two were meant to complement one another and the quest to separate both cannot be without negative consequences for the nation.

The first president of the United States, George Washington, stated that religious morals are the major ingredients for good governance. While preparing to step down as president after meritorious service to the nation, Washington said in his farewell address to the American people on September 17, 1796:

> Of all the dispositions and habits, which lead to political prosperity, Religion and Morality are indispensable supports. In vain would that man claim the tribute of Patriotism, who should labor to subvert these great pillars of human happiness, these firmest props of the duties of Men and Citizens.

> The mere politician, equally with the pious man, ought to respect and to cherish them. A volume could not trace all their connexions with private and public felicity. Let it simply be asked, where is the security for property, for reputation, for life, if the sense of religious obligation desert the oaths, which are the instruments of investigation in Courts of Justice? And let us with caution indulge the supposition that morality can be maintained without religion. Whatever may be conceded to the influence of refined education on minds of peculiar structure, reason and experience both forbid us to expect that national morality can prevail in exclusion of religious principle.[101]

It is therefore a gamble for any nation who wishes to progress to elect anyone who has no regard for God. Anti-God leaders would only bring further decay into a decaying society. No godless leader has the capacity to proffer good solutions to the myriad of political, social and economic problems of the nation.

Though there appear to be many who are trying to destroy the Christian historic heritage of America, there are evidences that those who ran this nation had reverence for God, and following are some of them.

Our Nation Thanked God

The need for godly reverence in the conduct and actions of government officials was important to early American leaders. As a result, they saw the hand of God and His support in the success of their endeavors. The leaders recognized God not only when there was trouble but also in thanksgiving after God had delivered them.

The American leaders of old devoted a day of national thanksgiving to thank God for the mercies extended to the nation in the previous year. This was not just a national holiday, but a day for every citizen to recognize the importance of God in the affairs of their society.

In 1789, President Washington issued a proclamation that gave America its first official day of Thanksgiving under its new constitution. Here is the full text of the historic proclamation:

> WHEREAS it is the duty of all nations to acknowledge the providence of Almighty God, to obey His will, to be grateful for His benefits, and humbly to implore His protection and favor; and Whereas both Houses of Congress have, by their joint committee, requested me to recommend to the people of the United States a DAY OF PUBLIC THANKSGIVING and PRAYER, to be observed by acknowledging with grateful hearts the many and signal favors of Almighty God, especially by affording them an opportunity peaceably to establish a form of government for their safety and happiness ...
>
> NOW THEREFORE, I do recommend and assign THURSDAY, the TWENTY-SIXTH DAY of NOVEMBER next, to be devoted by the people of these States to the service of that great and glorious Being who is the beneficent author of all the good that was, that is, or that will be; that we may then all unite in rendering unto Him our sincere and humble thanks for His kind care and protection of the people of this country previous to their becoming a nation; for the signal and manifold mercies and the favorable interpositions of His providence which we experienced in the course and conclusion of the late war; for the great degree of tranquility, union, and plenty which we have since enjoyed;—for the peaceable and rational manner in which we have been enabled to establish Constitutions of government for our safety and happiness, and particularly the national one now lately instituted;—for the civil and religious liberty with which we are blessed, and the means we have of acquiring and diffusing useful knowledge;— and, in general, for all the great and various favors which He has been pleased to confer upon us.

And also, that we may then unite in most humbly offering our prayers and supplications to the great Lord and Ruler of Nations and beseech Him to pardon our national and other transgressions;—to enable us all, whether in public or private stations, to perform our several and relative duties properly and punctually; to render our National Government a blessing to all the people by constantly being a Government of wise, just, and constitutional laws, discreetly and faithfully executed and obeyed; to protect and guide all sovereigns and nations (especially such as have shown kindness unto us); and to bless them with good governments, peace, and concord; to promote the knowledge and practice of true religion and virtue, and the increase of science among them and us; and, generally to grant unto all mankind such a degree of temporal prosperity as he alone knows to be best.

GIVEN under my hand, at the city of New-York, the third day of October, in the year of our Lord, one thousand seven hundred and eighty-nine.

(Signed) G. Washington[102]

On June 20, 1676, the governing council of Charlestown, Massachusetts, held a meeting to determine how best to express thanks to God for the good fortune that had enabled their community to become securely established. By unanimous vote they instructed Edward Rawson, the clerk of the House of Deputies, to proclaim June 29 as a day of thanksgiving.

The thanksgiving celebration ordered by the early Pilgrims under Governor William Bradford, which was aimed at showing a heart of gratitude to God for the year's harvest, is believed to be the true beginning of the present-day Thanksgiving Day.

Reference to God in Speech and Actions

Our early leaders did not hide their love for God. President Abraham Lincoln showed his submission to the Lord Jesus Christ at the battle of Gettysburg, which claimed about 60,000 American lives. In his famous Gettysburg Address, the president said:

"When I left Springfield [to assume the presidency] I asked the people to pray for me. I was not a Christian. When I buried my son, the severest trial of my life, I was not a Christian. But when I went to

Gettysburg and saw the graves of thousands of our soldiers, I then and there consecrated myself to Christ. Yes I do love Jesus."[103]

Many of the past American presidents ended most of their public speeches with the prayer 'God bless the United States of America' or prayers to God to guide their administration. It is a show of love for God and indication that they knew that for a nation to succeed, God's hands and interventions are required.

See some of the examples of the convictions of American's past leaders:

"And may that Being who is supreme over all, the Patron of Order, the Fountain of Justice, and the Protector in all ages of the world of virtuous liberty, continue His blessing upon this nation and its Government and give it all possible success and duration consistent with the ends of His providence." —President John Adams, Inaugural Address, Philadelphia, PA, Saturday, March 4, 1797

"I shall need, too, the favor of that Being in whose hands we are, who led our fathers, as Israel of old, from their native land and planted them in a country flowing with all the necessaries and comforts of life; who has covered our infancy with His providence and our riper years with His wisdom and power, and to whose goodness I ask you to join in supplications with me that He will so enlighten the minds of your servants, guide their councils, and prosper their measures that whatsoever they do shall result in your good, and shall secure to you the peace, friendship, and approbation of all nations." —President Thomas Jefferson's Second Inaugural Address, Washington, DC, Monday, March 4, 1805

"I shall look for whatever success may attend my public service; and knowing that "except the Lord keep the city the watchman waketh but in vain," with fervent supplications for His favor, to His overruling providence I commit with humble but fearless confidence my own fate and the future destinies of my country." —President John Quincy Adams' Inaugural Address, Washington DC, Friday, March 4, 1825

"In this dedication of a Nation we humbly ask the blessing of God. May He protect each and every one of us. May He guide me in the days to come."—President Franklin D. Roosevelt's First Inaugural Address, Washington, DC, Saturday, March 4, 1933

".....to believe that together, with God's help, we can and will resolve the problems which now confront us. And, after all, why shouldn't we believe that? We are Americans. God bless you, and thank you." —President Ronald Reagan; First Inaugural Address, Washington, DC, Tuesday, January 20, 1981

"We have changed the guard. And now, each in our way, and with God's help, we must answer the call. Thank you and God bless you all." —President William J. Clinton, First Inaugural Address, Washington, DC, Wednesday, January 20, 1993

"God bless you all, and God bless America." —President George W. Bush First Inaugural Address, Washington, DC, Saturday, January 20, 2001[104]

Other Evidences of God in American Government

The nation's original pledge of allegiance did not include the words "under God." These words were added through the initiatives of the Board of Directors of the Knights of Columbus, who adopted a resolution to the effect in New York City on April 22, 1951. The initiative triggered the recommendation to Congress of the United States of America on August 20, 1953. The 83rd Congress passed a bill amending the pledge of allegiance to include the words "under God" in February 1954.

President Dwight D. Eisenhower signed the bill into law on Flag Day, June 14, 1954 as Public Law 396. In a statement by the president upon signing the bill, he said:

"FROM THIS DAY FORWARD, the millions of our school children will daily proclaim in every city and town, every village and rural school house, the dedication of our nation and our people to the Almighty. To anyone who truly loves America, nothing could be more inspiring than to contemplate this rededication of our youth, on each school morning, to our country's true meaning.

Especially is this meaningful as we regard today's world. Over the globe, mankind has been cruelly torn by violence and brutality and, by the millions, deadened in mind and soul by a materialistic philosophy of life. Man everywhere is appalled by the prospect of atomic war. In this somber setting, this law and its effects today have profound meaning. In this way we are reaffirming the transcendence of religious faith in America's heritage and future; in this way we shall constantly strengthen those spiritual weapons which forever will be our country's most powerful resource in peace and war."[105]

On August 17, 1954, the president sent a message of praise to the Knights of Columbus, who contributed immensely to this idea. He said:

"We are particularly thankful to you for your part in the movement to have the words "under God" added to our Pledge of Allegiance. These words will remind Americans that despite our great physical strength we must remain humble. They will help us to keep constantly in our minds and hearts the spiritual and moral principles which alone give dignity to man, and upon which our way of life is founded. For the contribution which your organization has made to this cause, we must be genuinely grateful."[106]

The Early American Court

The court, which is the third tier of government in the presidential democracy of our nation, also acknowledged the supremacy of God in the dispensation of justice.

John Jay was the first chief justice of the Supreme Court of America. He was appointed by President George Washington, and is believed to be among America's eminent scholars in the art of law and constitution. Justice Jay played a major role in crafting the American Constitution. He said, "Providence has given our people the choice of their rulers, and it is the duty as well as the privilege and interest of our Christian nation to select and prefer Christians for their rulers."[107]

The early court adhered to the Christian faith and was committed to Christian values. In *The People v. Ruggles,* 1881, Justice James Kent, the chief justice of the Supreme Court of New York, said:

The defendant was indicted...in December 1810 for that he did on the 2nd day of September, 1810...wickedly, maliciously, and blasphemously, utter and with loud voice publish, in the presence and hearing of divers good and Christian people, of and concerning the Christian religion, and of and concerning Jesus Christ, the false, scandalous, malicious, wicked and blasphemous words following: "Jesus Christ was a bastard, and his mother must be whore," in contempt of the Christian religion....The defendant was tried and found guilty, and was sentenced by the court to be imprisoned for three months, and to pay a fine of $500.[108]

The court responded to this case:

The jury...finds a malicious intention in the speaker to vilify the Christian religion and the scriptures, and this court cannot look beyond the record, nor take any notice of the allegation, that words were uttered by the defendant, a member of a debating association, which convened weekly for discussion and mutual information....

That there is an association in which so serious a subject is treated with so much levity, indecency and scurrility...I am sorry to hear, for it would prove a nursery of vice, a school of preparation to qualify young men for the gallows, and young women for the brothel, and there is not a skeptic of decent manners and good morals who would not consider such debating clubs as a common nuisance and disgrace to the city....

It was the out-pouring of an invective, so vulgarly shocking and insulting, that the lowest grade of civil authority ought not to be subject to it, but when spoken in a Christian land and to a Christian audience, the highest offence contra bonos mores; and even if Christianity was not part of the law of the land, it is the popular religion of the country, an insult on which would be indictable.[109]

In addressing the defense, the court went on to say:

We will first dispose of what is considered the grand objection—the constitutionality of Christianity—for, in effect, that is the question. Christianity, general Christianity, is and always has been a part of the common law…not Christianity with an established church…but Christianity with liberty of conscience to all men.

Justice Kent declared, "We are a Christian people and the morality of the country is deeply engrafted in Christianity."[110]

This goes to say that all levels of our society, executive, legislative and judicial, at foundation recognized the importance of God to the progress of the nation. And God was with them in their activities as they piloted America to a land of opportunities for the world. It was no doubt why the United States became the most powerful nation of the world. The source of American strength of character has been God.

God Is Referenced On the American Economy

The economy of America was also at the early days managed by people who acknowledged God and His providence in the affairs of the nation. The managers sought the leading of God in their handling of the nation's economic affairs. The currency of the United States of America, the main legal tender for trade and commerce, bore the words "In God we trust." This motto was placed on US currency in 1861.

Notable citizens have expressed support for this national emblem. The Secretary of Treasury (direct evidence of a man of God in the nation's economic management) expressed this sentiment in a memo to James Pollock, Director of the Mint at Philadelphia, dated November 20, 1861:

"No nation can be strong except in the strength of God, or safe except in His defense. The trust of our people in God should be declared on our national coins.…You will cause a device to be prepared without unnecessary delay with a motto expressing in the fewest and tersest words possible this national recognition."[111]

"In God we trust" was accepted by the United States as the motto on the currency when the resolution of the nation's 84th Congress was signed into law by the president on July 30, 1956.

Former US president Ronald Reagan once said, "Our nation's motto—'In God We Trust'—was not chosen lightly. It reflects a basic recognition that there is a divine authority in the universe."[112]

The modern-day economists who depended on mere human intellects to put the economy on the path of growth have not succeeded because of the dependence of the managers on only human knowledge. The absence of God in any management cannot produce good results. The economy of the United States was strong not because of the economic management alone but because those who were managing the economy counted on the wisdom of God to achieve their goals.

In the Bible, King David said, "Blessed is the nation whose God is the Lord, the people he chose for his inheritance" (Psalm 33:12). The words of God as expressed in the Bible are infallible, the reason America will continue to be great so long we do not stop acknowledging God. It was not an accident of history but a reflection of the early Americans' reverence and love for God.

But Satan is never happy when the people love and show their reverence to the Creator. Satan would usually influence the hearts of people to step up opposition to the things of God. And he is gradually succeeding in our nation. America, who was known all over the world for her love for God, has suddenly found herself in antipathy towards the things of God.

Why the Sudden Change

In all good systems in the world, there is a word of caution for people and operators to be alert that no good organization can be free from being subverted. The people of God (the church in America) became conceited with the godly system that was built. They forgot that Satan and his angels are all over the place to destroy any godly heritage. This is the reason why watchfulness is an essential part of a sustained system. Paul warned the church at Corinth, "So, if you think you are standing firm, be careful that you don't fall" (1 Corinthians 10:12). So watch and pray.

The moral foundations on which the founders built the nation were soon undermined by those who Satan used to infiltrate the system to destroy it. The Bible says, "For lack of guidance a nation falls" (Proverbs 11:14a). "How the mighty have fallen!" (2 Samuel 1:19). It is usually hard to sustain what is good because the devil's business daily is to bring down the tower of righteousness.

The United States of America has a robust system of government based on the understanding that the opinion of the majority counts. Representatives elected by the populace are to express and defend public opinions, interests, beliefs, and convictions. This is government of the people, for the people, and by the people. While everyone has a say in governance, no individual or group of individuals is to lord their opinions on the majority. And the representatives were expected to be men who have through the system learnt the fear of God.

The architects of the democratic system of government deliberately introduced checks and balances between the various arms of government so that no branch would subvert the wishes of the people. It was meant to place the public interest above the individual wishes. The care for the good of the general public was uppermost in their hearts.

The three tiers of government—executive, legislative, and judiciary—work together. It was thought they would be people of the same mind. The executive arm is responsible for the implementation of the policies of government. The legislature is responsible for the making of laws for the good of society. The judiciary is responsible for the arbitration and interpretation of the law. None of the three arms is to be superior to the other, but rather to complement one another for the good of the society.

Laws are principles and regulations formulated to guide relationships among people in the society, and they are to be obeyed by everyone without exception. The objectives of law in society were to regulate and make stable the condition of societal environment. Once godlessness, the manifestations of the sinful condition of the human heart, is introduced to the management of democracy, it would show apparent dysfunctions.

The system cannot be successful unless all the three arms of government are run by persons with the same values. Those who make the laws must be people of high moral character who will help citizens live decent and orderly lives. The executives who promote and enforce the law have to be people of proven integrity and character. Good executive and legislative arms also nominate and confirm respectively the judicial officers who reflect godly faith and character. And such a judicial arm would be guided by the objectives and intentions of the lawmakers in furtherance of the good of society.

But if an arm is not properly constituted with societal values, the likelihood that other arms would do well is not guaranteed. At best there would be rancor between the arms of government resulting from disagreements. The misunderstandings slow down the progress of governance and may also retard and destroy past achievements.

The pervading godlessness in the American society can be traced to such development. One would have expected the judiciary that was in the vanguard of protecting righteousness in society to continue. But such is not the case. On the contrary, the opinions of the majority are now often subverted. The judiciary, instead of merely interpreting the laws, rewrites them. Usually, the interpretations reflect the personal opinions of the judge, even when that goes against the popular acceptance.

For example, in November 4, 2008, the majority of citizens in California cast their ballots under Proposition 8 restricting the definition of marriage to opposite-sex couples. But on August 4, 2010, U.S. District Chief Judge Vaughn R. Walker overturned Proposition 8 through a suit, *Perry v. Schwarzenegger,* filed in the Federal District Court.

Earlier, in 1947, some judges waged war against the cherished values of the American people. The judges ruled that prayers in the public places, specifically in our public schools, were against the provision of separation of church and state in the nation's constitution as amended. Several cases were decided based on interpretations that were inconsistent with the character of Christians who fear God. A few examples are as follows:

In the case of *Everson v. Board of Education,* 330 U.S. 1(1947) the court declared what is now regarded as separation of church and state. Justice Hugo Black led a majority opinion for a sharp separation between government and religion. The opinion led to several other court decisions with negative policies involving matters of religion, which has had a major effect on Christianity, which had shaped our nation's values. Justice Black ruled that:

"A verbal prayer offered in a school is unconstitutional, even if it is both voluntary and denominationally neutral."

Prayer was since then stamped out of schools by the cases of Engel v. Vitale, 370 U.S. 421 (1962), Abington School District v. SCHEMPP,

374 U.S. 203 (1963), and Commissioner of Education v. School Committee of Leyden, 358 Mass. 776 (1971).

In Reed v. Van Hoven 237 F Supp. 48 (W. D. Mich, 1965); in the opinion of the court, it is Unconstitutional for kindergarten students to recite: "We thank you for the flowers so sweet; We thank you for the food we eat; We thank you for the birds that sing; We thank you for everything." Even though the word "God" is not contained in it, someone might think it is a prayer.

Per decision of court in case of State Board of Education v. Board of Education of Nectcong, 108 N.J. Super. 564 (1970).

"It is unconstitutional for students to arrive at school early to hear a student volunteer read prayers which had been offered by the chaplains in the chambers of the United States House of Representatives and Senate, even though those prayers are contained in the public Congregational Record published by the US Government."

In Graham v. Central Community School District, 1985

"It is unconstitutional for a school graduation ceremony to contain an opening or closing prayer"[113]

Stein v. Oshinsky, 1965, and Collins v. Chandler Unified School District, 1981, dictated that students could no longer practice or profess Christianity or their religious beliefs. "Freedom of speech and press is guaranteed to students unless the topic is religious, at which time such speech becomes unconstitutional."

Lowe v. City of Eugene, 1969, concluded: "It is unconstitutional for a war memorial to be erected in the shape of a cross."............

Per court ruling in DeSpain v. DeKalb County Community School District, 384 F. 2d 836, 838-840 (1967);

It is unconstitutional for kindergarten students to recite: 'We thank you for the flower so sweet; we thank you for the food we eat; we thank you for the birds that sing; we thank you for everything.' Even though the word God is not contained in it, someone might think it is a prayer."[114]

The judiciary became both the interpreters of law and the makers of law. And with such enormous power at its disposal, it became more or less a dictator. The members of the judiciary seem to exercise authority without considering the people's opinions. Public decisions are subject to the personal discretion of a judge. The good intentions of the early Americans were reversed by unanticipated imperfections in the system.

But truth cannot be destroyed. Chip Brogden said, "The one who buries the Truth in the ground for safekeeping will lose it, while the one who does something with the Truth will receive more Truth. This is why some grow spiritually and some do not."[115]

Ironically, the war of separation of church and state is targeted at the Christian faith that the founders of America so labored to entrench. All other religious beliefs are freely expressed in the public schools. While the Bible is being censored, various profane literatures are given to students without restraint. Christmas celebration may not be allowed in schools, but Halloween and Kwanzaa are celebrated and even inculcated in some school curricula.

It is an issue for concern that children may graduate from schools without knowing God. Tomorrow's leaders are therefore lacking the wisdom that makes for a great nation. Our problem is in our failure to defend the gospel and consequently the morality of the nation. The preaching of undiluted words of God is critical to change in our society. Not only that, our lifestyle as Christians should not be different from what we preach. The society is tired of our talk without the practical demonstrations of what we say. We can only raise an army of upright men and women when we pray and talk and also match our talks with actions appropriately.

The moral setbacks in our nation are meant to spur us for vigorous spiritual campaign and awakening. And we should take up the challenge of our time in good stride like Paul, who was not discouraged but rather, believed that the misfortune that befell him was for the good of the church. He said, "Now I want you to know, brothers and sisters, that what has happened to me has actually served to advance the gospel" (Philippians 1:12).

We therefore need to be motivated and not give up training our young generations about God. The Jews were told by God to teach the people the word of God because that is the only way for a great nation. "Only be careful, and watch yourselves closely so that you do not forget the things your eyes have seen or let them fade from your heart as long as you live. Teach them to your children and to their children after them" (Deuteronomy 4:9).

We should not be scared of telling the truth because truth will survive in all generations. Søren Kierkegaard said, "There are two ways to be fooled: one is to believe what isn't so; the other is to refuse to believe what is so."[116] And in the words of Karl Barth, "Man can certainly keep on lying…but he cannot make truth falsehood. He can certainly rebel… but he can accomplish nothing which abolishes the choice of God."[117]

As King Solomon in the Bible said, "I know that everything God does will endure forever; nothing can be added to it and nothing can be taken from it" (Ecclesiastes 3:14). America's godly heritage will be revived again. But it requires the boldness of the Christian believers to speak out and to act.

It is evident that nothing will change the fortune of this world other than the undiluted word of God.

Thoughts

Satan is the enemy of God and to that extent, the enemy of man because man and woman are created in the image of God. Satan is full of deceptions and he makes us feel he exists only in our imaginations. He has succeeded in making some individuals believe there is no Satan, just as they hold to the error that God does not exist. But we often find ourselves in issues that we would not believe we can be involved in. Satan leads us to a point of no return and by the time he finishes with us, our lives have been completely shattered.

We need to recognize early in life that Satan is not our friend. And our spirit cannot exist in a vacuum; we need God in our lives. God created us and He would not leave us to suffer.

CHAPTER 8

THE DILEMMA OF RUINED EDUCATION

The task of the modern educator is not to cut down jungles
but to irrigate deserts. The right defense against false sentiments is to inculcate just sentiments. By starving the sensibil-
ity of our pupils we only make them easier prey to
the propagandist when he comes. For famished nature will
be avenged and a hard heart is no infallible protection
against a soft head.[118]
—C. S. Lewis

THE REMOVAL OF God from our public places has resulted in
outright godlessness and moral decadence, with attendant consequences
on society. The political, economic, and social lives of the people have
been gradually destroyed because the new generation did not have any
good examples after which to model their behavior.

Our lives are filled with knowledge gaps created through the deliberate suppression of God's Word in our public institutions, resulting in
a serious decline in morality. The state of human minds, our conducts
in homes, at jobs, in and outside of societies is dictated by our inner
developments through the exposures we have had in life. We are faced
with crisis today at all levels of our societies because the environment in

the world does not make for uprightness because of the absence of the words of God, the rock and foundation of good education.

As a result of this, the following critical aspects of human endeavor are destroyed:

The Family (An Important Organ of Society)

The family is the nucleus unit of any society. Families in disarray are indicators of a nation in confusion.

Satan knows the importance of the family to the growth, development, and sustenance of a nation. Thus, he has made the family his major target. The devil sows seeds of discord into families by causing divisions within them.

A united family unit with a sense of direction and purpose will result in societal orderliness and good governance. Satan cannot enter successfully into a society with strong moral values. He therefore seeks to destroy the platform on which a sound upbringing is developed: the home.

In God's creation, the purpose of family is intimacy, love, and trust. It is meant to be a place of warmth, tenderness, and understanding. Unfortunately, many families today do not live up to that description. This is because lack of proper education has denied us the capacity of meeting the requirements of a good family. Because of the absence of God's knowledge, members of the family are controlled by evil, which adversely affects society.

Family Structure

There are three important members of the nuclear family: the father, the mother, and the child. The unity, love, and devotion shared among these members make the family successful. A strong family supports and sustains its members, ensuring continuity. This cohesion helps reduce the effects of conflict.

To underscore the importance of family and its leadership in the management of society, the apostle Paul advised Timothy to be careful not to allow those who could not rule their own homes properly to emerge as leaders in the church. In his letter to Timothy, Paul said:

Here is a trustworthy saying: Whoever aspires to be an overseer desires a noble task. Now the overseer is to be above reproach, faithful to his wife, temperate, self-controlled, respectable, hospitable, able to teach, not given to drunkenness, not violent but gentle, not quarrelsome, not a lover of money. He must manage his own family well and see that his children obey him, and he must do so in a manner worthy of full respect. (If anyone does not know how to manage his own family, how can he take care of God's church?)

—1 Timothy 3:1–5

Paul's intention was not only to stop certain individuals who failed in their responsibilities at home from being leaders in the church. He also sought to encourage persons who could lead by example, those whose lives could be mirrored by the rest of society. Such people can be trusted to lead a church…or a nation.

Entrusting the running of society to those who are far removed from the knowledge of God is like a case of 'the blind leading the blind'. It would do further damage to the people. Jesus Christ said this about the leaders of the Jews (the Pharisees) who led the people but did not know God: "Leave them; they are blind guides. If the blind lead the blind, both will fall into a pit" (Matthew 15:14).

Divorce: A Destroyer of Family

One of the greatest assaults of Satan against family, and by extension the society and the nation, is divorce. This devastating seed sown by the devil has affected many homes in this country. Yet this silent killer of society has become an accepted norm. The marriage vow of 'for better for worse' is gradually rubbished because our minds have been completely taken over by Satan.

Judith S. Wallerstein, a researcher on divorce in America, in her book *The Unexpected Legacy of Divorce*, writes:

When I began studying the effects of divorce on children and parents in the early 1970s, I, like everyone else, expected them to tally. But as time progressed, I grew increasingly worried that divorce is a long-term crisis that was affecting the psychological profile of an entire generation.

I caught glimpses of this long-term effect in my research that followed the children into late adolescence and early adulthood, but it's not until—when the children are fully grown—that I can finally see the whole picture. Divorce is a life-transforming experience. After divorce, childhood is different. Adolescence is different. Adulthood—with the decision to marry or not—is different. Whether the final outcome is good or bad, the whole trajectory of an individual's life is profoundly altered by the divorce experience.[119]

Satan does not allow us to see the effect and damages done to society through divorce because he has replaced the true knowledge of God in our hearts with lies. He gives us the impression that our immoral conduct is just the easy way out. Paul said, "They are darkened in their understanding and separated from the life of God because of the ignorance that is in them due to the hardening of their hearts. Having lost all sensitivity, they have given themselves over to sensuality so as to indulge in every kind of impurity, and they are full of greed" (Ephesians 4:18-19).

It is the same strategy Satan used in the Garden of Eden "'You will not certainly die,' the serpent said to the woman. 'For God knows that when you eat from it your eyes will be opened, and you will be like God, knowing good and evil'" (Genesis 3:4-5). Human eyes were since opened but to calamities.

Satan's assurance that we would not die was not true. The nation is gripped with the spirit of death. Life is now much threatened because the families have been thrown into disarray through divorce.

Divorce Is of Satan

In the early days of America, the only legal grounds for divorce were adultery, cruelty, or physical harm to one of the parties. But this has changed. The most common grounds for divorce today are "irreconcilable differences." It is called "no fault" divorce; the parties do not need to prove any issue to make their case for separation.

Governor Edmund G. Brown of California, on May 11, 1966, set up a commission to address the issue of divorce in the state. He tagged the set-up of the commission a "concerted assault on the high incidence of divorce in our society and its often tragic consequences." In his charge to the commission, the governor said:

> Whatever the cause of the growing divorce rate—the anxieties in our world, a society of rootlessness and increasing mobility, an erosion of the moral absolute—divorce produces not only broken homes but broken lives. It erodes the very foundation of our society, the family....Society is paying an almost intolerable price for this breakdown of family life—in terms both of human misery and of public financial resources.[120]

In spite of the devastating effects on children and parents, divorce is now socially accepted because Satan has taken control of our systems and he is on the rampage to destroy all known values within our society.

Divorce is Contrary to God's Design

Jesus Christ addressed the issue of divorce when He physically lived on earth. He taught the people to know that God does not have pleasure in divorce. The Jewish people and their leaders observed that Moses, who received the Ten Commandments from God, had allowed a law permitting people to divorce their wives on the grounds of infidelity. But Jesus told the people this was not the original plan of God. He said, "Moses permitted you to divorce your wives because your hearts were hard. But it was not this way from the beginning" (Matthew 19:8).

Jesus said this in difference to the widely held views that if one of the couple was found unfaithful, the partner was in order to go for divorce. He told them Moses came up with the law on divorce because it became necessary to check the growing rates of couples' separation in society. He taught the people to know that the intention of God was that married couples should remain together until death. Divorce is not only a separation of the couple but also a violation of the vow they made before man and God.

A marriage vow is not an ordinary contract which can be broken recklessly. It is a relationship in which God is involved. That is the point Jesus made when He said, "Therefore what God has joined together, let no one separate" (Mark 10:9).

God in the Home

By God's arrangement, the father is to be the leader of the family. "For the husband is the head of the wife as Christ is the head of the church, his body, of which He is the Savior" (Ephesians 5:23). The man has the main responsibility for loving and giving guidance. He sets the tone for a strong family. He supplies the needs of the children. He helps the family meet its objectives of unity, cohesion, and moral growth. He plays an active part in his children's lives. Because he loves his wife and children, there is no bitterness in the home.

Caring for the children includes appropriate discipline when a child does something wrong. "Start children off on the way they should go, and even when they are old they will not turn from it" (Proverbs 22:6). "Fathers, do not exasperate your children; instead, bring them up in the training and instruction of the Lord" (Ephesians 6:4). These are part of the instructions of the Lord which makes for perfect education.

The mother is the bedrock of the family system. She prepares food for the family. Solomon describes a noble wife as worth "far more than rubies." He said, "A wife of noble character who can find? She is worth far more than rubies. Her husband has full confidence in her and lacks nothing of value. She brings him good, not harm, all the days of her life" (Proverbs 31:10-12). She obeys her husband in accordance with the biblical injunction, "Wives, submit yourselves to your husbands, as is fitting in the Lord" (Colossians 3:18).

Father and mother work together to ensure that their children know God and are prepared to face life's many challenges.

The Bible also encourages children to honor their parents. "Children, obey your parents in everything, for this pleases the Lord" (Colossians 3:20).

These are the perfect arrangements for families, designed by God.

A breakdown in the family order began when Satan introduced to the world his idea of home arrangement. Satan's alternative negates God's plan and is usually destructive. The option the devil sold to us has led couples not to accept their individual roles in the home, resulting in uncontrolled conflicts and consequently separation.

We need to get back the original God-designed idea of home. The husband and the wife are to be helpers to one another. The wife, no matter her success, was meant to submit to her husband, and the husband must deal with the wife with unconditional love. Unfortunately, the church that is supposed to champion the course of true marriage is also enmeshed in divorce. And the society either assumes that marriage is not pleasant or that there is nothing bad in divorce. Worse still, some take to a wrong concept of marriage by people of the same sex taking the marriage oath.

Conflicts Resulting in Child Abuse

It is the plan of God that parents train their children to do what is right. The Bible says, "Whoever spares the rod hates their children, but the one who loves their children is careful to discipline them" (Proverbs 13:24). "Do not withhold discipline from a child; if you punish them with the rod, they will not die" (Proverbs 23:13). "Folly is bound up in the heart of a child, but the rod of discipline will drive it far away" (Proverbs 22:15).

However, discipline was to be exercised from a heart of love for the children and the desire to make them better human beings. The Bible says, "Fathers, do not embitter your children, or they will become discouraged" (Colossians 3:21). But because godlessness has dominated the society, some parents, rather than being leaders in the home directing the children in the path of progress, have become child abusers.

The law on child abuse was made to protect innocent children from satanic handling by ungodly parents. But often the law, rather than help solve problems, creates additions to the conflict and sometimes complicates already bad situations. Good as the law on child abuse is, it has been misapplied to create fear among parents who appropriately discipline their wards. The social welfare officer acting on the law on child abuse sometimes tends to believe what the child says rather than the explanations of the parents on why the child was disciplined.

And the American children who do not want to be disciplined exploit the situation, while they rot away in bad behavior. Stubborn kids in America now hide under the law on child abuse to disobey their parents and often threaten to call police when parents exercise authority to discipline them. Discipline of children has thus become a nightmare for parents in our society. Many social problems, robbery, drunkenness, and drug abuse result from the inability of parents to give appropriate discipline to their children. Parents have the right and responsibility to put their children on the proper path when they go astray. But not a few parents have surrendered completely to the fear of the child abuse law and are no longer willing to discipline their children.

The perception of society on relationship within homes has further eroded the confidence of the individuals in the family for one another. Not all parents are abusers. There are errors and genuine mistakes in family interactions and that should not be misinterpreted. Misrepresentation of the good intentions of some good parents may discourage others from doing the best they could because they do not want other people to see them in a bad light.

For instance, the media attacks on Joe Jackson in June 2009, after the death of his son Michael, appear not proper. Joe was said to have abused Michael when his son was still young, per alleged statements credited to the king of pop music when he was alive. While no one would support child abuse, some credit should be given to Mr. Joe Jackson, who is believed to have contributed to the great music talents of his children. The fans of the late Michael Jackson owe a debt of gratitude to Joe Jackson for doing his job as a father. His involvement in his children's lives resulted in the development of Michael Jackson's talents. Whatever mistake in the process should be pardoned because it must have been with good intentions.

The point is that while the law is created for the good of the society, we should not give room to Satan to exploit the law to create fear among the people. When the devil succeeds in creating fear in the human heart, the objective of the law may often not be achieved.

Results of Dysfunctions in the Family

It is a fact that godlessness in the society has seriously impaired the family system. When a family is dysfunctional, the development of the children is left to the schools and teachers. These children often see school as a better alternative to their homes. They view teachers as parental figures they can talk to and trust. And often the teachers are not any better, because they are also products of the same society that inhibits the knowledge of God.

Mistrust ensues in the home and many parents are eager to get their children out of the house in the name of "attaining adulthood," even when those teenagers are not capable of living on their own. When they are forced out too early, they won't make the best choices for their lives.

Because of poor relationships in the home, many parents suffer deprivation in their old age. The care they may have expected from their adult children becomes lacking. Some parents are abandoned to old folks' homes, not because the children are incapable of caring for them but because of disharmony in the family relationship. An old folks' home is not an acceptable alternative to the loving care that family members owe one another.

The Importance of the Bible in Children's Training

The Puritans insisted that education be accompanied with knowledge of the Bible, which would lead to good family values and the survival of the society. School administrators emphasized quality in teachers. They equipped students with moral and religious books that would help shape their lives. Christian teaching was considered a vital part of education.

C. S. Lewis said, "One of the reasons why it needs no special education to be a Christian is that Christianity is an education itself. That is why an uneducated believer like Bunyan was able to write a book that has astonished the whole world."[121]

In the early days of Great Britain, when government was run by the Word of God, Britain prospered. C. S. Lewis observed the disaster in the political and social life of Britain. He said:

The decline of "religion" is no doubt a bad thing for the "world." By it all the things that made England a fairly happy country are, I suppose, endangered: the comparative purity of her public life, the comparative humanity of her police, and the possibility of some mutual respect and kindness between political opponents. But I am not clear that it makes conversions to Christianity rarer or more difficult: rather the reverse. It makes the choice more inescapable. When the Round Table is broken every man must follow either Galahad or Mordred: middle things are gone.[122]

Today, jihadists abound in the British land that once boasted that all citizens, including the king, were believers who honored the living God.

Effects of Family Destruction on National Leadership

Political leadership emerges from people within a society. The society deserves the leader it has chosen. A society with good moral values will produce leaders with purpose and wisdom.

Some leaders have taken their societies to the Promised Land; others have not. The common denominator is the values those leaders have gotten from their society to offer the people.

Removing the Bible from our schools has robbed our nation of future leaders with proper upbringing and focus. We need to be concerned because the education and type of exposure our children have shape their views as future leaders of our society.

Politics is now dominated by those who do not have a reverence for God. Because of the disappearance of a biblical value system, the political process is no longer based on character but on cunning and dishonest means. Politics is not based on principles of forthrightness anymore. The priority of most politicians is to beat their opponents, rather than what they have to offer the people.

Thomas Jefferson noted that an effort to build a nation on a footing other than God's perfect will would always fail.

> Can the liberties of a nation be sure when we remove their only firm basis, a conviction in the minds of the people that these liberties are the gift of God? That they are not to be violated but with His wrath? Indeed, I tremble for my country when I reflect that God is just; that His justice cannot sleep forever, that a revolution of the wheel of fortune, a change in situation, is among possible events; that it may become probable by supernatural influence! The Almighty has no attributes which can take side with us in that event. [123]

Most modern-day politicians see the world of politics as a game. Their goal is not to get society to embrace a good value system but to attain or retain power. They stoop to double-talk during campaigns in order to win the election. A strong political system requires men and women with strength of character, clarity of purpose, and a measure of trustworthiness. These virtues are in short supply today because our society is being developed on godless principles.

The purpose of government is to maintain law and order and to ensure justice. The successful attainment of this objective will depend on the election of God-fearing leadership by the people. Anyone who aspires to lead our nation should be led by God. Those who do not know and fear God will lead our country into further conflict, chaos, and anarchy.

Democratic election of good leaders is dependent on the availability of godly candidates and the right choice by the voters. If the majority of people fear God, and there are godly candidates on the ballot, the probability of electing a leader with strong moral values is high. But if most of the people do not know God, or there are no godly candidates, a godless leader will emerge.

The nations of the West who have had the early days of closeness to God are strategically in a better stead to put the world right. The future of our world depends on the leaders of Europe and America. However, the knowledge of God is being gradually eroded in these nations, including our country, the United States of America. The world cannot be guaranteed peace if ungodly leadership is in place. But that is the tragedy of the present world.

According to Paul Kengor, in his book *God and Ronald Reagan,* former American president Ronald Reagan said, "The real crisis we face today is a spiritual one; at root, it is a test of moral will and faith. Whittaker Chambers, the man whose own religious conversion made him a witness to one of the terrible traumas of our time, Hiss-Chambers case, wrote that the crisis of the Western World exists to the degree in which the West is indifferent to God…"[124]

It is an unfortunate series of ripple effects. The actions and inactions of political leaders greatly impact the economic and social life of a nation. The nation is in trouble when she does not have a God-fearing leader who will put the interests of the society first and subjugate his personal ambitions. A godly leader judges his actions by the measurement of God's expectations of him. He will consult with God and his constituents to ensure that every step he takes is in accordance with the wishes of God and the people.

A leader who does not know God will not consult with Him in the management of the affairs of society, but will act based on his personal interests. Even if he consults with the people, he will always have a personal agenda that his advisers must align with. Leaders who do not know God are influenced by Satan. The Bible says, "He [the Devil] has come to steal, to kill and to destroy" (John 10:10). The actions of godless leaders often lead to the destruction of society.

The breakthrough we need in our quest for peace, economic progress, and social order in the world cannot be achieved as long we continue to have leaders who are removed from God's touch. This is why past efforts at overcoming conflict have not achieved the desired results.

Examples of Past Efforts

After the Second World War, leaders were concerned about the waste of human lives and resources. They believed war could be avoided, human carnage could be averted, and man could live in peace. These leaders saw the need for the world to live and work together in harmony. Their concern resulted in the birth of the United Nations in 1945.

The objective of the UN was to facilitate cooperation in international law, international security, economic development, social progress, human rights, and the attaining of world peace. The UN gave birth to several efforts and initiatives to further the attainment of those objectives. Peace-keeping, education, health, and economic branches were initiated.

But not much has been achieved since its onset. World leaders have continued to live in suspicion of one another. They make landmark decisions, but never follow through.

Similarly, the Organization of African Unity was formed in 1963 with the aim of promoting the solidarity of African states. It was aimed at the growth of social, economic, and political cooperation, promotion of human rights, and raising the standard of living.

But this initiative didn't work. The continent witnessed various kinds of conflicts, political upheavals, social degeneration, and economic stagnation.

In July 2002, thirty-nine years after its institution, the African Leaders led by former South African president Thabo Mbeki replaced

OAU with the African Union (AU). The leaders thought the problem was in the name of the organization. But the problem was the men who operated it.

Solutions to Conflict

Dialogue between countries is considered by many to be a positive answer to the conflicts that have engulfed the world. Discussion is a good recipe for peace. Communication is a viable tool for dealing with conflict. But the conflicts of the world cannot be fully resolved by dialogue alone among men. There has to be dialogue with God at the center of man's discussions. He is the Creator and the maker of the human heart. He alone understands the heart, and He is the only One who can change it. Solomon said, "The king's heart is in the hand of the Lord; he directs it like a watercourse wherever he pleases" (Proverbs 21:1).

Dialogue among people fails because it is based on human philosophies and intellect. The issue of the heart is spiritual, and only spiritual formulas can resolve conflicts that originate from the heart. Philosophy without God is deceptive and at best produces only temporary results because the root cause of the problem, usually within the human heart, is not addressed.

The chaotic situations of the world can always be traced to the degenerate condition of the human heart. The Bible says, "The heart of man is deceitful above all things and desperately wicked" (Jeremiah 19:9). This is the reason for undiluted education in the fear of the Lord among the people so that every area of our lives, economic, social, and political, can be managed in the fear of God. When God is removed, we definitely have Satan in control and the devil offers only evil.

America's Foundation

The reason America has towered above all others in the midst of a myriad of conflicts is that our foundation was built on the righteousness of God. It is an insult to the memory of the founders of the American nation when people say this country is not a Christian nation. President Barack Obama, in his 2008 campaign, said that America is not a Christian nation.[125] The same sentiment is expressed from some church pulpits in America as well.

America is a Christian nation just as Saudi Arabia is regarded as a Muslim nation. The first amendment of our Constitution prevents the government from making any law respecting an establishment of religion. It guarantees the free exercise of religion or no religion. The Supreme Court has interpreted this amendment as preventing the government from having authority on religion. This is fine.

However, a society is not known by individual opinions. The opinion of a bigger cross-section of people within a society determines what that society is. Saudi Arabia, Iran, Iraq, and Egypt are considered Islamic nations because the majority of their citizens are Muslims, even though people of other religious views live in those countries.

OABITAR, a nonprofit educational organization, states that 75 percent of Americans profess Christianity, either as Protestants, Evangelicals, or Catholics. The rest are Jewish, Buddhist, Muslim, and those who hold no religious views.[126]

Based on these demographic statistics, as well as the declarations of American founders, America is safely referred to as a Christian nation. The fact that other views are accommodated in the Constitution does not make this nation any less Christian. Again, we would not have to debate this reality of what America is vis-a-vis our Christian values if the knowledge of God which was bequeathed to this nation were not being destroyed by those who just cannot accommodate the Christian faith.

The point here is that while one can pardon a non-Christian or a non-committed Christian expressing anti-God sentiments about our blessed nation America, it is unacceptable for those who aspire as church leaders to use the church pulpit to make such ungodly statements. It is a disservice to the nation and the memories of those who labored to build a Christian foundation for the country.

The fact that we are witnessing a gradual crumbling of our Christian values as a nation does not suggest that we are no longer a Christian nation; we are. Besides, Christianity is founded on FAITH and not by what we see. And faith is calling those things that be not, as though they were (Romans 4:17). The Bible says, by reason of Abraham's faith, "it was credited to him as righteousness" (Romans 4:22). It is an act of faithlessness for Christians to make pronouncements that America, known in all nations of the world as 'God's own country,' is not a Christian nation. Such individuals, if indeed they are Christians, require asking for mercy and forgiveness of God.

The American Dream

One of the main goals of the founders of the United States of America was to share the good of the land with other nations. They risked their lives to build this country. Their mission of continuing to receive immigrants was intended to help the poor and give liberty to the oppressed people of the world. They demonstrated their love to everyone, regardless of their views. But they were able to do this without attaching any conditions to it because of their Christian faith. Citizens of other nations saw America as a land of opportunity, where hard work was rewarded with success.

The reason America has so many diverse religions is that the nation's founders believed in love and tolerance. Christians tolerate other beliefs because they want to show love to those who do not share their views. They do not use force. Jesus Christ's teachings are based on the free will of people. The majority of Christians in America desire to live in harmony with others and, through love, to reach out to them.

Over the centuries, the open door as provided by the founders of America has been abused by immigrants who came to America wanting to impose their foreign cultures and to pull down the godly foundations laid by early Americans.

The issue of separation of church and state in the American Constitution was not intended to deny the reality of our being a Christian nation, but to protect the rights of individuals to personal beliefs. However, modern interpretation of this tenet has been used maliciously to isolate the church from society. I believe the reason is because the church is the only institution that teaches righteousness and warns against evil.

Atheism and other views such as Halloween are accorded free expression in our public places. Public schools and job places freely celebrate Halloween, and without any consideration to Christians who do not favor the practice. But any appearance of Christianity is considered unlawful based on the interpretation of separation of church and state. For example, in October 2009, at a school in Paramus, New Jersey, an eighth-grade student named Alex Woinski was sent home on Halloween for dressing like Jesus, in sandals, a robe, fake beard, and a crown of thorns. Five hundred other students participated in the school's celebration. Alex's costume was considered offensive while the horror outfits (depicting Halloween) of other students were deemed acceptable.

The interpretations of separation of church and state has become a singular war against Christianity and what it stands for in America. Our children and new generations do not have the connection with God, and the moral upbringing which sustains a strong nation is therefore lacking in their lives.

John MacArthur, Jr., in his book *Alone with God*, wrote:

> The greatest opposition to Christ's kingdom, and the greatest opposition to Christian living, is the kingdom of this present world, which Satan rules. The next time you begin to resent the latest victory for the ungodly agenda in our country, consider the source. The essence of Satan's kingdom has always been opposition to God's kingdom and God's people.[127]

Satan is at war in America. His agenda to capture the nation is being pursued and he appears to be gaining wider acceptance. Our leaders know that moral values are essential in running a society. They just refuse to acknowledge this fact for political reasons. The challenge we face in all these is the destruction of the nation's godly heritage.

Failure of the Economy

Our economic future is gloomy because it is dependent on human intellect. Without the fear of God we can produce no success. Governance based on the Word of God used to fuel the growth of the nation's economy. The removal of God led to a drastic reduction in people who loved the truth and the rise of those who lacked sincerity in government.

It is always easy to blame the economic woes only on the leaders. But the financial problem we are in today was created by all the economic managers who are part of our growing population of godless in society.

In 2008, George W. Bush was blamed for the nation's economic woes. The opposing party used this perception in the presidential election. Anyone who opposed Bush would win because of the drastic decline in the economic fortune of the nation. The same trend happened with President Obama in the mid-term elections in November 2010. All the economic failures of the country were blamed on the government.

But we are all responsible for the economic misfortune in which we find ourselves. It stems from our appetite for evil. In the past, people were satisfied with their income as long as their basic needs were met. But greed has overtaken the hearts of both leaders and followers. Our attention is now on self rather than society. Corruption and fraud have become an epidemic.

This same trend has occurred in the underdeveloped nations of the world. Nigeria, for example, is blessed with abundant human and natural resources. But it is one of the poorest nations of the world. More than three fourths of the population cannot afford the basic necessities of life. This poverty is the result of corruption and mismanagement over decades.

According to Transparency International, the global coalition against corruption, Nigeria ranked as the 134th most corrupt nation in the world in 2010.[128] Many other countries that should be wealthy based on their natural endowments are also in this tragic situation.

The economic trouble around the world is a direct result of abuse and fraud resulting from corruption. Under-the-table dealings in both public and private sectors are killing big industries and creating unprecedented unemployment.

Sudden downturns in the employment market make people unable to pay their debts or buy new products. Manufacturing companies cannot sell in a dull market, so they have lower revenue. This leads to decreased profits, which results in an inability to pay workers. Management then decides to cut costs, including reduction of the workforce. This perpetuates the cycle of unemployment.

This situation cannot be redeemed unless we appeal to the human heart. The best economic experts cannot fix the situation if the heart situation is not corrected. This is why our early educational system, which was accompanied with the moral Christian teachings and has sustained our efforts in managing our political and economic issues, must be revived. If we allow the damages to continue to a total destruction, the future of the nation cannot be good.

Formulas That No Longer Work

A common modern trend is to stimulate the economy in times of distress. This process works when all things (economic parameters) are equal, including the economic environment that is being stimulated. However, stimuli will not show appreciable impact in a corrupt economic environment. The benefits will be eroded through dishonest implementation.

People also believe that the situation in society requires better laws to improve. Laws are good because they set the standard for people's behavior. The law levels the playing field for all men and women. But we will continue to have need to change, review, or create new laws for a society that is gone or going into godlessness because people do not regard law when the fear of God is lacking in their hearts.

In 2002, in response to the high-profile Enron and WorldCom financial scandals, Senator Paul Sarbanes and Representative Michael G. Oxley co-sponsored a bill that would prevent fraudulent practices in American corporations. This act addressed issues concerning public companies' accounting oversight boards, auditors' independence, corporate governance of officers, and audit committees' responsibilities. The Sarbanes-Oxley Act was signed by President George W. Bush and went into effect on July 30, 2002.

This law was expected to protect the public from being defrauded by white-collar criminals. But in December 2008, massive financial fraud in Wall Street was uncovered by American Federal Investigators of the FBI. Bernard L. Madoff was charged with securities fraud, investment advisor fraud, mail and wire fraud, money laundering, and other financial malpractices. He was sentenced to 150 years in jail and fined a whopping $179 billion.

According to research conducted by the Association of Certified Fraud Examiners (ACFE), US organizations lose an estimated 7 percent of annual revenues to fraud. Based on the projected US Gross Domestic Product for 2008, this percentage indicates a staggering estimate of losses around $994 billion among organizations, despite increased emphasis on anti-fraud controls and recent legislation to combat fraud.[129]

According to an ACFE publication, the cost of fraud and abuse rose from $400 billion in 1996 to $994 billion in 2008 (over 100 percent). These situations consumed about $3 trillion in 2010, despite many changes in the regulations.

President Barack Obama's administration believed that the nation's struggling financial system required regulatory reforms. The government believed that the laws guiding Wall Street were outdated. According to ABC World News with Diane Sawyer on April 22, 2010, "President Obama took on Wall Street today from a nearby New York City college where he renewed his push to convince Main Street and Capitol Hill of the need for sweeping financial regulations."[130] The president believed the system needed to be overhauled to take care of the loopholes that have been created in our financial system.

The president made a good point, but the problem is not only the outdated laws; it is the growing wickedness (godlessness) in our society which the law could no longer control. Good as it is, reforming the law cannot permanently resolve our economic, social, or political problems because wicked acts resulting from the human heart continue to increase unabated.

Paul, in his letter to Timothy, said, "We know that the law is good if a man uses it properly" (1 Timothy 1:8). Law alone cannot solve societal menace, including sabotage to economic development, because the human heart has been conditioned by sin to do what is not right. Violators find ways to beat the law no matter how many laws are created. We will not achieve the objective of the laws, which is deterring evil in our society, even when our jails are overcrowded.

Paul referred to this when he said, "The former regulation is set aside because it was weak and useless; for the law made nothing perfect" (Hebrews 7:18–19). He affirmed that law is not made for the good but for the wicked.

"We also know that the law is made not for good men but for law breakers and rebels, the ungodly and sinful, the unholy and irreligious; for those who kill their fathers or mothers, for murderers, for adulterers, and perverts, for slave traders and liars and perjurers and for whatever else is contrary to the sound doctrines" (1 Timothy 1:9–10).

A perfect society needs no laws to operate successfully because everyone would do what is just. But law is required in a wicked environment. And wickedness is a condition of the human heart.

Law works by controlling the criminals and keeping them away, often in jail houses, from creating further harm to society. There are two issues here; the first is that we often create law out of experiences of past inappropriate activities of the people. The second issue is that the law created to combat certain activities of criminals is only relevant to the extent to which the people have developed other ways of offending the law.

And what we require for a peaceful society is not new laws or revisions of outdated ones. If we had done what is right by appealing to the hearts of the people, some of those in jail would probably have been saved from the problem. The plausible way to achieve a peaceful society is to motivate the hearts of the people to live a life with fewer tendencies for evil.

The problem is that laws cannot change the human heart. Godliness is the key to law and order in any society. Our economic, political, and social travail cannot be corrected by law. We need a change of heart more than reformation of laws. Only the law that is in the heart can produce the desired result of right social order, economic fortune, and political uprightness. That is why God said concerning the Jews, "I will put my laws into their minds and write them on their hearts. I will be their God, and they will be my people" (Hebrews 8:10).

The point is that when a man or woman surrenders his or her life to God, the spirit of God rules such a heart, and the heart naturally follows the moral principles without any fear of law because doing the right thing is obedience to God. That is why when a person becomes a Christian (born-again), the old pattern of life is changed because the conscience is now governed by the Holy Spirit. "Therefore, if anyone is in Christ, the new creation has come: The old has gone, the new is here!" (2 Corinthians 5:17).

The failure we are witnessing is a result of human hearts that need to be reformed. Satan has taken the world captive by giving the impression that people have the capacity to fix the problems without God.

Therefore, if we desire an upright and just society devoid of the current political, social, and economic problems that we are experiencing today, unemployment, surge in huge national debt, hyperinflation, and corruption, etc.; we need to go back to where our nation's founders began, and build on their foundations of Christian truth. We have to teach this Christian truth to our children and children after them. When leaders and people reverence God, their actions bring peace and prosperity to the nation.

Thoughts

Do we have any remedies for the catastrophes resulting from our ruined education and pervading godlessness in our society? To an ordinary natural mind, hope is lost. But a man filled with the spirit of God would know that "with God all things are possible." "Jesus looked at them [bewildered people who have lost hope of eternal life] and said, 'With man this is impossible, but with God all things are possible'" (Matthew 19:26).

It is only an honor when God depends on our contributions to fix the conflicts in the society. We should count it as a privilege, and what we are required to do is to depend on God for wisdom and strength to perform the responsibilities He has committed to us. If we work with God, godliness will be restored in our nation and we will reverse the collapse of the values America is known for.

CHAPTER 9

CAN GOD STOP EVIL?

One thing God has spoken, two things I have heard:
"Power belongs to you, God."
—Psalm 62:11

MOST OF THE human race has not recognized God and are not able to understand our relationship with Him. Our concept of God has become distorted due to a lack of understanding of who He is. Thus man has come up with a variety of opinions about the creation of man and the world in order to explain away the notion of God. The existence or non-existence of God is an issue in the world and has led to many unanswered questions in the conduct of human lives.

The dictionary definition for God is "a being conceived as the perfect, omnipotent, omniscient originator and ruler of the universe, the principal object of faith and worship in monotheistic religion."[131]

Though some people deny the existence of God, many concepts have been formulated about Him. Even people who claim not to believe in God use expressions such as *godly, godless, godfather, godforsaken,* etc. These concepts have been part of the English vocabulary as far back as the use of language.

God and Scientific Claims

One common human characteristic is that we question our own existence. We ask, "Who am I?" and "How did I get here?" While we look for answers, the acceptable opinion is often that which does not acknowledge God.

Scientific theories of human inventions opposed to, or that query the theory of God's creation, are generally considered credible because they are supposedly backed with "proofs," that is, evidence on which their theories are based. They are also popular because Satan, who took the control of world affairs, would always promote anything anti-God.

However, science has a serious drawback in that its instruments of verification are part of God's creation. Therefore, the outcomes of scientific research cannot be conclusive because all inventions are discovered, not created; that is, they were already in existence before science.

As commendable as the works of science are, they have not been able to fully resolve the problems of the world as to creation and human existence. Many unanswered questions remain. And more difficult questions abound as we struggle to find answers for those we already have.

Charles Darwin was a great scientist. He believed that humans developed over time from other things already in the world. One major flaw in Darwin's theory was the inability to answer pertinent questions. For example, if man developed from amoeba, how did amoeba come into being? And why has human development been static and unchanged over the past several centuries?

The theory of evolution and others which are argued against creation by God as written in the Bible do not explain how various human behaviors, races, cultures, and languages changed over time.

The Problem with Charles Darwin

Darwin's observations were not all wrong, but he veered into error because his knowledge of science was not mixed with the knowledge and fear of God. Knowledge that excludes God will usually end in confusion. He was right that the human body is a product of earth. God made man from the dust. The Bible says, "The Lord God formed man from the dust of the ground and breathed into his nostrils the breath of life, and the man became a living being" (Genesis 2:7).

When Adam and Eve sinned in the garden of Eden, God reminded them that they came from dust. He said, "By the sweat of your brow you will eat your food until you return to the ground, since from it you were taken; for dust you are and to dust you will return" (Genesis 3:19).

However, the body is not the man, but a component made by God to house the man. When God made Adam, He breathed into his nostrils the breath of life, which turned the clay into a living being made in His image. God is not dust; therefore, dust cannot represent His image. "God created mankind in his own image, in the image of God he created them; male and female he created them" (Genesis 1:27).

When a human being's time on earth is over, the house (clay) in which he or she dwelled is buried or cremated, but the real person will return to God. King Solomon said, "The dust returns to the ground it came from, and the spirit returns to God who gave it" (Ecclesiastes 12:7).

The point is that in our efforts to disprove God's existence, we often fall into the trap of using God and His creations to disprove Him. In the end, we are actually proving His works, because we cannot make any new thing. All human theories must make reference to what has been. The Bible says, "All things were made by Him and without Him was not anything made that was made" (John 1:3).

Darwin's work in the area of evolution added significantly to the confusion in the world, as his theories contained more questions than answers. And yet, modern-day science teachers make great efforts to convince students that Darwin's theories of evolution are fact. *That is what the science textbook says, and you must accept it if you wish to make progress in your academic pursuits.*

Bruce Bickel and Stan Jantz, in their book *Creation and Evolution 101*, wrote:

"Darwin's theory has survived and flourished since he proclaimed it in 1859. It is taught as a fundamental precept of biological science without any disclaimer or mention of anomalies or ambiguities. So it must be correct, right? Wrong. Darwinism is not so obviously true that it should be accepted as fact instead of theory. Although Darwin's theory has had almost 150 years to be proven by scientific findings, significant problems remain."[132]

Though numerous questions about the theory of evolution have not been satisfactorily answered, the human heart gets excited about anything that seems to disprove God's work. We want God to prove who He is. But God does not owe us any explanation. Neither does He need to prove who He is to us because our belief and non-belief does not change who He is.

The only theory on the origin of man that has not changed is the truth of God's creation. This is the only theory that can help us to have our sanity in our thoughts on creation. We will be free from self-inflicted mental torture when we learn to believe God and who He is. The Bible says, "Then you will know the truth, and the truth will set you free" (John 8:32).

The Human Heart: Obstacle to Truth

We have the choice whether or not to believe in the existence of God. Often, even those who profess trust in God sometimes doubt their conviction. But disbelief does not change reality. Human argument cannot prove that God does not exist. The knowledge of God is beyond proof of science; it is a fact that has never been disproven.

When the people of Israel questioned their origin, the prophet Isaiah told them, "You turn things upside down, as if the potter were thought to be like the clay! Shall what is formed say to the one who formed it, 'You did not make me'? Can the pot say to the potter, 'You know nothing'?" (Isaiah 29:16).

The prophet was provoked to anger by continued human reservations about creation and the work of God. He pronounced curses on those who engaged in the fruitless exercise of challenging God. Isaiah said, "Woe to those who quarrel with their Maker, those who are nothing but potsherds among the potsherds on the ground. Does the clay say to the potter, 'What are you making?' Does your work say, 'the potter has no hands'?" (Isaiah 45:9).

Intellect is a talent given by God for the benefit of society. Many intelligent people have used their God-given talents for the service of humanity. Their inventions have added to the social well-being of the people. But intelligence becomes simplistic when it is used as evidence that man has attained such great heights that he no longer has any need for God and thus holds Him in contempt.

The Certainty of God

The Bible says, "The heavens declare the glory of God; the skies proclaim the work of his hands" (Psalm 19:1). The intelligent arrangement of the universe is evidence that there is a power beyond human ability.

All bodies of knowledge put together have not succeeded in explaining life's mysteries. The only answer to these questions is God. We must accept this gap in our knowledge; otherwise, we make fools of ourselves.

Proof of God is all around us. Nature shows beyond reasonable doubt that there is a higher being in control of this universe. The sky, the earth, and the sea are all beyond human comprehension. Those people who think they can comprehend the sky, earth, and sea had better re-examine their brains. Some people spend their entire lives studying these unique wonders but till date no one has successfully proved the creations of the planets. Yet some people hold the theory of 'no God'. The Bible says, "The fool says in his heart, 'There is no God'" (Psalm 14:1).

Former president Ronald Reagan said, "Sometimes when I'm faced with an unbeliever, an atheist, I am tempted to invite him to the greatest gourmet dinner one could ever serve and, when we finished eating that magnificent dinner, to ask him if he believes there's a cook."[133]

For many decades, we have engaged in the explorations of the universe. We are still exploring the moon. We have not so much thought about explorations of the sun and the stars. Yet, we still do not have clues. It is an evidence of a greater being.

Evils in Our Society

Some individuals base their argument against the existence of God on the prevalence of evil in the world. They argue that if there is a God, nothing horrendous should ever happen. And that if God is such an all-powerful being, He should eradicate all wickedness.

A young lady in a trying experience doubted the existence of God because she was physically abused. She could not believe that God would allow her to pass through such an ordeal. From an earthly perspective, she was right to seek an explanation for this. But human beings are limited in our understanding. True knowledge can only come from the Creator. The young lady's bad situation as it were, in a God-fearing heart would have led her to solicit for God's mercy.

Equally unexplainable are societal ills such as terrorism, war, and criminal acts such as murder, rape, and stealing. In addition, we experience natural disasters such as earthquakes, floods, and tornados. No one has all the answers to why these things occur. But that does not negate the fact that someone superior to human beings is in control of the situations in the world. A colleague of mine in a job place scandalously said that God has failed the world as the chief executive. My response to him was that none of us has the power to give God a target on which He could be measured as having failed or passed.

Denial of the existence of God does not change the fact of God's existence. We can indulge or plume ourselves in a feeling of pride, but it is all temporary. All men and women will ultimately have an appointment with God on His judgment seat at the appropriate time.

Testimony of an Atheist

Former president Ronald Reagan, at the annual convention of the National Religious Broadcasters Association on February 1, 1988, told the story of a young Russian soldier who found God on his last day on earth. Reagan had received a letter from a woman in Wisconsin whose husband was killed in World War II. She enclosed in her letter a prayer her husband had sent her:

"Hear me, Oh God; never in the whole of my lifetime have I spoken to you, but just now I feel like sending you my greetings. You know, from childhood on, they've always told me you are not. I, like a fool, believed them. I've never contemplated your creation, and yet tonight, gazing up out of my shell hole, I marveled at the shimmering stars above me and suddenly knew the cruelty of the lie.

Will you, my God, reach your hand out to me, I wonder? But I will tell you, and you will understand. Is it not strange that light should come upon me and I see you amid this night of hell?

And there is nothing else I have to say. This, though: I'm glad that I've learned to know you. At midnight we are scheduled to attack. But you are looking on, and I am not afraid.

The signal. Well, I guess I must be going. I've been happy with you. This more I want to say: As you well know, the fighting will be cruel and even tonight I may come knocking at your door. Although I have not been a friend to you before, still, will you let me enter now, when I do come?

Why, I am crying, O God, my Lord. You see what happens to me: Tonight my eyes were opened. Farewell, my God. I'm going and not likely to come back. Strange, is it not, but death I fear no longer?

The president said that young man did die in that attack, and that prayer was found on the body of a young Soviet soldier who was killed in combat in 1944."[134]

The young soldier embraced God in his dying days. His experience was similar to that of the thief on the cross with Jesus, who cried out to God for help just before he died and was promptly assured of paradise (Luke 23:43). The soldier's travail stems from growing up in an environment opposed to the truth of the existence of God.

And we may not all have same opportunity this soldier had in getting to reconcile with God before he passed on. It is instructive therefore for those who are opposed to acknowledging God to change and make things right with God while there is opportunity to do so, because we all have a date with the Lord.

Reasons for Evil in Society

One reason we have had little reprieve from the evil in the world is that we refuse to acknowledge our human limitations. We are responsible for much of the wickedness around us because of our bad choices. We have the ability to choose, which makes us responsible for the decisions we make. Ironically, we often hold God responsible for the evil we voluntarily choose while we expect God to stop the effects on us.

Human choice is an issue of life. Our success or failure in life is derived from our personal choices. If we all make good choices, our society will have peace and we will individually live useful and fulfilled lives. Robert F. Bennett said: "Your life is the sum result of all the choices you make, both consciously and unconsciously. If you can control the process of choosing, you can take control of all aspects of your life. You can find the freedom that comes from being in charge of yourself."[135]

Human beings have the power to choose between good and evil, and we have continually chosen evil. We have a big appetite for evil. Yet everybody blames someone else, and no one wants to take responsibility for his or her own actions.

When negative situations occur, people are usually quick to apportion blame. Yet those who are quick to condemn others, if given the same situations, would usually end up committing the same mistakes they blamed others for.

For instance, the issue of slavery was blamed on white men who bought blacks as slaves. But are the sellers free from blame? If there were no sellers, would there have been buyers? The point is that evil is universal; it is a malaise of the human race.

And the reason for the prevalence of evil is the absence of the knowledge of God. The knowledge of God produces fear and reverence for God, which ultimately keeps people away from evil. The proportion of evil in any environment is determined by the knowledge the people have of God.

God wants His children to always choose good, and not evil. The Bible says, "He has shown you, O mortal, what is good. And what does the Lord require of you? To act justly and to love mercy and to walk humbly with your God" (Micah 6:8). The Lord directed the prophet Amos to tell the people, "Seek good, not evil, that you may live. Then the Lord God Almighty will be with you" (Amos 5:14), and in the next verse, "Hate evil, love good" (Amos 5:15).

Everything a person does is a personal choice. The choices we make in life determine who we turn out to be. When our time on the earth is over, we will be remembered for whatever good or evil we have done. Balaam, a wise man of the Bible, said, "Let me die the death of the righteous, and may my final end be like theirs" (Numbers 23:10).

Human Submission to Satan

God has not put us in the dark concerning the originator of evil. Lucifer, also called Satan, is the source of all wickedness. According to the Bible, he was an archangel in heaven and lived in God's presence like other angels before he rebelled against God. He was then sent out of heaven and cast down to the earth. He has since gained control of the world. (See Isaiah 14:12–18.)

Satan's objective is to destroy the human race because we are created in the image of God. Satan is opposed to God, and the only way he thought he could hurt God was to destroy His beloveds created after God's image. So we have become the target of Satan. The devil knows the depth of God's love for mankind, and that He does not want anyone to perish.

God made an unparalleled sacrifice when He offered His Son, Jesus Christ, for the redemption of mankind from the consequences of sin. Jesus was nailed on the cross for our sin. He died (an ignoble death) but rose on the third day as a sign of victory over human conflict. For ages, Satan has fought to destroy this truth. But God's words cannot be destroyed.

Satan continually urges and leads mankind into evil thoughts and actions. However, the goodness of the Lord remains with us. Everything Satan does is an attempt to convince people to deny God. But everything God does is for the good of mankind.

Men Who Made Good Choices

When Satan threatens to overcome the world with wickedness, God raises individuals to stand up against Satan's evil plans. Many such situations abound, and here are a few examples.

Slavery is one of the worst examples of man's inhumanity to man. One person's calamity became the other's prosperity. Many protagonists of the slave trade believed they were making good business decisions. The feelings of the slaves weren't considered. The slave-trading industry guaranteed the survival of the strong over the weak.

Many saw slavery as necessary for their welfare and existence. Other people, however, rose up to fight this evil. They committed all their resources, including their liberty and their lives, to stop it.

William Wilberforce

William Wilberforce was one of such people who chose to honor God. He was born into a prosperous merchant family and entered Parliament at the exceptionally young age of twenty-one years. He was a talented orator who was not committed to any particular cause.

But shortly after he became a Christian, his perspective about life changed. He viewed politics from a moral perspective and desired to reform societal behavior. He doggedly fought slavery until finally he saw the bill [abolition of slavery] with royal assent in March 1807.

Wilberforce confronted stiff opposition from England's allies and England's amity with Napoleon and France, who were staunch supporters of the dastardly trade. Mr. Wilberforce came, saw, fought, and conquered, leaving the world a better place than he met it.

Abraham Lincoln

Abraham Lincoln recognized that he was an instrument in the hands of God. At the end of America's Civil War, on a presidential mission to inspect the ruins of battle, he refused to be praised by the crowd of African Americans who had surrounded the president to praise him for his efforts at freeing the slaves. Instead Lincoln directed the attention of the people to God, who had used him to accomplish His purpose.

"Lincoln stepped off a rowboat on the Richmond shoreline, and walked unannounced into the city. No conqueror entered a captured city with less pomp and circumstance. Within minutes, an elderly newly freed slave stepped forward to squint at the tall stranger in the black stovepipe hat. "Bless the Lord! There is the great Messiah!" he shouted. "Glory, Hallelujah." …

A crowd of African Americans quickly surrounded the president, weeping, shouting and cheering. When some dropped to their knees, Lincoln, now in tears himself insisted: "Don't kneel to me. You must kneel to God only."[136]

The history of the ending of slavery in America cannot be complete without reference to President Abraham Lincoln.

John Brown

John Brown was a white man born in comfortable surroundings. But he was full of anger at the way slaves were being treated. In 1859, John witnessed the brutal murder of Elijah Lovejoy, a journalist who had devoted his life to fighting the slave trade prevailing in the south of the United States. He was cut down by the bullets of assassins who hated him for it.

John Brown attended a special service in honor of Elijah at the Congregational Church in Hudson, New York. At the service, John renewed his commitment to fight injustice. He declared, "Here before God, in the presence of these witnesses, I consecrate my life for the destruction of slavery."[137]

John chose to fight a guerrilla war against the slave masters and to free the slaves he knew in America. His children who joined him in this war all died in the battle. John was arrested, tried, and condemned to death by hanging for treason against the state of Virginia, and for murder and conspiracy. He was executed in December, 1859.

John Brown paid the supreme price. His efforts to end slave trade and help slaves to freedom wiped out all his children as well. John saw a war he could not ignore, and he went down in history as a man who fought and died for what he believed.

Men Who Made Bad Choices

Despite God's concern and use of individuals to fix societies' issues, Satan does not relent in using some other individuals to further his evil cause. Again, these are matters of human choices; there were those who by their choice were used by Satan to do evil against the people. They preferred to be remembered for killing and destroying the society. They had the opportunity to do good or evil but chose to do evil. They were people the world would wish it never had in its history.

Adolph Hitler

Adolph Hitler came from a humble background. He was an Austrian peasant who worked as a construction worker but was fired by his bosses after other workers refused to work with him. His attempts to enter art school failed. He was homeless and impoverished. He barely survived as a poster artist but God showed him mercy. He joined the German army and rose to the rank of corporal.

He was blessed by God with the talents of popular leadership, like Abraham Lincoln, and powerful oration, like William Wilberforce. He could have used those talents to bless the world. But he chose otherwise. Hitler's sixty-one-year sojourn on earth cost the world millions of lives, including about seven million Jews, in war and genocide. In 1948, he committed suicide.

By the time he left the world, the people believed it would have been better for the world if Hitler had never been born.

Mahmoud Ahmadinejad

Iran is currently under United Nations sanctions because of its nuclear program. The government of Iran, under President Mahmoud Ahmadinejad, is in a battle with the rest of the world. Few nations are comfortable with this prospective danger.

Ahmadinejad has publicly revealed his hatred for the Jewish nation. His attitude is a major source of concern for other world leaders as it is similar to Hitler's.

Muammar Gaddafi

When Muammar Gaddafi seized power in his country, Libya, in 1969, he abolished the Constitution of the nation. He became a dictator who together with his relatives controlled the economy of the oil-rich African state. Gaddafi eliminated all opposition in the country and during his forty years of totalitarian rule of Libya, a large section of the country's population have had their lives reduced to below poverty level while President Gaddafi's family members live in excessive affluence.

Gaddafi started several unnecessary wars and acquired chemical weapons. The Arab nations were not comfortable with his reign, while African nations were always suspicious of every move of Gaddafi. He was known to be prone to igniting political and religious troubles in any country he had access to. The religious and terrorist problems being experienced in northern Nigeria were often linked to him. He once advocated for the break-up of Nigeria, the West African country, where the Hausa-Fulani Muslims dominated the north but which has more Christians in the southern part of the country. The United Nations referred to Libya as a pariah state under Gaddafi.

Godless leaders often appear to be working for the good of their societies, but those without the fear of God do not do any good. The forty-two years of the tyrannical rule of the Gaddafi ended in 2011 after he had plunged Libya into an avoidable civil war which claimed the lives of thousands of innocent citizens. On October 20, 2011, Gaddafi was killed by Libyan freedom fighters that rose against his government.

The Third Choice

The third choice is to sit or stand by and watch while the world goes into flames. It is the worst choice, but a common one. Each of us can choose whether to be a builder or a destroyer. But some people spend their years on earth neither destroying nor fighting destruction. They live in complacency. They do not care and do not realize that they are created to fulfil a purpose for the good of society. A destroyer is bad for society, but equally bad is the carefree who cannot be bothered whatever went wrong.

In his article "A Presidential Handshake," James R. Kessler quoted former president Jimmy Carter as saying, "I hate to see complacency prevail in our lives when it's so directly contrary to the teachings of Christ."[138] We are part of the problem if we aren't part of the solution.

Words of Reason

The above three categories of human actions are matters of individual choices. We are not robots, as it was not the intention of God to create us that way. He made us to have intelligence to make choices. And God has continually played His role as our Creator, guiding us not to destroy ourselves. We do the evil we do because we disregard the words of God. And we are fully accountable for the choices we make.

As a toddler, I loved to touch flames of fire because flames looked attractive to my eyes. And my mother was always concerned I would harm myself, because fire burns. But because of my insistence all the time when I saw flames of fire to touch it, my mom left me on one occasion and I got burnt and learned from the experience that fire can harm. Thereafter, I would not go near fire anymore.

However, there were other kids who got burnt many times but were still not deterred from self-inflicted harms. No one can blame the parents of such disobedient children when they hurt themselves because the parents have done their job of teaching them to know that fire harms. The disturbing aspect of such disobedience is that often, the disobedient child who plays with fire may not only burn himself but other people and properties when his or her actions get uncontrolled.

God has not left us in doubt as to His ability and willingness to check the activities of the devil in the world. God's interventions have prevented the world from self-destruction resulting from the manipulations of Satan and his evils. Our choices therefore cannot be blamed on God, and He cannot be held responsible for the evils we bring on ourselves. Rather, we are accountable to God as our Creator. God is sovereign.

The Role of Christian Believers

The glaring evils in our societies notwithstanding, God expects Christian believers to surrender themselves for the use of God to fix issues in societies. The requirement is the willingness and obedience by Christians to humbly submit self to the services of God to fix issues created by the devil within the society. With that, the church would be fulfilling the purpose for its existence in society. The world is in dire need of persons who are willing to give from the talents God has blessed them with for the promotion of peace and good life around the world.

The social and economic troubles in our nation can be fixed with selfless individuals, who are not seeking for personal pride or political gains. When the motive for such service is right, the totality of our input and output will be based on truth.

The society can be impacted, and it requires minimum efforts if we rely on God and the wisdom from the words of God. The society would witness drastic reductions in the unbelievable number of homeless people in our society. Those who are struggling with addictions foisted on them by the spirit of Satan would be delivered. With the words of God and power of prayers, the church can challenge the evil that we consider reprehensible within our society and work to change the situation.

Beyond that, as in the days of early American missionaries, we can also tackle Satan around the Third World that is being ravaged by poverty and starvation, and has become breeding societies for terrorism, human trafficking, child abuse, and other serious social vices.

Need for a Change of Heart

The condition of the human heart is the obstacle to achieving the purpose of God for us, and to fixing issues in society. Our hearts therefore need to be purified by the words of God to do useful service to ourselves and to our communities. It is always in the human selfish nature to act based on our individual and personal interest. But when the spirit of God fills our hearts, like William Wilberforce, our priorities in life will change to please God and to serve the common good.

We have tried to fix our problems but have not succeeded because our efforts are not mixed with the fear of God. For instance, governments have initiated many ways to protect the lives and property of people from terrorists, but we are not winning the war. Amazing high-tech gadgets intended to detect security threats at airports often fail to track the activities of suspicious people, and terrorists still find their way to accomplish their malicious acts. The reason for the failure is also human. No matter how good our machines and infrastructures are, they are operated by people. The common good is compromised when the fear of God is not in their hearts. A society that does not fear God cannot protect itself with gadgets.

For example, at the Los Angeles International Airport (LAX), in California, one of the busiest but adequately policed airports in the world, the security was compromised. The TSA officer who manned the security gadgets at the airport compromised his professional ethics, which led to free access for marijuana and illegal drug dealers at the airport.

On October 18, 2011, *Daily Breeze,* a South Bay newspaper in California, carried the news headline, 'Ex-fire Chief's son, and security agent arrested at LAX'. According to Art Marroquin, *Daily Breeze* staff writer, Millage Jonathan Peaks IV, 23 passed through the heavily fortified LAX airport checks with the dangerous drugs, and was not caught. Millage was aided by Dianna Perez, a Transportation Security Officer (TSA).

The criminal activities were blown open because an employee of the airline in which Millage was travelling smelled the marijuana on him, and he was arrested by the FBI. And this was not the first attempt; there were several successful such illegal deals in the past. "Perez …admitted to being paid $3000 for assisting Peaks and several of his friends to carry drugs onto several other flights."[139]

The point is that the objective of policing and investments in security gadgets can only be achieved when the hearts of our people are transformed, and are good. When the loyalty of men and women in our society has been shifted away from God because of lack of the knowledge of the words of God, they will be loyal to the devil.

Why Good People Suffer

The tragedy of the situation, however, is that good people suffer in the midst of the conflicts they never created. These are questions we have no answer to. But something is certain: God is God and God is good. For example, Job in the Bible, despite his uprightness, was faced with hard times. In response to Job's genuine complaint, God answered Job with these rhetorical questions: "Where were you when I laid the earth's foundation? Tell me, if you understand" (Job 38:4). "Will the one who contends with the Almighty correct him? Let him who accuses God answer him!" (Job 40:2).

Job had no answer to God's questions, and he humbly responded: "I am unworthy—how can I reply to you? I put my hand over my mouth" (Job 40:4). It is foolhardy to argue with the Lord Almighty. We do not have the qualifications or intelligence to so do. God is not our equal. He is the object of our worship and reverence. Only the wise understand this.

David, a former monarch in the nation of Israel, said:

Lord my God, you are very great; you are clothed with splendor and majesty. The Lord wraps himself in light as with a garment; he stretches out the heavens like a tent and lays the beams of his upper chambers on their waters. He makes the clouds his chariot and rides on the wings of the wind. He makes winds his messengers, flames of fire his servants. He set the earth on its foundations; it can never be moved.

—Psalm 104:1–5

Agur, son of Jakeh, said:

Surely I am only a brute, not a man; I do not have human understanding. I have not learned wisdom, nor have I attained to the knowledge of the Holy One. Who has gone up to heaven and come down? Whose hands have gathered up the wind? Who has wrapped up the waters in a cloak? Who has established all the ends of the earth? What is his name, and what is the name of his son? Surely you know! Every word of God is flawless; he is a shield to those who take refuge in him.

—Proverbs 30:2–5

God has unlimited power. He is awesome and there is no wrong or fault in His actions. Whatever He does is right. The apostle Paul summed up the power of God thus:

What then shall we say? Is God unjust? Not at all! For he says to Moses, "I will have mercy on whom I have mercy, and I will have compassion on whom I have compassion." It does not, therefore, depend on human desire or effort, but on God's mercy.

—Romans 9:14–16

When C.S. Lewis lost his wife, Joy, he said:

"When I lay these questions before God I get no answer. But a rather special sort of 'No answer'. It is not the locked door. It is more like a silent, certainly not uncompassionate, gaze. As though He shook His head not in refusal but waiving the question. Like, 'Peace, child; you don't understand'. Can a mortal ask questions which God finds unanswerable? Quite easily, I should think. All non-sense questions are unanswerable. How many hours are there in a mile? Is Yellow Square or round? Probably half the questions we ask-are like that."[140]

Yes, we cannot understand why, but yet our revolt should not be to God because we cannot move Him. What we require after all the experiences, bad or good, is the mercy of God. He is the God of order and makes no mistakes in all His plans.

Paul Johnson, in his book *The Quest for God,* said, "Ours is not a chaotic universe but a universe of laws, and they include moral laws. We ignore them individually at the risk of our immortal souls, and mankind ignores them collectively at the risk of its social health and even its existence."[141] We cannot hurt God when we perpetrate evil; we only hurt ourselves and our society.

But God is ever merciful and patient. His program, in the light of the world's circumstances, is clear to Him. The sensible thing for us to do, therefore, is to accept what we cannot change: that there is a God and we surely need Him.

Thoughts

Do we truly find answers to all the questions of human life? No. But does that change the nature and position of God? Not a bit. Our arguments, our belief and unbelief, cannot change the person of God. We should also be sure that when our time on earth is over, we have an appointment with God, for we will be held accountable for all our deeds on earth. Paul counseled the church in Corinth, saying: "We must all appear before the judgment seat of Christ, so that each of us may receive what is due us for the things done while in the body, whether good or bad" (2 Corinthians 5:10).

CHAPTER 10

THE ROLE OF THE CHURCH IN SOCIETY

We wonder if God can still redeem our society and bring
about a nation characterized by righteousness. Is anything too
hard for God? At the appointed time, if we remain faithful
and serve Him in obedience and understanding, He will
reestablish righteousness in our land and He will do it by His
word and through His Spirit, beginning in His church.
—Pastor Rod and Joni Parsley

THE CHURCH IS an assembly of persons called Christians, whose
collective voice and behavior identify with and match the pattern and
character of Jesus Christ. Jesus is the founder of the church. The early
believers were called Christians because they were often mistaken for
Jesus Christ, even when it was known that He was no longer physically
on earth.

Jesus began His ministry by fixing conflicts within society. He told
the world that He came so humans could live good lives. He said, "The
thief [the devil] comes only to steal and kill and destroy; I have come
that they [people] may have life, and have it to the full" (John 10:10).
And throughout His stay on earth, everyone that came to Him got relief
for their problems.

At the inception of His ministry, He declared to the public what they should expect from Him. He said, "The Spirit of the Lord is on me, because he has anointed me to proclaim good news to the poor. He has sent me to proclaim freedom for the prisoners and recovery of sight for the blind, to set the oppressed free, to proclaim the year of the Lord's favor" (Luke 4:18-19).

The founding of the church by the Lord Jesus Christ was in furtherance of His mission in the world. He created the church for the purpose of fulfilling and accomplishing what He came to the world to do: deliver the people from the hands of Satan and establish a just and peaceful society.

The Church: An Instrument of Change

The church is an important instrument for change in society. Its birth was to put an end to the activities of Satan among the people. While introducing the church, Jesus said to Peter and others, "And on this rock I will build my church, and the gates of Hades will not overcome it. I will give you the keys of the kingdom of heaven; whatever you bind on earth will be bound in heaven, and whatever you loose on earth will be loosed in heaven" (Matthew 16: 18-19).

The church was empowered to oversee the affairs of the world with a view to rescuing people from all manner of conflicts which have ravaged the society. Before Christ departed from the earth, He instructed His disciples and those who would believe in Him to continue resolving the conflicts that would arise within society. Because the devil is here on earth and his time has not come when he will be forever chained, God placed the church in the position to repair whatever Satan destroyed.

Jesus gave His authority to the church after His resurrection. This was reaffirmed in His parting words to the disciples before He ascended to heaven. He said:

"All authority in heaven and on earth has been given to me. Therefore go and make disciples of all nations, baptizing them in the name of the Father and of the Son and of the Holy Spirit, and teaching them to obey everything I have commanded you. And surely I am with you always, to the very end of the age" (Matthew 28:18–20). The church therefore becomes the catalyst for change in the world.

This is the great commission with the full authority and the power to deliver the world from conflict. If any group of people has the responsibility and capacity for proffering solutions to the current travails of society, it is the church. The church is the anchor prepared by Providence for this purpose. The church is responsible for ensuring orderliness and peace among people, to the extent to which it is possible in this present world.

And the church has fared well. The early apostles and missionaries did a good job. Philippi, a Roman colony and the leading city of the district of Macedonia, was in uproar for the good job the apostles did. Lives of people were changed for good. Satan recognized the work of God through the apostles. The devil also praised the men of God. In that city, a lady possessed of the devil said, "These men are servants of the Most High God, who are telling you the way to be saved" (Acts 16:17).

Satan was nevertheless uncomfortable because his activities were stopped. Paul and Silas were later arrested and charged for creating uproar in the city. The Bible says, "They brought them before the magistrates and said, "These men are Jews, and are throwing our city into an uproar" (Acts 16:20).

The Church's Tool for Change

The church is empowered through the Bible, the words of God. The Bible for decades has been instrumental for change in the world. It is the strongest and most dependable weapon to accomplish the lofty goal of changing the behavior, thoughts, and characters of nations. And the Bible is available in abundance and is changing lives of those who want to be guided by the words of God. But it is also a problem for people whose hearts have been completely darkened by Satan. Some individuals do not want to go near the Bible because it judges their hearts; they equally do not want people to see it because they know the Bible has the power to change lives for good. David in his songs of Psalms said, "Your word is a lamp for my feet, a light on my path" (Psalm 119:105).

The Word of God, the Bible, is supported by the Holy Spirit to transform the hearts of men and women. It is a venerable tool that the early apostles carried everywhere they went. Paul said, "I am not ashamed of the gospel, because it is the power of God that brings salvation to everyone who believes: first to the Jew, then to the Gentile" (Romans 1:16). Conflicts are resolved as parties to the disagreement receive the undiluted (genuine) words of the Lord from the Bible.

The Bible is also the only reference book in the world that has never been revised or become outdated. Some of the books of the Bible are believed to have been written between 586 and 538 BC. A translation of the Bible into English was completed in 1611 through the initiative of King James of England. Since then, the Bible has been translated into numerous other languages. But nothing in the content has changed. Jesus said, "Heaven and earth will pass away, but my words will never pass away" (Matthew 24:35). Many thanks to young and old folks in different countries of the world who are in the business of translating the Bible into the local languages so that people can have readily the words in the language they understand. The success in this endeavor is the hope of the world. The world will change when the majority of the people can have access to the Bible and understand the words of God.

There are constant attacks on the Bible by the agents of Satan who do not wish the world well. They are people who want the society to remain in darkness because they profit from disorderliness. Conflicts among the people give such individuals opportunity to lord their wishes on the society. The truth of the words of God liberates the minds of the people and they can choose what is right in their efforts to please God. However, despite the attacks, the Bible remains the only book that can be measured not only by its popularity judged by its continuous rise in sales all over the world, but by its efficacy in resolving human problems.

The Bible and Science

Satan tried to use science to disprove the words of God, but science has not disproved the genuineness of the Bible. On the contrary, many branches of science—archeology, astronomy, geology, paleontology, meteorology, biology, anthropology, and physics, for example—have provided proof of its accuracy and infallibility. Scientific inventions and knowledge are blessings of God to human generations. God gave such knowledge to benefit the people but not to disprove His power or existence.

Though written by men, the Bible was not created out of human imagination. The Bible says, "For prophecy never came by the will of man, but holy men of God spoke as they were moved by the Holy Spirit" (1 Peter 1:21 NKJV).

Great scientists confirmed the indispensability of God in this world. Sir Isaac Newton, an English physicist, mathematician, astronomer, natural philosopher, and alchemist was an accomplished scientist on this planet. He acknowledged the power of God in his achievements.

Mitch Stokes said of Newton, "In fact, when it came to science generally, Newton cared far more about the knowledge itself than for its application in technology. For him, knowledge of God was all-important, and scientific knowledge was simply part of knowing God-knowing God through his works."[142]

George Washington Carver, another erudite scientist, accomplished academic, and agriculturist whose researches and inventions in agriculture benefited the world and farmers, acknowledged God in his scientific successes. He believed he could have faith both in God and science and integrated them into his life. He often said that his faith in Jesus Christ was the only mechanism by which he could effectively pursue and perform the art of science.

Albert Einstein was another successful scientist. A German-born Jewish professor of physics, he was credited with many laurels, among which was the Special Theory of Relativity (1905). In his book, *The World as I See It*, he laid credence to the fact that no one, not even a successful scientist, could doubt the existence of a higher Being. He said, "A knowledge of the existence of something we cannot penetrate, of the manifestations of the profoundest reason and the most radiant beauty, which are only accessible to our reason in their most elementary forms—it is this knowledge and this emotion that constitute the truly religious attitude; in this sense, and in this alone, I am a deeply religious man."[143]

Those who think science has replaced God and God's words are simply suffering from internal disorders. I tried early in my life to query the creation and the existence of God inside of my head. But when the light of the word of God came into my heart, I recognized my folly as I got back to my senses and good reason. I reasoned that if I were not created, I would not have the opportunity to query my maker. The Bible came to my rescue.

The Word of God remains the only cure for the disorders of the human heart. Paul said:

> The word of God is alive and active. Sharper than any double-edged sword, it penetrates even to dividing soul and spirit, joints and marrow; it judges the thoughts and attitudes of the heart. Nothing in all creation is hidden from God's sight. Everything is uncovered and laid bare before the eyes of him to whom we must give account.
> —Hebrews 4:12–13

Opposition to the Church

The role of the church in society has come under severe and fierce attack not because the people do not appreciate the church, but for the fact that the church is a constant check on the unrighteousness within the society. The church serves as an indictment of the human tendency for evil.

Critics of the church portray Christians as people who see no good in others and people who are out nosing the affairs of the world where they are not concerned. Their reasoning appears logical but is often not true. The fact is that no Christian, in the true sense of Christianity, condemns other people based on differences of opinions. Christians are human, subject to the same issues of life. The difference is that a true Christian trusts his or her life to Jesus Christ and God's Holy Spirit to meet the required standard of behavior expected by God. Paul said, "The life I now live in the body, I live by faith in the Son of God, who loved me and gave himself for me" (Galatians 2:20). We therefore have nothing to glory in.

The people of the world are not comfortable with Christians because the standard of Christian life is a challenge to the human heart. The conduct of the world has been destroyed by Satan through sin, and man cannot live an upright life until his heart is changed by the words of God. An upright life therefore sends huge guilt into an ordinary human heart.

The Holy Spirit, the main power behind the church, also exposes the activities of Satan in society. Jesus had predicted that the world would not be comfortable with the work of the Holy Spirit He sent to the church. Jesus said, "When he [the Holy Spirit] comes, he will prove the world to be in the wrong about sin and righteousness and judgment: about sin, because people do not believe in me; about righteousness, because I am going to the Father, where you can see me no longer; and about judgment, because the prince of this world now stands condemned" (John 16: 8-11).

It should then be expected that those who want to live an upright life must be prepared for the opposition of Satan because Satan and his followers are constantly being judged by the operations of Christian lives. The church cannot therefore shy away from its calling because of antagonists. Engagement of the church in the nation's public lives is therefore a necessity if the church would fulfill its purpose on earth.

The Difficulties the Church Faces

The importance of the church to the world is huge. Satan, who is aware of the importance of the church and the damage the church would do to his kingdom, creates obstacles against the church and church ministries. Satan is the reason why people are opposed to anything that has to do with Christ or the cross.

A serious challenge Satan poses to the church is the counterfeiting of Christian lives through the activities of impostors. The counterfeit Christians have caused misrepresentations of the church in the world, ranging from distortions of the Bible's truth and personal conducts, thus creating image issues for the church. This is not new and the world needs to understand that not all who claim they are Christians have their certification, Born Again (BA).

Some people also mistakenly assume that all individuals who teach the Bible are Christians, which is not true. Jesus said, "Not everyone who says to me, 'Lord, Lord,' will enter the kingdom of heaven, but only the one who does the will of my Father who is in heaven" (Matthew 7:21).

Paul warned Titus about those in the church who represent Satan. "Their minds and consciences are corrupted. They claim to know God, but by their actions they deny him. They are detestable, disobedient and unfit for doing anything good" (Titus 1:15–16). The Apostle told Christians to avoid such people (2 Timothy 3:5).

Unfortunately, the hypocrites are often louder in society than the honest believers. Self-proclaimed Christians who possess the power of oratory eloquence can lead many astray. Their misrepresentations have confounded the genuine work of God's elect. This is why it appears as if the church is no longer vibrant and effective in its role of salvaging the destructions unleashed on the people by Satan. But despite the rise in the numbers of Christian frauds in the world today, they cannot change or destroy the Word of God.

The world must be wary of persons who give the impression that they are Christians but who undermine the course of the gospel. Paul said, "Such people are false apostles, deceitful workers, masquerading as apostles of Christ. And no wonder, for Satan himself masquerades as an angel of light. It is not surprising, then, if his servants also masquerade as servants of righteousness. Their end will be what their actions deserve" (2 Corinthians 11:13–15). The good news, however, is that God promised to separate them from the real Christians sooner than later. The Bible says He will clear the weeds that have grown in the midst of good seeds (Matthew 13:24–30).

There are also concerns about Christians who are gifted in Christian teachings but do not walk worthy of their calling. Their conduct and lifestyles are at variance with their teachings. The contradictions in their lives give the agents of Satan cause to blaspheme the name of God and the church. These are serious challenges for the church of God.

Michael McCabe, in his article "The Role of the Church in Civil Society: Some Theological Orientations," stated:

> There is a glaring gap between the official teaching and the actual practice of the church and its official leaders. What is done in practice tends to become the acceptable teaching and the official teaching become more and more like rhetoric: unrealistic, incredible and (for many) honored "more in breach than in the observance" (Shakespeare).[144]

Also, Bruce Bickel and Stan Jantz, in their book *I'm Fine with God… It's Christians I Can't Stand,* write, "It's bad enough that some Christians project such a morally superior attitude, but their offense is at its worst when they don't live up to the standards they are trying to impose on the rest of us."[145]

The church cannot deny these failures. The behavior from the pulpit and the general assembly do not represent the victory that Jesus had on the cross, setting us free from the captivity of the devil. The situation is affecting the progress of the gospel because the people of the world no longer take the Christian seriously.

Bruce Bickel and Stan Jantz, in their book *I'm Fine with God,* wrote:

> Can we start with the premise that Christians are not held in high regard in society? According to my purely anecdotal research, Christians have managed to slide down the societal acceptability chart to a position that is slightly below telephone solicitors and personal injury lawyers. For each notch they move lower on the chart, Christians raise the respectability of some other annoying segment of society. So by contrast, they keep looking progressively worse.[146]

The church, however, is not lost because the Founder and Proprietor, Jesus Christ, is alive, and He said the gates of hell cannot prevail against His church. The Christians are human and are not yet in heaven. Christians do not ascribe to themselves a state of perfection. Denial of failures would put the Christian believer under curse. The Bible says, "Whoever conceals their sins does not prosper, but the one who confesses and renounces them finds mercy" (Proverbs 28:13). We are people who daily progress in our faith in the Lord Jesus Christ and His power to make us perfect.

The reason for the seeming contradictions is not difficult to discern. Often, in our attempt to cling to our friendship with the world and also remain Christians, we become inconsistent with our profession. We cannot cling to the truth and at the same time compromise with or tolerate falsehood. Jesus said, "No one can serve two masters. Either you will hate the one and love the other, or you will be devoted to the one and despise the other. You cannot serve both God and money" (Matthew 6:24).

And John expanded on this, when he said, "Do not love the world or anything in the world. If anyone loves the world, love for the Father is not in them" (1 John 2:15).

Christians always find themselves on the spot when they make the mistake of doing anything contrary to the Bible. Peter the great apostle was rebuked by Paul. Peter was often pleased to be in the company of the Gentiles (the Gentiles were the non-Jews), but not when any Jew was around. The Jews and Gentiles had both racial and religious discrimination. Paul said, "When Cephas (Peter) came to Antioch, I opposed him to his face, because he stood condemned" (Galatians 2:11).

Peter was delivered from hypocritical life because there was a brother like Paul to call him to order. The church and the Christian leaders should be bold to condemn sin when and wherever it is found. Sin is a reproach to the cross. The church should also accept criticisms, good or bad, constructive or destructive. Either of them should spur us for good deeds. We should be prepared to suffer for the gospel of Christ but not to suffer as evildoers (1 Peter 4:15).

Friendship of the World, Enemy of God

The reason why our light is not shining is because of our continued compromise with the world. And our attitude of compromise has often led us into trouble. The church is modernizing its approach to the gospel and thereby using the methods the world uses in ordinary daily life. The Christian has become vulnerable and culpable by doing the work of God using the techniques the world is known for. The style of Jesus on the gospel has not changed. Jesus loves sinners, of whom I am one, but Jesus hates sin.

For example, some of our leaders, wanting to be the friends of all, are gentle on homosexuality, drunkenness, divorce, etc. The church leaders should be careful not to confuse their tolerance of people with the tolerance of sin. Jesus loves everyone, including the lady who was caught in adultery. But Jesus was hard on every appearance of sin. The Lord hates sin. The reason for our incessant failure is because we often fail to condemn sin. The modern-day church leaders play with iniquity and often fall into the tragic state of compromise. It is therefore not difficult for a clergyman or a bishop to be invited to a gay wedding. In the old-time Christian religion, no one would contemplate informing a man of God that he's gay. To invite the minister of God to such a program would be inviting the wrath of man and of God. We are today completely mixed up with the world, and people often confuse our lives with the world's style. Christian leaders have no excuse to be meddling with evil desires.

Peter had these words of advice for Christians: "Dear friends, I urge you, as aliens and strangers in the world, to abstain from sinful desires, which war against your soul. Live such good lives among the pagans that, though they accuse you of doing wrong, they may see your good deeds and glorify God on the day he visits us" (1 Peter 2:11-12). Peter further said: "Live as free men, but do not use freedom as a cover-up for evil; live as servants of God" (1 Peter 2:16). We cannot do the work of God or be identified with Jesus Christ and expect to please the world. Jesus told His disciples, "You will be hated by everyone because of me, but the one who stands firm to the end will be saved" (Matthew 10:22).

The Lord also forewarned the Christians that they would not be accepted by the people of the world. He said: "If the world hates you, keep in mind that it hated me first. If you belonged to the world, it would love you as its own. As it is, you do not belong to the world, but I have chosen you out of the world. That is why the world hates you" (John 15:18-19). A Christian leader whose popularity soars among the people of the world needs to have some inward checks.

The Church Can Make a Difference

Much as these negative perceptions may be based on genuine reasons, most critics do not understand what the church stands for. Some individuals have a phobia for the truth that the church represents. The truth of the Bible is hard, but it is able to change the immoral situations in our society and also fix the mirage of conflicts Satan has surrounded the world with.

Our attitude toward the calling of God on our lives must not be pressured by any other issues. We should look to Jesus Christ alone. Paul advised:

Since we are surrounded by such a great cloud of witnesses, let us throw off everything that hinders and the sin that so easily entangles. And let us run with perseverance the race marked out for us, fixing our eyes on Jesus, the pioneer and perfecter of our faith. For the joy set before him he endured the cross, scorning its shame, and sat down at the right hand of the throne of God. Consider him who endured such opposition from sinners, so that you will not grow weary and lose heart.

—Hebrews 12:1–3

The people of the world are greatly agitated and are opposed to the truth. Satan is in control of the political, social, and economic life of nations. The leaders of the world call for change and the people yearn for change, but change is never going to be realized unless the human heart is changed. The church is the only beacon of any good change that can occur to humanity.

When Christianity is mentioned in the public arena, the usual thought is 'social morals'. Christianity is beyond morals, it is a totality of the original life, and the original life is life at its best when God created man and woman. The Bible says, "God saw all that he had made, and it was very good" (Genesis 1:31). So when we bring our faith to public places, we are not about to convert the executive power in the government house, or change congress to, preaching pulpit, but we bring our body of knowledge into public services with righteousness and upright behavior. The fear of God is lacking today in public governance and the nation is completely grounded for burden of social and economic failure.

C. S. Lewis said, "Christianity has not, and does not profess to have, a detailed political program for applying 'do as you would be done by' to a particular society at a particular moment. It could not have. It is meant for all men at all times and the particular program which suited one place or time would not suit another. And, anyhow, that is not how Christianity works. When it tells you to feed the hungry it does not give you lessons in cookery. When it tells you to read the Scriptures it does not give you lessons in Hebrew and Greek, or even in English grammar. It was never intended to replace or supersede the ordinary human arts and sciences: it is rather a director which will set them all to the right jobs, and a source of energy which will give them all new life, if only they will put themselves at its disposal."[147]

As believers, we are the bible the public reads. Our conduct indicates that the Bible is true or that something is amiss. Unethical behavior that contradicts the gospel sends wrong signals to the world. Our biblical values and integrity should be employed in our public and private lives. This will in turn impact the progress of our society. The church should not be seen as a group of religious bigots who nose into peoples' private affairs; rather, society should look to Christians for righteous leadership.

The church leaders today are more concerned about the size of church membership. The quest to maintain the crowd of worshippers often affects the way the truth is preached. Sin is no longer called its name so as not to offend the congregation. Sermons are preached to suit the ears of listeners as pastors are scared to lose members. The early church was not judged only on the basis of numerical strength but on righteousness and upright living and leadership in society. The apostles exemplified disciplined and sacrificial lives. We would do well to emulate their example.

Salt and Light

An effective church must be salt and light to society, because that is the reason it was founded. "You are the salt of the earth. But if the salt loses its saltiness, how can it be made salty again? It is no longer good for anything, except to be thrown out and trampled by men" (Matthew 5:13).

Salt is an important ingredient in the home. It is a seasoning and also a chemical used to preserve food, on which a family depends for physical survival. It is therefore guarded from anything that would render it ineffective, including exposure to sun, rain, and air. Once the savor of salt is lost, it becomes useless. This is the value the church adds to society. Problems result when Christians are not in their right forms in society.

"You are the light of the world. A city on a hill cannot be hidden. Neither do people light a lamp and put it under a bowl. Instead, they put it on its stand, and it gives light to everyone in the house. In the same way, let your light shine before men, that they may see your good deeds and praise your father in heaven" (Matthew 5:14–16). Light allows people to see, work, and make progress. It is also the embodiment of divine truth, which helps to transform the social system of a society. Darkness is a curse to people, because atrocities are easily perpetrated in darkness, creating fear, stress, and discomfort for innocent people. The issues of chaos and violence in society are evidences that the light of the church is not shining. A light that does not shine is not useful. The lives of Christians should be like arrows piecing the hearts and judging the conscience of the world.

The relevance of the church will be terminated when these two fundamental social needs for salt and light are not being met.

Missionary Efforts

The early American Christians engaged in the nation's governance with great success and they also contributed to the spiritual awakening in the world. The relative peace in some areas of the world today is the result of the efforts of European and American missionaries. The missionaries took the gospel to the farthest corners of the world. Many great men of faith sacrificed their lives for this cause. Some died because of the dangerous environmental conditions they exposed themselves to. They gave their intellects in academics, economics and politics to the use of the world. They were teachers, agriculturists, and so on in rural and urban areas of nations of the world in order to reach the people with the light of the gospel.

For example, in 1893, three men in their twenties—Rowland Bingham, Walter Gowans, and Thomas Kent—went to the interior of Sudan in Africa. They embarked on that mission not for money or personal wealth but to bring light to parts of Africa that were languishing in spiritual darkness.

They were faced with challenges that threatened their lives, including dangerous animals, hostile people, and killer mosquitoes. At the onset of their missionary trip, they were dissuaded by people. A Methodist minister based in Lagos, Nigeria, told them they were on a mission to nowhere. At a dinner table with the young missionaries, the minister told them, "I would be neglecting my duty if I did not tell you that you are on a fool's errand. You will never see Sudan."[148]

In spite of the discouragements, they were determined to reach Sudan. Their efforts resulted in the planting of one of the biggest churches in Nigeria. The Evangelical Churches Winning All (ECWA) trains Christian teachers, preachers, and missionaries to engage in God's work all over the world. Its headquarters are in Jos, Plateau State of Nigeria, which has the largest concentration of Christians in the country. The organization has about 2.5 million members. It is made up of six thousand churches with more than five million faithful Christians in attendance. ECWA also sponsors a university named after Rowland Bingham near Abuja, Nigeria's federal capital. The university focuses on science and research.

Though two of these kind-hearted and purpose-driven men did not make it back home from Sudan, their work saved millions of souls. And Nigeria is just one example of how God has used European and American Christian missionaries to bring the light of the gospel to other lands.

Other Efforts of Early American Believers

The people of United States have contributed immensely to financing the gospel of Jesus Christ all over the world. American Christians have been committed to giving of their substance to the cause of evangelization. Millions of dollars are donated every year by Americans who believe the light of the gospel should reach everywhere.

One example is the Gideon International, a Christian business and professional men's organization, which devotes funds to the printing and distribution of Bibles, given freely in hotels, hospitals, schools, and jail houses all over the world. The organization was started in 1889 by three American business travelers, John Nicholson, Samuel Hill, and W. J. Knights, who were determined to get the Bible into the hands of people in all walks of life. They got this idea in their spirits from God. The efforts of these three visionary individuals have grown big. More than two billion Bibles and New Testaments have been distributed around the world.

The purpose has been largely achieved with testimonies of several people who, by God's providence, came in contact with Gideon Bibles and had their lives turned around for good. Testimonies abound on the website of the Gideons International (see gideons.org). The Gideons International is currently in 194 nations of the world with the goal to be in all countries of the world to impact the lives of the people with the words of God through the Bible.

Other Christian organizations in Europe and America have initiated numerous projects for the relief of poverty and control of diseases in underdeveloped nations of the world and have in the process furthered the gospel of Christ all over the world.

One of the reasons why America is a target of the terrorists is because of the impact American Christians have had in spreading the light of the gospel in the world. The role of Americans in helping other nations of the world to have access to Christian gospel which gives them light has become a concern for the leaders and sponsors of terrorist movements. They aim to cripple the system of nations that are sympathetic to Christianity, especially America. The objective is to make it easy for the jihad against the "infidels" of the world. Islamizing the world is difficult as long as America is standing. They also consider America as a stumbling block to their plan to destroy the Jewish nation.

How Do We Respond?

The church has three options on how to respond to the challenges the decaying situation in the world has posed to it:

- Do nothing
- React negatively
- Act positively

Do nothing

Doing nothing is often a popular choice. The common question has always been, "What can we do about the problems of the world?" The world is already in a mess and we did not create the mess. We have our own problems, so we care less about the situation in society. We therefore do nothing, leaving the next generation to deal with the calamities that have been created.

People are discouraged and have given up. They blame their lukewarmness on the belief that society is lost and cannot be redeemed. Some often justify the progressive evils in the world with prophesies of old in the Bible. They opine that the evils in the world were prophesied in Scripture and cannot be changed. So they sit on the fence, wishing God would fight His own battles. God certainly is capable of winning battles; however, He chooses to use people to lead the fight.

The idea that we cannot do anything about godlessness in our society is a deceit from Satan. The devil uses lies to make people believe that he doesn't exist. We therefore require alertness against the subtle devices of Satan. The devil knows that as soon as his identity is unveiled, he can no longer deceive people. Doing nothing does not help our cause but rather creates more problems for the church and what the church stands for. Besides, the Bible says, "If anyone, then, knows the good they ought to do and doesn't do it, it is sin for them" (James 4:17).

It is irresponsible to sit idle while Satan is using his followers to change the systems around us. Satan has his foot soldiers in all areas of our endeavors, changing our laws, tampering with our public schools' curriculums and exposing our children to teachings that would not further their moral growth. Satan is destroying all that we stand for as a church.

Reacting negatively

We could also react negatively, like the disciples of Jesus Christ who became angry with the people of Samaria and wished them dead. Jesus, the master, was set to go to Jerusalem and would pass through Samaria. The Samaritans, who were not friends of Jews, didn't want Jesus to pass through their home to Jerusalem. James and John were mad and requested of Jesus, "Lord, do you want us to call fire down from heaven to destroy them?" But Jesus rebuked them, reminding them that He came to the world to deliver people from destruction. (See Luke 9:51–55.)

The people who do us bad are used by Satan. We cannot respond to people who are being used by Satan in the same way they deal with us because we have the spirit of God in us. We have to reach out to them in love; otherwise, we contradict the purpose of the church, which is reconciliation of every nation to God. The advice to Christians is: "Do not be overcome by evil, but overcome evil with good" (Romans 12:21).

Act positively

Our response as Christian believers to the numerous attacks on us should be positive all the time. We must pray and explore ways to get the world to reason with God. When our response is led by the Spirit and words of God, we will win the battle. The battle is not ours but the Lord's. Here are some suggested responses which are cardinal principles of the church since its inception.

1. Share the Word of God with neighbors and fellow citizens. Sharing should be done with love and compassion. The gospel may often be resisted, but resistance is no excuse for not sharing the Christian good news. "Whosoever shall call upon the name of the Lord shall be saved. How then shall they call on him in whom they have not believed? And how shall they believe in him of whom they have not heard? And how shall they hear without a preacher?" (Romans 10:13–14).

Disseminating the gospel has never been an easy task. "From the days of John the Baptist until now, the kingdom of heaven has been forcefully advancing, and forceful men lay hold of it" (Matthew 11:12). The disciples went through more fierce opposition, but they never gave up. They said, "We cannot but speak the things which we have seen and heard" (Acts 4:20).

2. Support our efforts with prayer, which is the power of the church to defeat Satan. God said, "If my people, who are called by my name, will humble themselves and pray and seek my face and turn from their wicked ways, then will I hear from heaven and forgive their sin and will heal their land" (2 Chronicles 7:14). Prayer for the nation cannot be overemphasized in the church, especially now, when God's elect are coming under spiritual attack.

Former president Ronald Reagan, at his presidential inaugural address on January 20, 1981, said, "I'm told that tens of thousands of prayer meetings are being held on this day, and for that I'm deeply grateful. We are a nation under God, and I believe God intended for us to be free. It would be fitting and good, I think, if on each Inaugural Day in future years it should be declared a day of prayer."[149]

Our faith is constantly challenged by economic, social, and political issues, and we have been bugged with denominational and liturgical differences. United prayers for the nation and its leaders will renew our society's hopes. People need a message of comfort that will help them remain in the will and plan of God. God listens to His people when they pray. The problems of our society are not beyond redemption when faithful believers pray.

3. Exhibit exemplary lives in words and deeds and provide fellowship. The church must participate in building communities. Our engagement in civic duties with our Christian values and characters will showcase to the world the change that a life in Christ can offer to society. We are also to provide fellowship through intimacies, mentoring, and development of societies' leaders through which people can be equipped for the task of nation building. The church is a place of refuge for society. Society looks to the church for solutions in the midst of economic, social, and political pressure. The people are seeking comfort and relief from the logjams created by conflicts. The purpose of fellowship is to provide the people comfort.

Fellowships in the early days of the church were for the purpose of sharing the good life and meeting personal needs. The early Christians shared in the teachings of the words of God, which empowers individuals to live victorious, purposeful and fulfilled Christian lives. They also took care of the needs of individuals by giving from the surplus of members to the needy in society.

The Bible says this about the people under the mentoring of the early apostles:

> They devoted themselves to the apostles' teaching and to fellowship, to the breaking of bread and to prayer. Everyone was filled with awe at the many wonders and signs performed by the apostles. All the believers were together and had everything in common. They sold property and possessions to give to anyone who had need. Every day they continued to meet together in the temple courts. They broke bread in their homes and ate together with glad and sincere hearts, praising God and enjoying the favor of all the people. And the Lord added to their number daily those who were being saved.
>
> —Acts 2:42-47

Church membership and attendance are good habits that can enable us to get regular teachings of the Word of God. The Bible says, "Not giving up meeting together, as some are in the habit of doing, but encouraging one another—and all the more as you see the Day approaching" (Hebrews 10:25). Also one-on-one contact with each other can meet the needs of members before things go drastically wrong. We should always be prepared to be the answer to someone's prayers for comfort, rescue, and deliverance. Personal privacy is good and should be respected, but it should not preclude us from reaching out to the people of God. We should explore ways to help people who are hurting in our job places and in our communities. A lifestyle patterned after "mind your own business" is not good for a proper role of church in society.

Paul counseled the Philippians on their role to one another. He said, "Do nothing out of selfish ambition or vain conceit. Rather, in humility value others above yourselves, not looking to your own interests but each of you to the interests of the others" (Philippians 2:3).

In our relationships with one another, we should have the same mind-set as Christ Jesus, "who, being in very nature God, did not consider equality with God something to be used to his own advantage; rather, he made himself nothing by taking the very nature of a servant, being made in human likeness. And being found in appearance as a man, he humbled himself by becoming obedient to death—even death on a cross" (Philippians 2:6–8).

The Church: a Place of Refuge

The question is not if God would change our society for good, the problem is if the church is prepared to make the change. The church is a place of refuge for the people. Isaiah and Micah, great prophets of the Lord, had this same message at different times during their individual prophetic service in the world:

> In the last days, the mountain of the Lord's temple will be established as chief among mountains; it will be raised above the hills, and people will stream to it. Many nations will come and say, Come, let us go to the mountain of the Lord, to the house of the God of Jacob. He will

teach us his ways, so that we may walk in his paths. The law will go out from Zion, the word of the Lord from Jerusalem.

He will judge between many peoples and will settle disputes for strong nations far and wide. They will beat their swords into plowshares and their spears into pruning hooks. Nation will not take up sword against nation, nor will they train for war anymore.

—Isaiah 2:2–4 and Micah 4:1–3

Thoughts

There is no alternative to the role of the church in society. The church filled with the Holy Spirit is the hope of the world. The church therefore has the enormous responsibility to live exemplary life in words and in deed. When the members of the church are at peace with one another, they will be in a position to showcase the true God who is the Prince of Peace. The conflicts in societies can be resolved by the collective determination of the body of Christ to work for righteousness in the land.

What our nation will be today and tomorrow depends on what we make of the opportunity God gave to us as a church in turning the situation around for good in our society. The freedom and the abundance of life that remain with us today were the efforts of our early Christians. They worked hard for it and we are responsible for its maintenance.

CHAPTER 11

CHRISTIANITY AND POLITICS

The idea that religion and politics don't mix was
invented by the devil to keep Christians
from running their own country.[150]
—Dr. Jerry Falwell, Baptist minister

ONE HUGE ISSUE in society is leadership. Leaders make or break society. A leader is known by his or her knowledge, skills, vision, and the capacity to realize the vision. The quality of a nation's leader determines where the country is heading. The problem in most underdeveloped nations of the world is largely leadership. The people want a leader whose skills, abilities, competencies, behavior, activities and personal life and style align with the aspirations of the society. And very often, the people do not have what they desire because the physical attributes are sometimes deceptive and do not show the true character of a person.

Samuel, the prophet of God, was asked to anoint a successor to King Saul, the first monarch in Israel, who was removed because he had failed God and the people. Samuel was persuaded by the physique of the candidates, the children of Jesse. "But the LORD said to Samuel, 'Do not consider his appearance or his height, for I have rejected him. The LORD does not look at the things people look at. People look at the outward appearance, but the LORD looks at the heart'" (1 Samuel 16:7). Oratory and physical charisma that often persuade some voters is a wrong test for choosing leaders.

The leadership of the nation should be a concern for the church. In a democratic society, government representatives and leaders are elected by voters. Politicians sell themselves and their programs to the electorate. The response of the people is determined by their convictions about the program and the amount of trust they have for the candidate. The people determine who will govern them by their votes. The nation gets a government by the will of the majority. Democracy gives power to ordinary people. This is why democratic countries, and international organizations such as the United Nations, devote time, energy, and human and material resources to the promotion of democracy all over the world.

Democracy appears to thrive in most developed nations of the West. But in many underdeveloped and developing nations of the world, there is no true democracy, and in places where they claim to be practicing democracy, the politicians are involved in the destruction of property and the shedding of innocent blood for political gains.

Autocracy is the opposite of democracy. An autocratic government does whatever it desires without the input of the governed. The leaders often suppress the rights of citizens, using their unquestioned power to kill, maim, and cause fear in society. Autocracy is synonymous with godlessness because human values are not regarded. The rights and liberties of individuals are restricted. This results in human deprivation, hunger, poverty, and social vices. In nations where autocracy is practiced, the government is regarded as a god that the citizens must worship.

Close to autocracy is the feudal system of government, which is based on obligations between the lord or king and his subjects. This is common in Islamic countries. In autocracy and feudalism, the law is often for the less privileged in society. But in democracy, everyone is equal before the law, though, this is also being gradually supplanted as godlessness takes over the system.

Unfortunately, over the centuries, as godlessness took over the hearts of people, politics became a game of abusive character assassinations. In politics today, everything but righteousness is practiced.

Most politicians cannot be trusted because they are deceitful. They are dishonest about their opinions and sometimes lie outright in their public pronouncements.

A political system can only be good if it is practiced in the fear of God. When God is removed from government, the society is thrown into darkness and trouble. The Bible advises rulers who wish to govern the nation successfully to imbibe God's fear. It says, "The fear of the LORD is the beginning of wisdom, and knowledge of the Holy One is understanding" (Proverbs 9:10).

Should a Christian Take Part in Politics?

Some Christians do not like to participate in politics for reasons that are obvious. Mindful of their goals in life here on earth, they do not want anything to get between them and heaven. So they decline the thought of any involvement in partisan politics.

There are Christians who have gone into politics and lost their moral bearings. They became a warning for believers who similarly nursed political ambitions. It is not impossible to find people who were committed, Holy Ghost-filled believers and leaders of Christian groups lose their connections with the Christian faith when they joined national politics.

Other 'Christians' have run political campaigns in the same manner as those who do not profess Christ. This constitutes an image problem for the church, as the world regard every 'Christian' as representing the church. The conducts and choice of words of Christians are supposed to be different from those who are not Christians or are opposed to Christian values. For example, Senator John McCain, in his campaign for the presidential election in 2008, used uncomplimentary language against one of the leading servants of God in America, describing his comment on the travails of the Jews as "crazy."[151]

Reverend John Hagee of Cornerstone Church in San Antonio, Texas, had said in a sermon that the Jews often suffered as a result of disobedience to God. This message was probably considered by Senator McCain as a negative statement against his potential voters. It could be scary seeing Christians throw caution to the wind in their campaign utterances. In most of the cases, the image of the church does not look good. However, I do not know if Senator McCain considers himself a Christian.

Roy Herron, a Christian senator from Tennessee, said, "The ugliest campaign attack I've endured came when a fellow Christian ran against me. His party's political operatives and some supporters spent many resources not promoting him but attacking my values and character. And this was a campaign between fellow believers."[152]

It is hard to think that Christians who backslide after venturing into politics had derailed from their Christian calling because they were not really Christians in the first place. While this is not impossible, it may not always be the case. A person's true faith is known only to God. Therefore, it would be wrong to presume that politicians who denied their Christian faith were not really believers. However, the abundance of apparent Christians backsliding from faith after entering into politics is sufficient to serve as a warning for others.

As difficult as the question of Christian participation in politics may be, upright believers are needed in government. Godly leadership is critical to the well-being of a nation. The players at the head are supposed to be custodians of the values of society, giving the society the right direction that will promote healthy relationships among the people. Those who lead the nation require some measure of wisdom. They are expected to possess qualities that only few others have.

King Solomon, the third Jewish monarch, as soon as he ascended to the throne, recognized that he needed something that could impact his character and that would distinguish him as a leader: wisdom. He therefore turned to God to ask for wisdom to direct the affairs of the nation. He said, "Give your servant a discerning heart to govern your people and to distinguish between right and wrong. For who is able to govern this great people of yours?" (1 Kings 3:9).

No doubt, Solomon was a great leader who knew the importance of reliance on God for wisdom. And the Lord was pleased with Solomon's request. God said to him, "Since you have asked for this and not for long life or wealth for yourself, nor have asked for the death of your enemies but for discernment in administering justice, I will do what you have asked. I will give you a wise and discerning heart, so that there will never have been anyone like you, nor will there ever be" (1 Kings 3:11–12). God delights in upright leadership because it engenders justice, equity, probity, and godly public policies. The people under a good leader receive correct directions and live good lives that glorify Him (God).

In the days of King Solomon, the economy and social life of the nation flourished. Israel was a revered nation. Under his leadership, the fame of the Jews was known all over the world. People were astonished at King Solomon's temple, the first of its kind on earth. It attracted tourists, including royal visitors.

The Queen of Sheba, who visited King Solomon, eulogized Israel by saying:

> The report I heard in my own country about your achievements and your wisdom is true. But I did not believe these things until I came and saw with my own eyes. Indeed, not even half was told me; in wisdom and wealth you have far exceeded the report I heard. How happy your people must be! How happy your officials, who continually stand before you and hear your wisdom! Praise be to the Lord your God, who has delighted in you and placed you on the throne of Israel. Because of the Lord's eternal love for Israel, he has made you king to maintain justice and righteousness.
>
> —1 Kings 10:6–9

When a society is governed by leaders who lack God's wisdom, it is like the blind leading the blind. Jesus said, "Leave them; they are blind guides. If the blind lead the blind, both will fall into a pit" (Matthew 15:14). Such nations often miss the plan of God for the people as they are overwhelmed with conflicts.

Importance of Politics

Politics is important to society because it is the only civilized means of emergence of leadership. The elected government is entrusted with the affairs of society, education, health, shelter, and other social services. How we fare on these important issues depends on the quality of leaders in power. The objective of government is also to sort out conflicts in society before they hurt the people. This is why voters want to be sure that those who lead them have the capacity to do so. The power to resolve conflicts depends on whether the leader who seeks to provide solutions to the problem understands the source of conflicts and knows the correct tools to effectively address them.

All political office gladiators always claim they have what it takes to resolve the nation's problems. And most of the time they are wrong because conflicts in the world are an issue of the human heart, and only God, who created the heart, possesses the tools to work successfully on it. It is therefore doubtful if those who do not know God would have the ability to deal with these problems.

The church is the major watchdog of society and cannot be indifferent to political issues. Critics of the church on politics in America have often harped on the separation of church and state. As have been reiterated in the earlier chapters of this book, the people cannot be separated from issues that affect their lives, one of which is politics, which produces leaders that govern them.

Pastor Rick Warren, pastor of Saddleback Church in California, was interviewed in August 2008 by Jeffrey Goldberg. Rick had then only recently hosted John McCain and Barack Obama, candidates for America's presidential election, for a well-televised interview in Saddleback Church. In Goldberg's interview tagged 'No Compromise with Evil', Rick said, "I believe in the separation of church and state, but I do not believe in the separation of politics from religion. Faith is simply a worldview. A person who says he puts his faith on the shelf when he's making decisions is either an idiot or a liar."[153]

No one would want to secure his family home and be indifferent to the hiring of a security guard for the home. The quality of services a security guard would render can be predicted by his character. Hiring a questionable character as guard is compromising the security of the family. Election of the nation's leaders are therefore a serious business for all reasonable adults. The church's stake in election of godly candidates in the country is high because of the importance of political leaders to the people and the effect of ungodly leadership on our Christian faith.

The early disciples of Jesus Christ, in the course of managing the affairs of the church, recognized the impact ungodly public servants would cause the body of Christ. In the course of their assignment, they were being bogged down by administrative and political issues in the community, and their spiritual work suffered. It was obvious that they could not serve church pulpits and administrative tables at the same time. They therefore determined to hold to their spiritual roles.

However, because of the importance and effect community politics could have on the health and growth of the church, the men of God did not consider it wise to leave the administrative responsibilities of society for fools or Satan's agents. So they prayerfully and with support of the church community elected men full of the Spirit of God and wisdom to take charge of the political affairs of their community (Acts 6). The individuals elected were men of moral values, integrity, and character, who were commissioned to lead the people. The church supported these leaders with constructive advice when required. The apostles and leaders of the church counseled the leaders and also prayed for them, obeying the words of Scripture:

"I urge, then, first of all, that requests, prayers, intercession and thanksgiving be made for all people—for kings and all those in authority, that we may live peaceful and quiet lives in all godliness and holiness. This is good, and pleases God our Savior" (1 Timothy 2:1–3). The church's prayer for government leaders cannot be overemphasized. The prayer support does not depend on partisan politics. Whichever party produces the nation's leaders, such leaders become the responsibility of the church for prayer support. It is a duty that pleases God and also could avert any negative consequences of the leadership's policies and decisions in governance.

America's founding fathers insisted that our society should be led by God-fearing people. They understood that only laws based on the principles of the Word of God can reform and transform the world. So they wanted those who recognize God and the laws of God to lead the nation aright. Their dream (the early Americans) for refuge for their souls would only be achieved, they believed, under godly leadership.

Former president Ronald Reagan summed it up this way: "It began in 1620 when a group of courageous families braved a mighty ocean to build a new future in a new world. They came not for material gain, but to secure liberty for their souls within a community bound by laws."[154]

The church has responsibility for the physical and spiritual well-being of the government and the governed. The attempt to exclude the church from governance because of her relationship with God is therefore a fallacy. This is the reason why leaders have not found clues to nations' myriad problems. Let no man think he can properly lead a society without God.

The Choices of Early Americans

Americans have been blessed in the past with godly leaders. This accounts for the strong foundation the nation was built on. But good leadership did not come easy; it was a demonstration of the will of citizens who chose upright persons to lead them. A couple of generations ago, the choice of political leadership in the United States was dependent on the character of the candidates. Their lifestyles mirrored the values that the American culture had developed. A successful election did not depend on persuasive talks but on past records, moral conducts, and success or failure in home management. Society wanted to see the hand of God in a candidate's life before giving him or her opportunity to lead them.

And the people were right in their selections. The issue is not that all past leaders were saints, but the people were determined to commit the fortune of the nation to individuals with transparent lives, at the helm of its governance. Most of the past presidents of this great country accepted that they needed God to help them to succeed in their leadership of the nation. Godliness is key to good leadership.

Ronald Reagan once said:

> The basis of [America's] ideas and principles is a commitment to freedom and personal liberty that itself is grounded in the much deeper realization that freedom prospers only where the blessings of God are avidly sought, and humbly accepted. The American experiment in democracy rests on this insight. Its discovery was the great triumph of our Founding Fathers, voiced by William Penn when he said: "If we will not be governed by God, we must be governed by tyrants." Explaining the inalienable rights of men, Jefferson said, "The God who gave us life, gave us liberty at the same time." The evidence of this permeates

our history and our government. The Declaration of Independence mentions the Supreme Being no less than four times.[155]

No nation whose leaders despise God would succeed. It may appear that they are progressing but such success is for a short time. Godlessness does nothing but destruction. As such a nation goes up godlessness brings it down the same way it went up.

Partisan Politics

People's involvement in politics varies. Most are in politics as civic duty but some are in partisan politics. The error of the propagandists of separation of church and state is that they forget that the members of the church have their civic duties. We cannot all be involved in partisan politics as we individually have our preferences in life. But we are all in politics with the responsibility to ensure we elect people we can trust to give good leadership to the nation. Pastors and clerics have their calling primarily to spread the gospel of Jesus Christ. They also disciple the people so that nation can be blessed with people of godly minds, both professionals and politicians, because these are people who influence the hearts and minds of the future generations and leaders. The clerics, like any citizen, and the church congregations, must exercise their civic responsibility of electing godly leaders.

Christians who are called into partisan politics should also be encouraged to be involved because in whatever vocation, we are ambassadors of the church and Jesus Christ. Any Christian man or woman in partisan politics should be clear that in and outside of politics, their loyalty is first and foremost to Christ. Those of us in the church who do not have the calling to go into partisan politics should therefore give support to our brothers and sisters who are called into political leadership.

It is the duty of all Christians to ensure that we are led by godly leaders. We cannot afford to be indifferent to this issue and we must not be divided in our spiritual judgment over the elections of those who will govern us. Satan has often succeeded in dividing Christian believers using things such as politics. The church ought to be united in matters of political decisions. We know that righteousness lifts up a nation. The desire for godly leadership in the society can only be achieved through voting people with godly characters into the nation's political offices.

Division in the Church

The greatest weapon of Satan against the church is division. Disunity is an effective tool in the hands of the devil to keep not only the church bound but also to hold captive the society that God has placed in the care of the church. We have been sharply divided in political choices and Satan has used the disunity to retain his hold on the nation's leadership and the people. The discord in the church has robbed the church of the power to install and maintain righteous leadership in America.

David Halton, in his article "Faith and Politics," said, "For more than three decades, the driving force behind the Religious Right has been the wide range of churches that call themselves Evangelical …the Southern Baptist Convention, the Assemblies of God…..The numbers are huge. More than 60 million American adults are Evangelicals who define themselves as "born-again-Christians", meaning they have accepted their sinfulness and established a personal relationship with Christ through conversion. One Evangelical group alone…the Southern Baptist Convention has more members than the Methodist, Episcopalian and Presbyterian churches combined."[156]

Politics is a game of numbers and the Christians in America have the numerical strength to bring about righteousness in this nation. The evangelicals, the Catholics, and the traditional or Orthodox churches put together cannot be upstaged politically in America. Besides, the church also holds the spiritual weapon of prayers to tell the nation to obey the voice of God. But the two powerful weapons of number and spiritual warfare have not worked for us. What then is our problem? The greatest challenge that has kept American Christians from fulfilling their calling of restoring society to righteousness has been division in our ranks. Nothing works unless the people agree together.

Plausible Reason for the Division

The National Association of Evangelicals (a group of evangelicals in America) thought one of the reasons the church has not shown its influence in the nation's politics was because "only half of all evangelical Christians bother to vote." It is possible that the political awareness for the average Christian believer may be lacking. Some naively believe that God will give us the best president even when they do not vote. Good as that faith is, we need to understand that God has given us the freedom to determine those who lead us.

We therefore cannot blame God if we allow those who do not have the fear of God to assume positions of authority in our nation. God's will for leadership is in our Bible; our responsibility is to pray and elect wisely individuals with the fear of God to be our leaders. We are the tools God uses to accomplish His purposes on earth, including righteousness in our land. If we continue to be indifferent to the political issues in our nation, Satan will take control of our leadership and install his servants. The church and the society cannot have peace under an ungodly leader.

But then our political problem is not the mere lack of awareness. A major issue among American's huge and politically vibrant Christian population is disunity. Satan exploits disunity among the men and women of God. It is in their disunity that he is able to manipulate them to do his biddings. American Christians are divided by race and political ideology. Though division in the church is a common issue all over the world, the dissension within the American Christian believers is troubling and has polarized us socially and politically. One major cause of division is race. It is a singular destroyer of the bond among the believers in America.

The Race Issue

In 2008, during the campaign for America's presidential election, a controversial sermon delivered by Rev. Jeremiah Alvesta Wright came under focus. The sermon that was condemned by not a few people was blown up for political gains. The cleric was quoted by ABC News Correspondence in one of his sermons as saying, "The government gives them the drugs, builds bigger prisons, passes a three-strike law and then wants us to sing 'God Bless America.' No, no, no, God damn America, that's in the Bible for killing innocent people," he said in a 2003 sermon. "God damn America for treating our citizens as less than human. God damn America for as long as she acts like she is God and she is supreme."[157]

But the outburst of the minister, condemnable as it is, was an issue that posed a serious challenge to the conscience of the nation and in particular the church. His action was a manifestation of the deep wounds in the body of Christ that cannot be easily wished away; they require a healing process that can only be achieved with a total dependence on God. The president, Mr. Obama, a candidate then, made clever political maneuvers to avoid the damage Rev. Wright's sermon could do to his campaign, but it nevertheless showed that the church was sharply divided by race.

Not many people understood where the reverend gentleman was coming from. Some of those who understood live under the delusion that slavery is not an issue anymore. Rev. Wright, a 1941 child in Philadelphia, Pennsylvania, grew up in a racially mixed section of the city called Germantown. He is an outspoken person not given to hypocrisy. His public outburst on his painful life experiences shows his transparency. Some other Americans are careful to make public their opinion and dissatisfaction with the past and with the system but in their privacy use the issue to damage peaceful coexistence in the nation, and in the body of Christ.

The relationship between the races in America, particularly among whites and blacks, could not be said to be smooth because of the past experiences of slavery and the prolonged discrimination between the blacks and the white majority. It was bad in the early days of America that blacks and whites had separate places of worship, and we still continue to have white and black churches until today.

But rather than acknowledge and confront the issue with efforts to proffer solutions to it, the Christian believers hope it will just go away. Some of us also feel that since it was the problem of our early fathers, we cannot be too concerned. But the problem has not left us. We are wrong if only we remember that the sins of Adam and Eve, the first generation on earth, are the root cause of the world's current travail. And we all individually have accepted to take steps to get ourselves out of the problem created by those we never got to know, by asking God for forgiveness. Though we were not in existence then, the sin became part of our lives.

We therefore cannot pretend that the issue of race does not exist; it is real. And does it affect our fellowship? Yes it does. And although it should not be the case, the reality is that it is, and this should not be allowed to continue. We need the healing process in the body of Christ not by formulating laws of non-discrimination, but by a deliberate process of forgiving one another in the church. The law is made for the world, but the love of Jesus is the law of the church. We require a determination to forge a common front by recognizing that Christ, who joined us together, is greater than the wrongs we have done to each other. Forgiveness is the tool for removing the damage Satan had done to us over the decades using race and segregations in our land.

Forgiveness is not only to heal our wounds; we are required to forgive one another so that our heavenly father may also forgive us our trespasses and that our prayers to God individually and corporately for our nation may not be hindered; because non-forgiveness within the body of Christ is an obstacle to prayers.

John Townsend, in his book *Beyond Boundaries: Learning to Trust Again in Relationships,* said, "But wounds should not stay wounds. They need to heal. A relational wound needs to be resolved so that you get back to normal life - that is, being in healthy connections, being freed from the past, and exercising your gifts and passions. And don't depend on the old proverb that says, 'Time heals all wounds,' because it's not true. Time, by itself, heals very little. Broken bones need more than time, as do homes in disrepair and lives that have had a troubled relationship. What you really need in order to heal is support. If it is relationship that wounded you, it is relationship that is required to heal you…"[158]

American Christians have been in this issue of relationship for too long. The third and fourth generations are suffering its effect and it is also not good for the nation that is going forward. We should stop talking down our brothers and sisters in our homes, white or black. When we do, we are killing the church. And also we do such wickedness especially in the presence of younger generations who are made to buy into the racial war that has passed. We have not allowed old wounds to heal and we keep passing bad legacies to the children when we tell them those negative things about others. The emerging leaders may continue to live their lives in bad relationship that has troubled the nation over decades. This is a result of errors in passing to the young ones a negative historic past which is militating against peace in our world. It is not the will of God that the church be divided for any reason.

Satan has exploited the issue of slavery and race segregation in America to divide the church in order to prevent the children of the kingdom from understanding one another. But in the midst of conflicts of slavery, there were white men like William Wilberforce, John Jay, and a host of others who spent their lives to fight for the freedom of slaves in the world. It is equally on good note that the civil rights leader, Dr. Martin Luther King, Jr. had the support of white Americans in the struggle for equality of life in the nation. It is important for Christians that we express and share more of the positive aspects of our relationship, which would engender quick healing of wounds in the process and bring the much-needed unity in the body of Christ.

Political Ideology

The bitterness of racial segregation also led to division in political understanding and political association among Christians. The dissension among Christians is so sharp that we seriously resent each other. We therefore prefer the candidates that belong to our race above others, forgetting that as Christians our race is heavenly.

Some people say proverbially that they are more comfortable dining with the devil than getting along with their neighbor because of race. We do have the right to make our choice, and the constitution allows individuals to deal with people they are comfortable with (as long as you do not use a public platform for discrimination). But the devil can never be an option to our relationship with each other in the church.

Our relationship in the Christian community cannot be likened to other ordinary world relationships. We are people who will live here together and remain together thereafter when the world as presently constituted is over. We are members of the same body and if any part of the body suffers, the whole body feels the pain (1 Corinthians 12: 27). Paul also told the Christians in Rome, "So in Christ we, though many, form one body, and each member belongs to all the others" (Romans 12:5). We may have our differences, but God expects us to be involved with one another.

The Bible says, "Love must be sincere. Hate what is evil; cling to what is good. Be devoted to one another in love. Honor one another above yourselves" (Romans 12:9-10). The devil is never a good alternative because he seeks to destroy us. The most reasonable thing to do when we wrong each other in the church is to reconcile and forgive one another so that we can move forward positively with our lives. As a black man and a Christian, I would dine with a Christian man or woman of any race, who shared my values. I would not for consideration of race put my trust in a black man or woman who does not fear and honor God.

Political ideology is the body of doctrine, myth, and belief that guides an individual, social movement, institution, class, or group. It also includes the political and social plan, along with the devices for putting it into operation. Political ideology identifies different political organizations. For example, the two dominant political parties in America, the Democratic and Republican parties, are known for their liberal and conservative agendas respectively.

Unfortunately, the church has also fallen for political ideologies and is sharply divided alongside. This has further polarized the body of Christ and has adversely affected our relationship as a church. We now have Christian Democrats and Republicans who are against each other on the political soapbox.

David Halton said about the Evangelicals in America, "Let me stress emphatically that Evangelicals do NOT form a monolithic political bloc. African American Evangelicals, for example, continue to be solidly in the Democratic camp and there are progressives who promote a generally liberal agenda."[159]

But the truth is that the church has only one ideology. Our doctrine as a church is to create the 'Kingdom of God on earth'. This may sound theological. The kingdom of God is simply justice, equity, liberty for all and peace on earth. Incidentally, every political ideology in the world, social, liberal, capitalist, or conservative, claims to be pursuing the same objectives, though not regarded as the 'kingdom of God' because of its religious connotation.

Each political party says they have programs aimed at improving the standard of living of the people, and promoting social justice in the land. However, advancement of social justice, liberty, and equitable life for the people cannot be achieved by mere propagandas of socialism or capitalism. Any ideology not accompanied with the fear of God will not achieve a useful purpose for the people. This is the reason why the church should be more concerned about the faith and values of the candidates, and not political ideology. Ideology becomes workable and beneficial to the people when the man or woman who will implement it is filled with the spirit and knowledge of God.

Election of our nation's leaders should not be based only on political ideologies of conservative or liberal agenda but on uprightness of the individuals who seek political office. We need leaders who have the knowledge and fear of God in them. The nation will get such leaders through prayer and support of the church. Our decision should not be entirely on the things we hope to gain from a political candidate but first and foremost our call of faith. "But seek first his kingdom and his righteousness, and all these things will be given to you as well" (Matthew 6:33). If we decide to put God out of our nation's politics and elect leaders based merely on intellect and our own choice, we should also not blame God for negative results because God was never consulted in our selections.

In 2008, the church of God was carried away by human ideologies and sentiments in our political choices. President Obama did not hide from us his views on issues such as traditional marriage and gays and lesbians, abortion, and similar stands that affect our Christian faith and our common destiny as a church. But we were determined about what we wanted politically, and nothing else mattered to us; we made our choice. The consequences of our actions will remain part of our history. And I could not say for sure if Christians really had any good options then, but we should not blame God if the president did anything negative to our collective faith.

For instance, one of the pillars of our Christian faith is prayer. It is the prayers of Christians that have protected and strengthened this nation. And that was the understanding of the early American leaders who brought prayers to the national polity. National days of prayer are part of the American heritage. Since April 17, 1952, when President Harry Truman signed Public Law 82-324, a national day of prayer has been observed in the White House. Prior to that time, the past leaders also recognized setting a day apart for thanksgiving by the nation as an act of gratitude to God. But in 2009 President Obama tampered with this tradition.[160]

Can a nation survive without prayer? President Reagan said:

> I grew up in a home where I was taught to believe in intercessory prayer. I know it's those prayers, and millions like them, that are building high and strong this cathedral of freedom that we call America; those prayers, and millions like them, that will always keep our country secure and make her a force for good in these too troubled times. And that's why as a nation we must embrace our faith, for as long as we endeavor to do good—and we must believe that will be always—we will find our strength, our hope, and our true happiness in prayer and in the Lord's will.[161]

At a breakfast prayer on February 5, 1981, in the Washington Hilton Hotel, Reagan explained the importance of God's support in leadership. He said:

> Abraham Lincoln once said, "I would be the most foolish person on this footstool earth if I believed for one moment that I could perform the duties assigned to me without the help of one who is wiser than all." I know that in the days to come and the years ahead there are going to be many times when there will only be one set of footprints in my life. If I did not believe that, I could not face the days ahead.[162]

No nation can succeed without God. Our political ideology must be driven by moral characters, which is the attribute of godly people. The ideologies of the world do not necessarily stand for the righteousness of the Lord. Human ideology cannot be detached from the condition of our heart. And every plan and effort of man is geared towards pleasing self first before consideration for others. Let's take a look at one of the ideological contentions in America for decades, the tax issue.

Politics of Taxation and the Unspoken Anger of the Rich

Tax is one of the political issues in American politics. Political campaigns, for many years past, have always been for or against increase in taxes. Payment of taxes is not strange to the world and people, including the church. Collection of taxes by governments into the commonwealth purse of nations are done to execute public programs. The spirit behind taxes is to ensure that the needy are taken care of from the public purse. This, however, can only succeed if done with understanding and in the fear and knowledge of the word of God.

The United States of America has one of the highest tax regimes in the world. The federal, state, local, and special purpose government jurisdictions impose taxes to fund their activities either fully or partly. There appears to be duplicity of taxes on the same income, property, or activity, very often without offset of one tax against another. The federal taxes sometimes could vary from 15% to 40%. And when considered in its duplicities, some tax payers pay more than 50% of income as taxes. There are different forms of taxes: income tax, payroll tax, property, sales and excise, estate and gift, and custom duties, etc.

High taxes may have the negative effect of killing initiatives and businesses, which many politicians in the recent times have argued would further worsen the economic situations, kill companies, and increase the unemployment rate. The congress is empowered by the constitution to make tax laws. High taxes look oppressive, and may lead people to sin or disobey the law because they find it difficult to cope with the system of high taxes. But the objective of taxes is that the less privileged and the poor in society will be taken care of, including the widows and the elderly, which God has put in our charge. And America is among the most humane nations of the world; it is the reason why many individuals are glad to be given opportunity to come and be part of this great nation. The point is that taxing ourselves is godly if the revenue is used judiciously to improve the lives of the less privileged in society.

The considerate culture of this country, which was developed based on the words of God, was used to initiate plans which would impact the people's welfare. One of the humane programs instituted by the early founders was the social security system. The social security system is funded through public taxes. It is used to take care of the less privileged, the old, and the disabled individuals in the society. This shows how seriously the early leaders took the words of God. For the Bible says, "Religion that God our Father accepts as pure and faultless is this: to look after orphans and widows in their distress" (James 1: 27), and Paul said, "We who are strong ought to bear with the failings of the weak and not to please ourselves. Each of us should please our neighbors for their good, to build them up" (Roman 15: 1).

Noble as the program of American government is of ensuring good life for all citizens, the system is failing because of the ungodly environment resulting from shutting out the knowledge of God from the people. The social security system appears to be abused with impunity. While the faithful tax payers are performing their civic responsibility in order to meet the needs of the less privileged, there may be some individuals who are capable of working but have depended on government social security. Not only this, there are individuals who should not ordinarily qualify for government stipends but may also be exploiting the system to satisfy their excesses.

What do I mean? The care for the needy becomes a big burden on some people because those who should have not been in the class of the needy are voluntarily turning themselves to one because they have found it an easy way of eating without working. Godlessness destroys everything that is good in society. The Bible teaches that if a man would not work, he should not eat, and here we have a society breeding individuals to be lazy because they are comfortable feeding on the government (tax payers') money. They do not consider such attitude as not fair because they have never known the way of the Lord. Besides, there are probably some individuals who are also defrauding the government through lies and wrong information about their condition in order to benefit from government largesse. All these are results of poor moral environment and ungodliness in society and are pulling the nation down.

The burden of government finances keeps climbing daily. And the government can only fund its operation either by borrowing or by raising taxes. The American nation's debt has become so huge that analysts are afraid that it may take many future generations to pay the debt. The rich people are revolting and are constantly rejecting any moves of government to increase taxes because they feel the funds are not being judiciously used. The rich have therefore mobilized politicians against increase in taxes.

While one can understand the sentiments of the rich that they are being overtaxed and are not sure of good use of the funds collected from them, they are also probably thinking more of their riches and less of the conditions of the poor. It takes a heart of God to share riches with the poor. Besides, the political and economic systems have been bedeviled by corruption and other abuses by public officers, because when a nation forgets God, the people chose evil.

The point is that we are all responsible for our troubles, both the rich and the poor in this nation, as we have allowed ungodliness to pervade our society. And in a godless world, nothing works for the good of the people. The failure of the political, social, and economic endeavor is an alert to Americans of the need to get back to God. The tax system requires overhauling to make it friendly and comfortable for people to work and do business. There is the need to identify the loopholes in the American tax system exploited by individuals who abuse the system, with a view to blocking these loopholes and lessening the financial burdens of government. But as we revise our laws, we should consider the limitations of law; the objective of any law, as earlier said, can only be attained when the people fear God. The knowledge of God must be returned to our young generations for the nation to have a future.

Division of the Church by Denominations

The prayer of the Lord Jesus Christ for His church is that we become one just as the heavenly hosts are one. Jesus said, "My prayer is not for them alone. I pray also for those who will believe in me through their message, that all of them may be one" (John 17:20-21). Paul also charged the church against divisions in the body. He said, "I appeal to you, brothers and sisters, in the name of our Lord Jesus Christ, that all of you agree with one another in what you say and that there be no divisions among you, but that you be perfectly united in mind and thought" (1 Corinthians 1:10). The Apostle further tells the church in Galatia, "So in Christ Jesus you are all children of God through faith, for all of you who were baptized into Christ have clothed yourselves with Christ.

There is neither Jew nor Gentile, neither slave nor free, nor is there male and female, for you are all one in Christ Jesus" (Galatians 3:28).

The Time has come for American Christians, Catholics, Evangelicals, Methodists, Presbyterians, Anglicans, and so on, to rise with one voice, forgetting the past issues that have divided us and moving forward because we have a common destiny. We are a big family and truly a family united by the blood of Jesus Christ. The Bible says, "For he himself [Jesus] is our peace, who has made the two groups one and has destroyed the barrier, the dividing wall of hostility" (Ephesians 2:14). We need to act with open confessions with one another, asking honestly for forgiveness for the past wrongs we have done to each other in race segregation for the sake of the kingdom of God.

Paul told the church in Corinth to be weary of the craftiness of Satan who brings strange issues of denominations into the body of Christ. He said, "My brothers and sisters, some from Chloe's household have informed me that there are quarrels among you. What I mean is this: One of you says, "I follow Paul"; another, "I follow Apollos"; another, "I follow Cephas"; still another, "I follow Christ." Is Christ divided?" (1 Corinthians 1:11-13).

Denominations are our own making, the early churches were known by their geographical locations. Many denominational issues arose from our differences in the interpretations of the scriptures. It is human to have such differences of opinion. But it should not be an issue to divide the Christian family because Jesus is the head of the church and none of us has the monopoly of interpretations of scriptures. Every church that identifies with the lordship of Jesus Christ, recognizes that He died and rose on the third day, and that He's coming back again to take the believers in Him to heaven. We are therefore one.

And I do not advocate the merger of the denominations, but we should desist from talking about one another's denominations as if one was superior to the other. We can correct one another with the words of God provided it is done in the spirit of love. We should stop condemning and ridiculing any part of the body of Christ. The Bible warns us against judging our fellow brothers; it says, "Who are you to judge someone else's servant? To their own master, servants stand or fall. And they will stand, for the Lord is able to make them stand" (Romans 14:4).

We therefore owe one another understanding, respecting the different views of those who profess the name of Christ, and we should pray for each other. A feeling of spiritual superiority is pride, and a proud heart is abominable in the sight of God. Our responsibility is to preach Christ. The Apostle Paul, in his letter to the Philippian church, said, "It is true that some preach Christ out of envy and rivalry, but others out of goodwill. The latter do so out of love, knowing that I am put here for the defense of the gospel. The former preach Christ out of selfish ambition, not sincerely, supposing that they can stir up trouble for me while I am in chains. But what does it matter? The important thing is that in every way, whether from false motives or true, Christ is preached. And because of this I rejoice" (Philippians 1:15-18).

Our wrangling over who is evangelical, Pentecostal, and Orthodox has continued to give the devil windows of opportunities to attack the church. We need to close ranks and encourage everyone to preach Christ. Our enemies are those who are against the cross of Jesus Christ. C. S. Lewis said, "The time is always ripe for re-union. Divisions between Christians are a sin and a scandal, and Christians ought to at all time to be making contributions toward re-union, if it is only by their prayers."[163]

We cannot achieve the goal of ensuring godly leadership when we are not united. If we have elected people who love and promote righteousness in our nation's Congress and executive arm, the nation will fare well and our spiritual aspirations will also be a smooth sail. We require leaders who will promote a godly environment where the hearts of people can be prepared to do what is righteous even when there is no law that would force them to do so. Therefore, American Christians must lay aside our differences and promote unity so that we may effect a godly leadership in the nation. Unity of the body of Christ is nonnegotiable.

David McCasland in one of the devotionals said: "One of the most beautiful aspects of the Christian faith is the unity among those who follow Jesus. Through His death on the cross, Christ has removed the barriers that so often separate people and has drawn us together in true friendship and love."[164] Those Christians who are so concerned about issues of life and human differences and cannot work together with other Christians need to re-examine themselves if truly they are in Christian faith.

It is the command of Jesus Christ that the church should occupy until He comes back to the world. But the world has silenced the church and the Christians no longer speak with one voice. The political representatives fear the world more than they fear the church. The church must make her voice heard. The politicians must see the church as consultant before they make any policy decision for the people.

For example, in 1987, President Ronald Reagan expressed his desire to the people in Congress to do the bidding of God by amending the law that prevents people from exercising their faith in any place. That was the intent of the heart of early American Pilgrims. In his address before the joint session of Congress on January 27, 1987, he said:

Let's stop suppressing the spiritual core of our national being. Our nation could not have been conceived without divine help. Why is it that we can build a nation with our prayers, but we can't use a schoolroom for voluntary prayer? The 100th Congress of the United States should be remembered as the one that ended the expulsion of God from America's classrooms.[165]

That did not happen. The president's prayers were not answered, because the 100th Congress of the United States did not attach importance to the issue of bringing God back into our nation's polity. Ronald Reagan was a voice representing the American majority. But he needed the support of elected representatives in Congress to change things.

It should be understood that the judges don't make laws. Judges are vested with judicial power specified in the Constitution to hear and decide cases brought before them on the basis of the supreme law—the Constitution—and federal statutes and treaties that conform to the Constitution. The judicial power involves interpretation of the law to make decisions in actual controversies that adversaries bring to the court. Human discretion is often seen in interpretations of laws.

Therefore, if the judicial arm of government has misinterpreted the intentions of the Congress on the issue of separation of church and state, the Congress could correct the court that the intention of the clause in the constitution was not to eliminate God in our system.

Amendments have been done to laws in the past, and this misinterpretation, or the deliberate intention of certain individuals to keep God away from our system with the excuse of separation of church and state, should not be an exception. The law separating the people of America from any references to God should not have been allowed to be sustained.

But the 100th Congress did not have enough people who were willing to stand on the side of God, or who were elected on the basis of their professed faith and commitment to Christ.

Who Will Lead the Church?

The church in America needs selfless leaders, individuals willing to surrender their liberty for Christ. It will require highly committed vessels of God to get America out of the current godless situation. And the nation does not lack such individuals. America is blessed with great men of God. God is waiting for a humble servant who will answer the Lord, "Here am I, send me." It is important to know that for the church to fulfill its purpose and to change the trend for evil in the world, we require spiritual leaders with strong character. Harold M. Marshall Shelley, quoting Russian poet Boris Pasternak, said, "It is not revolutions and upheavals that clear the way to new and better days but ...someone's soul, inspired and ablaze."[166]

It is an issue of personal choice to be used of God. American Christians need to come together as one. The war against iniquity in America can be won. The choice before all American Christians is clear; we need to answer the question Jesus posed to Peter the Apostle, "Simon son of John, do you love me more than these?" (John 21:15). The war requires people who would disregard the empires they presently superintend to lead the church of God. I challenge the men of God, the clerics, bishops, pastors, evangelists, and Christian leaders of thought in America, white and black, to rise to this challenge. Our efforts for the unity of the body of Christ leading the church to speak with one voice would reverse the trend of ungodliness in our society.

The current damages to righteousness in America, perpetrated daily by Satan, using people whose hearts he has occupied with anti-god spirits, can be stopped. The members of the entire church also need to lend support to the emerging leaders without reservation, by words of encouragement and intercessory prayers.

Warning

The nation's foundation and gains over the years are at risk and may not be sustained with the rate at which ungodliness is taking control of the affairs of the country.

Sodom and Gomorrah were once so prosperous they attracted many people, including Abraham's nephew Lot. But the land was overtaken by acts of wickedness, and the moral values of the people collapsed. The city became so enmeshed in evil it brought down the wrath of God.

Patriotic citizens in Sodom and Gomorrah could have rescued the land by championing the rebuilding of the society through godly leadership, but it did not happen. Sodom remained morally desolate. By the time Abraham interceded for the city, God could not spare them. All the inhabitants, except Lot, perished. (See Genesis 13:10–11; 19:1–25.)

The inferno created by the sins of the unjust consumes not only the sinners; the upright often get caught up as well. Lot lost his wife to the calamity of Sodom and Gomorrah. The righteous must not keep silent when wickedness is being done.

Thoughts

Satan entered into politics to prevent the emergence of godly leaders of society. He is also building up his army for the calamitous end of the world. He is in the process of engaging his agents and servants to take over the political leadership of the world. If he succeeds, as it appears currently, godlessness will grow in every area of the lives of nations. We will not have peace, and the growth of the church may be retarded. The Bible warns of the dire consequences of Satan taking control. For then there will be great distress, unequaled from the beginning of the world until now-and never to be equaled again. "If those days had not been cut short, no one would survive, but for the elect those days will be shortened" (Matthew 24:21-22). The leadership of the nation should be entrusted to only those who know the Lord and do His will.

CHAPTER 12

REBUILDING THE WALLS

Unless the Lord builds the house, the builders labor in vain.
Unless the Lord watches over the city, the guards stand watch
in vain.
—Psalm 127:1

THE MOST RATIONAL thing to do when a building dilapidates, cracks, or collapses is to repair or rebuild it. It is significant when the building is the home of a family because a home is the security for life and property. No one would ignore such issues because a family living in a collapsed home is exposed to different kinds of environmental hazards of weather, sun, rain and storms. The family may also become vulnerable to risks resulting from willful attacks of criminals, enemies, predators and other similar abusers of mankind.

In August 2005, Hurricane Katrina, one of the deadliest and costliest natural disasters, hit the city of New Orleans in the State of Louisiana. Thousands of individuals were dangerously exposed because their houses were washed away by the flood. It was an issue of concern to many people, friends, relations, country men and women and kind-hearted individuals. By September, a few days into the disaster, the re-building of the city began because the victims needed to be secured.

Groups, and organizations rallied, one example was the voluntary organization, "Rebuilding Together New Orleans". The organization, in cooperation with local government and community leaders, made significant strides in aiding homeowners to return to their communities and rebuild their lives.[167]

Jesus told people, "Destroy this temple, and I will rebuild it in three days" (John 2:18-21). The people, though, did not understand what He meant. He was teaching them that His mission on earth was to re-build the values of God in the people that Satan has destroyed. Jesus later died and rose from grave the third day as He accomplished the liberation of human hearts from the captivity of Satan.

The United States of America was known for her Christian values. The values were the anchor for her development and greatness over the years. It determined the nation's character and was the cord that held the people together despite their diversities. The values were the home builder through which the people were securely living together. But the values are fast disappearing because successive generations in our nation have been deprived of the knowledge of God that promoted and maintained the system.

The foundations on which the nation's values were built have come under severe attack from those opposed to Christian faith. The knowledge of God's words has suddenly become foreign to a cross section of American people because the platform on which they would have heard the word of God is being destroyed. We are therefore also witnessing what is common to the irreverent societies. Bribery, corruption, bigotry, poverty, and other forms of social injustices are part of America's present-day realities.

Open Attack on American Values

Some people say that the foundation upon which America was founded was not necessarily Christian. They argue that the core values in our society are not attributable to Christianity. They claim that such principles were in existence before Christ came to the earth.

S. K. Eleton, in his article "Christian Values," argued that there was nothing known as Christian values. He believed the characteristics of love, honor, charity, kindness, family, etc. are just good values which he supposes anyone could have and not Christians alone. He therefore thought it was an insult to the two-thirds of humanity who are religious but not Christian [statistics his], who have these characteristics, to hear someone call these traits Christian values. S. K. Eleton, a self-proclaimed Theocracy Watch, is just one of many individuals out there who believe there are good values but do not agree that these good values have their origin anywhere.

He said,

> It is insulting to non-Christians everywhere to continue claiming those as Christian values. You are, in short, insulting a full two-thirds of humanity, many of whom are religious but not Christian. To be consistent with my principles, however, I will maintain that, if this is a true statement, that these are indeed Christian values, then whether it is insulting is irrelevant. Truth isn't and can't be based on who gets their feelings hurt. The third objection I have to using this phrase [I believe he means Christian values] ad nauseum is just that: it isn't true. These are simply not properly defined as Christian values.[168]

Mr. Eleton said further that, "It is simply not necessary to have love, charity, honor, kindness, family values, and so forth. Although this has throughout the ages become associated by many with their love of Christ, they are not absolutely required."[169]

Those who are of Eleton's school of thought argue that doing good is not the sole preserve of Christians. It's true that some people who do not hold Christian views are involved in good deeds. But Christians are to be known by their good deeds. C. S. Lewis saw the issue this way:

"The question before each of us is not 'Can someone lead a good life without Christianity?' The question is, 'Can I?' We all know there have been good men who were not Christians; men like Socrates and Confucius who had never heard of it, or men like J. S. Mill who quite honestly couldn't believe it. Supposing Christianity to be true, these men were in a state of honest ignorance or honest error....

But the man who asks me, 'Can't I lead a good life without believing in Christianity?' is clearly not in the same position. If he hadn't heard of Christianity he would not be asking this question."[170]

Men and women of Eleton's persuasion lack a proper understanding of who God is (if they believe in God at all). They are perhaps people who don't acknowledge that God created the human race. They may also be people who disagree on the biblical account of God's creation.

I accept the biblical account of creation. I believe that God created people in His image (Genesis 1:27), so we carry the attributes of God within us. The values we hold come to us from God because only God is good. But those who do not believe in God may think the good they possess is of their own making and not attributable to anyone else. And we should respect such individuals' views. Christians do not claim to know it all. The difference between us and others in society is that we daily seek after God for understanding of what purpose we are required to accomplish by our Creator because we totally depend on Him.

When God finished His acts of creation, He affirmed that all was good (Genesis 1:31). But when Adam and Eve disobeyed God in the Garden of Eden, sin became part of humanity's character. The disobedience of Adam and Eve removed from us the attributes of God. The dominant life of sin is the source of all wickedness and conflict in the world today.

Godliness and Goodness Compared

There is a difference between being good and being godly. Not every good person is godly. You can choose to be good for reasons other than godliness. Some people are good to others; they give from their substances for purpose of receiving the praise of people. Others also are good in order to get benefits that go with it. For example, many wealthy Americans give to charity not because they desire to do so voluntarily but because it is one of the easy ways to take advantage of annual tax deductions. There is no doubt that some people are good. But the Bible says, all the good of man and woman are like filthy rags in the presence of God (Isaiah 64:6).

The best human actions and intents are often laden with motives right and wrong, but very often with wrong motives. When we love, it is with wrong motives; when we assist others, it is with wrong motives, but all the same we call ourselves good, because that is what any other human can see or understand. The Lord sees the heart. If the two thirds of humanity are as good as S. K. Eleton would have us believe, the world would be a better place. And there would be no need to talk about change of heart, which Christianity represents. But that is not the case; evil pervades our world.

However, all godly people are good. They are good not because of the good things they do but because they have a good God inside of them. Godly people do what they do because it is in the character of God inside their hearts to do good. So they do not consider themselves as the operators of good deeds but as tools in the hands of the operator. The operator is God. Paul said: "I have been crucified with Christ and I no longer live, but Christ lives in me. The life I now live in the body, I live by faith in the Son of God, who loved me and gave himself for me" (Galatians 2:20). The apostle was reiterating what he told the Roman church, that man cannot on his own do anything good. He said: "For I know that good itself does not dwell in me, that is, in my sinful nature" (Romans 7:18). What makes a godly man good is his reliance on the good God who does good all the time.

We can achieve the condition of doing good when we accept the offer of Jesus' reconciliation of man and woman with God. Jesus Christ died to reconcile us to God and thereby return to us the character and attributes of God that we lost through Adam and Eve's transgression.

Paul the Apostle said:

Just as sin entered the world through one man, and death through sin, and in this way death came to all people, because all sinned....

But the gift is not like the trespass. For if the many died by the trespass of the one man, how much more did God's grace and the gift that came by the grace of the one man, Jesus Christ, overflow to the many! ...

For if, by the trespass of the one man, death reigned through that one man, how much more will those who receive God's abundant provision of grace and of the gift of righteousness reign in life through the one man, Jesus Christ!

—Romans 5:12, 15, 17

So the damage we are experiencing today in our values was done thousands of years back by Satan. Jesus came down to the world to effect the repairs and rebuilding. But Satan keeps inflicting wounds on the nature of God in us to do good.

Isaiah, a Hebrew prophet in the kingdom of Judah (c. second half of eight century BC) thought he was good enough until he saw God in the spirit. 'Woe to me!' I cried. 'I am ruined! For I am a man of unclean lips, and I live among a people of unclean lips, and my eyes have seen the King, the LORD Almighty'" (Isaiah 6: 5). And when he saw God, he repented and decided to follow God.

It is therefore not true, and presumptuous to say that nothing can be done about our collapsing world. We do not need to remain in the sinful nature we found ourselves. Our inappropriate behavior is often blamed on the fall of Adam and Eve. But a remedy for sin was provided by God. The Bible says that while we were yet sinners, Christ died for us. Our responsibility is to accept the offer of grace to us by God. Once we receive Jesus Christ as our savior, our sins are forever forgiven.

Jesus told Nicodemus, a Jewish lawyer, that he needed to be born again in order to see the kingdom of God. The great attorney of his time recognized that God had done what was required to save mankind. Nicodemus also realized that he had personal responsibility to accept or reject the offer of God for salvation. He sought Jesus for salvation.

The Bible records this incidence:

> Now there was a Pharisee, a man named Nicodemus who was a member of the Jewish ruling council. He came to Jesus at night and said, "Rabbi, we know that you are a teacher who has come from God. For no one could perform the signs you are doing if God were not with him."
>
> Jesus replied, "Very truly I tell you, no one can see the kingdom of God unless they are born again."
>
> —John 3:1–3

So we must make personal efforts and by choice return to God and also get our society back to God so that it can be well with us. When we come to God, we are given a new heart which enables us to do the good deeds we were originally created to do.

Christianity offers, but does not guarantee, a crime-free society, because the people must accept and embrace the offer of life in Christ. However, Christianity assures a morally conscious nation in which the people live with the understanding that there is a God who would live His good life in and through them. While Christians do not claim to be good, they live their lives in the fear of God and work for a peaceful nation. Their conscience is alert and always ready to repent of wrong doing, and is always prepared to move their community forward.

When we get born again, we are changed back to the image of God. "Therefore, if anyone is in Christ, the new creation has come: The old has gone, the new is here!" (1 Corinthians 5:17). The rebuilding of our nation starts with the reformation of the people's hearts. A man whose heart has been transformed by the words of God, acts for the good of society. Vices in society will reduce when the hearts of many people within the nation are changed and occupied by the Spirit of God.

Nehemiah: An Example of a Builder

Nehemiah the son of Hachaliah was an example of a committed nations rebuilder. He demonstrated this virtue when Israel sinned against their God and were visited with calamities of great magnitude. Throughout the history of the Jewish nation, whenever wicked leaders ascended to the throne and misdirected the nation against God, misfortune came upon the people. God allowed Satan to torment them for their disobedience. And usually the people suffered the consequences of sin.

About 445 BC, the Jews disobeyed God and were conquered by the Babylonians. Some were enslaved in their own homes. Many others went into exile.

In 539 BC, Artaxerxes, the king of Persia, showed favor to the Jews by granting them freedom to return to their land. Nehemiah remained in Shushan, the capital of Persia, because he occupied a position of honor and trust in the king's palace: the king had appointed him as his cup bearer.

Hanani, one of the exiled Jews who visited Jerusalem, returned to Babylon with sad stories of what had become of Jerusalem, the city of

God. The wall of the city had fallen and the gates had been devastated by fire. The remnants of the Jews were exposed to aggression by hostile forces. The people were in great affliction and reproach because of the fallen wall of the city.

Nehemiah, though comfortable in the king's palace, and having no reason to be concerned about the plight of Jerusalem, was grieved by the situation. He knew the greatness of the nation Israel, her potential, and the reason for her current travail. And he knew someone needed to assume responsibility for rebuilding so the nation could get back on her feet.

Nehemiah cherished the work of the nation's founders in their struggle to serve and obey God. He also valued the covenant God had made with Abraham, the Jewish patriarch, which made the nation great.

Nehemiah knew that if nothing was done to avert the deterioration, his society and people was at risk of perpetual suffering in the hands of the enemy and possible extinction. He said, "When I heard these things, I sat down and wept" (Nehemiah 1:4).

Nehemiah went to the king and said:

> Why should my face not look sad when the city where my ancestors are buried lies in ruins, and its gates have been destroyed by fire?… If it pleases the king and if your servant has found favor in his sight, let him send me to the city in Judah where my ancestors are buried so that I can rebuild it.
>
> —Nehemiah 2:3, 5

Nehemiah was not a trained politician, pastor, or soldier. He was an ordinary member of society willing to be used for the common good. When God chose him to be an instrument for the rebuilding of the collapsed walls of Jerusalem, he resolved in his heart to face the challenge and take the people to victory.

Rebuilding the wall of Jerusalem was an overwhelming task, but Nehemiah knew the job was doable. He did not look at the impossibilities; instead, he prepared strategies to confront the challenges. He knew that any failure in the processes would only show better ways of accomplishing the ultimate purpose.

For Nehemiah, Israel represented hope for generations to come. The God of the Jews had assured this people that He would answer them whenever they called on Him. God said, "Before they call I will answer; while they are still speaking I will hear" (Isaiah 65:24). "Call to me and I will answer you and tell you great and unsearchable things you do not know" (Jeremiah 33:3).

Nehemiah had absolute faith that the God of Israel would not fail in any of His promises. He believed that God would provide all the resources and assistance required for the task.

He achieved the objective. The ruined wall of Jerusalem was rebuilt. But how did he do it? He was a man like us, or any others of his time. He had his personal struggles, with ups and downs in life. But he made a commitment to do the work of rebuilding of the wall of Jerusalem. The patriotism in him arose not out of human pride but out of the need to fulfill the purpose of God for his life.

Emulating the Virtues of Nehemiah

There are people who have worked for the reformation of their societies borrowing from the experiences of Nehemiah. John Knox was a man who had passion for change in his country, Scotland. He lived in the days of Queen Mary of Scotland, when corruption and immorality was destroying the country and the people. The church as represented by the Catholic faith was also not spared from the ravaging sin. The nation was at its brinks. John was burdened and in secret, he prayed passionately, "O God Give me Scotland or I die."[171]

The Queen of Scotland confessed that she feared the prayers of Knox more than all the armies of Scotland. John knew the importance of the reformation of the heart of the people for a change in the bad situation in Scotland. His flourishing ministry in Geneva was put on hold to enable him to contribute towards the rebuilding of Scotland.

"He was prevailed upon in May, 1557 by certain people to return to Scotland and help to build the nation, Lords Lorne, Glencairn, Erskine, and James Stewart who were of four protestant Scottish nobles. A strong desire, accordingly prevailed-so the letter indicated-that the Reformer would return to Scotland, to advance the cause by his presence."[172] John, like Nehemiah, was consumed with passion for his country and he was prepared, if possible, to die for this cause. The history of the transformation of Scotland cannot be accurate without the name of John Knox.

The passion of John Knox reminds one of Moses, the leader of the Jewish exodus out of Egypt. God was angry at a time with the Jews because they chose to worship a lesser god and God was going to punish them. Moses was troubled about the implications of God's wrath against the people. He preferred to be personally held responsible and punished instead by God for the salvation of his people.

Moses said to God, "Oh, what a great sin these people have committed! They have made themselves gods of gold. But now, please forgive their sin—but if not, then blot me out of the book you have written." (Exodus 32:31-32). Blotting a man or woman's name out of God's book of salvation meant that they would suffer eternal damnation. But he did not mind the consequence if only that would save the nation Israel from the wrath of God. That was an unrivalled commitment that a man could have for his nation.

The Pessimistic Church in America

Unlike Nehemiah, our church today is pessimistic. The men and women of God in our society today wonder if there is anything we can do about the growing godlessness in our nation. They have given up on the anti-God stance in society, for they think it is too late to get the people back to God. Christians have lost faith in themselves and in their God and have become disillusioned about the possibility of reversing the moral bankruptcy of our society.

The popular opinion is that the problems around the world and the godlessness in our country have defied any previous solution, so the world simply has to live with them. Confrontations with sin are therefore compromised in the name of peace and political correctness.

Since 1947, when Justice Hugo Black of the United States Supreme Court, in the case of *Everson v. Board of Education,* ruled that our children could no longer pray in public schools, Christians have accepted the verdict and quietly bemoaned our situation. New generations of Americans are growing up in our public schools without the knowledge of God, putting our society at risk of complete moral bankruptcy.

And because the church was indifferent to the issue when Judge Black dropped the salvo years back, it has become an accepted pattern for other anti-God elements to attack the nation's Christian heritage. Satan has used people with lawsuits to destroy our commitment at restoring righteousness into the social, political, and economic systems of the nation.

Sadly, some church leaders have become apostles of the separation of church and state, using that as a defense against their lukewarmness on the prevailing iniquities in the land. We are therefore intimidated and settle for compromise and our burden for rebuilding our nation has evaporated. This confirms the words of Jesus about the last days. "Because of the increase of wickedness, the love of most will grow cold" (Matthew 24:12). The warning of the Lord could have been used by the church to maintain our stand in the face of the stiff opposition in the land. But alas, it did not.

On September 14, 2001, Dr. Billy Graham, the revered father of World Christian Evangelism, spoke at the memorial service for people who had lost their lives in the tragedy of September 11, 2001. Dr. Graham said:

> Yes, our nation has been attacked. Buildings destroyed. Lives lost. But we have a choice: whether to implode and disintegrate emotionally and spiritually as a people, and a nation, or whether we choose to become stronger through the entire struggle to rebuild a solid foundation. And I believe that we are in the process of starting to rebuild on that foundation. That foundation is our trust in God. That's what this service is all about. And in that faith we have the strength to endure something as difficult and horrendous as what we've experienced this week.[173]

The admonition of Reverend Graham was that Christians should brace up for the nation's rebuilding. The church must be careful not to lose its relevance because our tepidness over the continuous assault on the Christian faith in America would lead to further decay and total destruction of our cherished values. The issues that were of serious concern to our Christian patriarchs no longer matter to us. We consider the present sinful conditions as the norm in modern society. Therefore, we have become ineffective in our ability to lead our society and ensure that righteousness prevails. We have been overrun by ungodliness.

Christians are called to a life of understanding, not compromise. This was the counsel of C. S. Lewis when he said:

> As Christians we are tempted to make unnecessary concessions to those outside the Faith. We give in too much. Now, I don't mean that we should run the risk of making a nuisance of ourselves by witnessing at improper times, but there comes a time when we must show that we disagree. We must show our Christian colors if we are to be true to Jesus Christ. We cannot remain silent or concede everything away.[174]

For example, in 1993, President Bill Clinton's administration came under intense pressure to support gays in the military. The law of "Don't ask, don't tell" was established. This was, however, not acceptable to the gay-rights movement. Activists have kept pressure on succeeding governments, employed the powerful, liberal mass media to make case of human rights for gay lifestyle. The gay communities lobbied the politicians and many politicians were won to their side.

The politicians who have become the friends and defenders of gays rallied to promote the law of hate crime against any opposition to gay life. This further created disquiet in the church. People became concerned about losing their jobs and relevance in society if they expressed their convictions about the gay lifestyle.

A cross-section of church leaders also is weary of speaking the truth of the word of God. Forthrightness on the stand of the church gave way to 'diplomatic' answers as clergymen and politicians of Christian calling evade answers to questions on gay issues in order to be accepted in society.

But Jesus Christ said, "If anyone is ashamed of me and my words in this adulterous and sinful generation, the Son of Man will be ashamed of him when he comes in his Father's glory with the holy angels" (Mark 8:38).

Where the Strong Fail, God Uses the Weak

But God is never at cross-roads. He is not man, that he would be worried by the human antics. He is not at our mercy to do what He will. By His words, the worlds came into being. So if you are positioned to defend the words of God and you are reluctant to do so, God may bypass you to use a lesser being to fulfill His purpose. Jesus told the Pharisees who were eager to stop people singing praises of Him that if the persons praising Him held their peace, the stones would take their place to praise God (Luke 19:39-40).

David in expressing his praises to God said, "Through the praise of children and infants you have established a stronghold against your enemies, to silence the foe and the avenger" (Psalm 8:2). David was expressing the power of God who could use the little ones to perfect His work when mighty men failed Him.

In 2009, Carrie Prejean, a young lady and Miss California for that year, treaded where pastors, reverends, bishops, and archbishops dared not go. The question those men of God parried or answered "diplomatically," this young lady answered forthrightly and according to the dictates of her faith.

During the 2009 Miss USA contest, Perez Hilton asked Carrie Prejean about her views on same-sex marriage. She answered, "We live in a land where you can choose same-sex marriage or opposite marriage. And you know what? In my country and in my family, I think and I believe that marriage should be between a man and a woman. No offense to anybody out there, but that's how I was raised. I think that it should be between a man and a woman."[175]

The opposition to her opinion was so severe she lost the Miss California crown. Courageously defending her faith also meant losing the Miss USA title. The young lady is an example of a direct message from God to the church and Christian leaders who are too careful to represent Him boldly in the midst of the conflicts of the world. God would replace them with ordinary faithful men and women if they continue to fail.

And The Gay Community Won the Battle

On December 18, 2010, seventeen years after the "Don't ask, don't tell" policy came into effect, it was repealed by Congress, which succumbed to political pressure. This was seen as a victory for the gay-rights movement because they would not give up what they considered as their rights.

But in contrast, the church is quick to abandon the cause of the cross, leaving our society to the rots of ungodliness. This was why Jesus Christ asked rhetorically, "When the Son of Man comes, will he find faith on the earth?" (Luke 18:8). The question arose because the followers of Jesus were fast giving up their faith in the face of difficulty. But in His response, "Jesus told his disciples a parable to show them that they should always pray and not give up" (Luke 18:1).

Damage Done by Christians' Lukewarmness

The unconcerned attitude of the church to the growing iniquities in our nation is doing incalculable damages to our society. While we do not care much about the restrictions put on our children in public schools to prayers and handling Bibles, those opposed to our faith go ahead to occupy our children with knowledge that is opposed to the knowledge of our God.

The gay-rights movement has tried to infiltrate our public schools with literature that promotes their liberal agenda. In Sacramento, California, it may soon become law for gay stories to be added to the social studies curriculum of our children. According to the Associated Press:

> Gays, lesbians, bisexuals and transgender people would be added to the lengthy list of social and ethnic groups that public schools must include in social studies lessons under a landmark bill passed Thursday by the California Senate. If the bill is adopted by the state assembly and signed by Gov. Jerry Brown, California would become the first state to require the teaching of gay history.[176]

This should grieve the church, but some leaders are indifferent provided it does not hurt the membership of their church congregation. The early church was not known just by numerical strength but by the power of God doing miracles and by righteousness that overtook the ungodliness in the land.

Wrong Optimism

Christians are often optimistic that it will turn out well even when they refuse to perform their responsibilities to promote righteousness in society. Our optimism is usually based on the fact that God will do His work with or without us. There is no doubt about the ability of God to put things right in our nation, but God is depending on the church as His ambassadors to do the work it is called to do. The purpose of the church is defeated if God has to descend again in another form of Christ to deliver the decaying world. This will not happen. When Jesus comes again, it is time for judgment.

The question therefore is not whether God can or will change our society from its current sinful situation to a godly state. The question is if you and I will put ourselves forward for the use of God for the purpose of reviving godliness in our nation. We can rebuild this nation into a godly path. We require commitment like Nehemiah's to accomplish the purpose of God for our lives on this planet.

We should stop carrying on us the Christian ego and optimism without faith. For example, in a recent conversation with a Christian friend, I asked if he ever thought about the possibility that America may one day elect a dictator. He dismissed the idea as impossible. After all, he and many others have fought valiantly for this country's freedom. Good as his sentiments are, such cannot be sustained if we keep having carefree attitudes towards the promotion of uprightness in our land. The current democratic system has endured because it was built on righteousness. The only guarantee of its continued support is the promotion of godly principles in our nation.

We therefore have to learn and appreciate how Nehemiah, John Knox, and others succeeded in changing the wrong directions their societies found themselves in. It is the will of God that our society be changed for good and we have to walk within God's will, that the glorious days of America may be back with us again. If we decide to do otherwise, it is to spend our sojourn here without accomplishing the purpose of our lives. As Charles Lewis said, "To walk out of His will is to walk into no where." We are therefore to pick our gauntlet to make the difference now;" but how?

A Call for Prayers

Nehemiah started with prayers. We cannot do God's service without consulting with Him. Prayer is an important aspect of a determined builder. John MacArthur, Jr. said, "For Christians prayer is like breathing. You don't have to think to breathe because the atmosphere exerts pressure on your lungs and forces you to breathe."[177]

Prayer is part of the makeup of a successful society-builder. Those who have succeeded in the past had their secret in either personal prayer or were blessed with a team of warriors who are constantly on their knees.

God made no pretense about the need for prayer for the nation by His children. He said:

> If my people, who are called by my name, will humble themselves and pray and seek my face and turn from their wicked ways, then I will hear from heaven, and I will forgive their sin and will heal their land.
> —2 Chronicles 7:14

Nehemiah talked to God about the onerous responsibility he was going to embark on. He praised God for His faithfulness, mercy, and unbroken covenant with the people of Israel. He then prayed to ask for forgiveness of the sins of his country so that God could answer his prayers of restoring the nation Israel back to Himself.

Nehemiah said, "LORD, the God of heaven, the great and awesome God, who keeps his covenant of love with those who love him and keep his commandments, let your ear be attentive and your eyes open to hear the prayer your servant is praying before you day and night" (Nehemiah 1:5-6).

John Wesley said "God does nothing on earth save in answer to believing prayer."[178]

Building is a Joint Effort

Nehemiah left us with no doubt that he needed people to rebuild the city of Jerusalem. He knew that the task could not be accomplished by him alone. The work required a collective responsibility of the people. Nehemiah stood out as a motivator and a mobiliser. He rallied the people to ensure that every section of the city of Jerusalem was put back in shape.

The contribution of everyone in all fields of righteous endeavor is important in ensuring our nation is restored back to the days when righteous living in our land was priority, and when sin was abhorred and people were afraid to commit crime. We may not be able to totally eliminate the influence of the devil in the world because he is in control of the apparatus of this earth, but we can reduce his effect to the barest minimum so that our people can have a good life. Jesus Christ died and rose again to ensure good life for us.

It is therefore important to have men of God in all works of life for the purpose of nation building. The teachers, lawyers, doctors, and the public servants have their parts to play as they render their different forms of service in the society. We need intelligent men on the table, but we require intelligence mixed with the fear of God to fix our society. When Christians render services as to God, there will be re-awakening of moral values in our society.

Unity of Purpose

Unity among the diverse people of God is a great tool to achieve the feat of national repairs. A cohesive church cannot be discountenanced by the society because it holds the keys to unlock all that is good and sound. The unity of the church would accelerate the re-building process of the moral values of the nation.

We have differences, and these differences must be recognized to the extent that we can adequately deal with them and move the nation forward. We should stop pretending there are no issues when we see them manifesting daily. The church must wage war against any forms of discrimination, for we are one, black, white, or any other color.

Our pastors and leaders should therefore teach the people in the churches to smoothen their relationship. It will be great when Christian leaders of diverse denominations and doctrines congregate together in a solemn assembly to pray for the revival of our nation. The day Christians no longer consider themselves by racial parameters and are able to place faith above all personal sentiments, America will be removed from Satan's agenda.

Importance of Home in Nation Building

The importance of the home cannot be over-emphasized for our nation's survival. Our attitude to parenting must change. We cannot depend on government, state, or school teachers to raise our children for us. We have to balance our children's secular training with their spiritual life. When attention is paid to secular education to the detriment of the moral education of our children, the foundation that can keep the child standing all through life will be missing, that is, the knowledge of God which results in society's values.

Whatever our children may become in their lives, doctors, engineers, teachers, athletes, musicians, etc., as desirable as these professions may be, they will not be effective when the moral foundation is lacking. The society will be near perfect when our political leaders, our doctors in the hospitals, our engineers in their various fields, and our teachers in their schools can seek to do the will of the Lord in their callings.

The point is that success at rebuilding our nation will continue to elude us until we recognize and accept God into our activities.

Thought

The problem of man is not in falling, but rather in not rising when he falls. The nation has been bruised; we can only sink if we fail to pick up from where we have fallen. The nation of Nineveh perceived the calamities that were going to befall their nation, and they repented. Everyone, small and big including animals wore sackcloth as a sign of penitence before God. And God forgave the people and spared the land. Jesus warned that "the men of Nineveh will stand up at the judgment with this generation and condemn it; for they repented at the preaching of Jonah, and now something greater than Jonah is here" (Matthew 12:41).

THE CHANGES THAT THE WORLD REQUIRES

No one calls for justice; no one pleads a case with integrity.
They rely on empty arguments, they utter lies; they conceive
trouble and give birth to evil.
—Isaiah 59:4

THE WORLD IS rapidly changing for the worse. Every day, life is getting scarier on all fronts. Good news is no longer common in the print and electronic media. Global warming, earthquakes, tsunamis, and other forms of natural disasters have become common occurrences. The world has witnessed in the last three years, 2008 to 2011, unprecedented natural disasters: Japan's earthquakes and tsunami, and Haiti's earthquake that claimed thousands of lives. In America, tornados, floods, and earthquakes have constituted high stress on the people.

On the political front, it is nothing but catastrophic, as the agents of Satan are taking control, changing the laws of God and replacing them with the laws of iniquity. Unrighteousness has pervaded the landscapes with corrupt, wicked, and ungodly leadership ruling nations with deceptions. It is certainly true that Bible prophesies are being fulfilled. The Bible says: "For false messiahs and false prophets will appear and perform signs and wonders to deceive, if possible, even the elect. So be on your guard; I have told you everything ahead of time" (Mark 13:22-23).

233

The believers in Christ are being persuaded by the oration of politicians. The tenets of Christian faith have become less important. Issues of economy, race, personal comfort and welfare are now priority and we have been completely overtaken by Satan.

On the socio-economic front, we have issues of falling standards of living of the people. The economy is failing because it lacks the right leadership in society. Because we do not have godly political leaders, plans are done in the absence of God and such plans have little chances of success. The Bible says: "The blessing of the LORD brings wealth, without painful toil for it" (Proverb 10:22). The truth is that if we plan and the blessings of the Lord do not accompany our plan, we will always fail. All our thoughts on the economy have not worked well, not because they were not good but because our intellect is not enough when God is omitted. Similarly, we continue to witness anti-social behavior on the increase because any social reforms and laws without the blessing of the Lord do not make positive impact in any society. Our relationship with one another has gone sour because individuals struggle to cope with the conflicts around us. People then result to criminal acts to get what they perceive they cannot have through honest and peaceful means. They therefore kill, maim, and destroy lives and properties. The conflicts around the world are overwhelming.

Obstacles to Change

Are things likely to get better in our nation and in the world? Most likely not, because the world is not prepared for change. We desire change, and talk about change in all spheres of our lives, but no one is prepared to pay the price for change. We have refused to ask, and are consequently unable to get answers to the fundamental questions of life. Where are we coming from? Where are we? And where are we going? These questions are critical to change in any society. These questions are important because they are the reasons why we continue to grope in darkness and have never found the appropriate strategies to move on to our desired destination.

Where are we coming from? There is no doubt about where we are coming from as a nation. The foundation of America was based on the words of God. The nation was governed from its inception by people who feared God and were ready to obey Him. The foundations they laid have kept the nation together until today. But the efforts of these past heroes in bequeathing uprightness to succeeding generations are being undermined. Some people have claimed that our past leaders were not Christians. Some individuals have tried to change history to discredit our Christian heritage because of their personal distaste for Christian life.

Our research and efforts for change have not often dwelled on the truth. When we research, we are opposed to the truth that may result from the research because truth is difficult for us to accept, and we consequently change the truth into lies. And truth is critical to changing the fortune of the world for the better. C.S. Lewis said, "The process of living seems to consist in coming to realize truths so ancient and simple that, if stated, they sound like barren platitudes. They cannot sound otherwise to those who have not had the relevant experience: that is why there is no real teaching of such truths possible and every generation starts from scratch."[179]

As the anti-God sections of the nation fight against the truth, they have gradually exposed our society to various forms of dangers. And we lack the capacity to stop or control the afflictions that is ravaging the world. We have reached our limits, except God comes to our rescue.

The Truth

The conflicts in the world today are the reflections and manifestations of the war in the human heart. We cannot win this battle unless we engage the heart of man. We are going nowhere with whatever ideas that we proffer to solve the menace around the world because the human is limited by the incorrigible condition of our hearts. We would never get any solutions to our problems with the absence of God's knowledge and fear in our dealings and actions. This is the reason why some theories have not worked for us. The communist theories and the socialist economies failed and became a source of tyranny because they were knowledge based on the supremacy of man, and man cannot be higher than his Creator.

Whittaker Chambers wrote, "Communism is what happens when, in the name of mind, men free themselves from God. There has never been a society of a nation without God. But history is cluttered with the wreckage of nations that became indifferent to God, and died."[180]

We have often heard theories of how past economic depressions in the country and the world were overcome. Some analysts said that the current economic trouble which began in 2008 has taken more time to recover than it did in the past. The reason why the economic downturn is increasingly becoming long and difficult to overcome is because the land has been completely overtaken by iniquities. It was not like this in the past; we are no longer conscious of God in our society and everybody does what is right in their eyes. If God is not in control, Satan is always on hand to exert control and this is why we are today experiencing the difficulties and have not recovered.

Also we entered into these troubles in the past not because economic depression is a necessary way of life but because the world found itself in wickedness and conflicts that led nations into such trouble, such as war which the world experienced in 1939. When we repented and the men of God in those days called upon God, He made things well for them. One would think we have learnt from the issues of yesteryears and should be able to manage ourselves so that we do not go through similar experiences again. But we will go back into the problems again and again because rather than recognizing the need for God in the situations of the world, we have moved further away from the knowledge of God. And the Bible says: "Righteousness exalts a nation, but sin condemns any people" (Proverbs 14:34). The only way to get out of these troubles, economic, political, and social, is to get our nation back to God.

America, the Last Standing Super Power in the World

The nation, America, is the last standing of the superpowers of the world. And Satan is on the offensive to get America. If America is brought under the control of the agents of Satan, the world will be in trouble. Britain has been overrun by the liberals and sharia agitators. Britain, the one-time mission station to the world, has seen churches converted to mosques or movie theatres. The younger generations have no touch with the knowledge of the true God. The political power of Britain has evaporated; the most stable economy in the world some centuries past has been gradually eroded and is now wobbling. It will be a miracle for the one-time number one leading nation of the world to rise.

Anti-Christian faiths of the world, particularly Islam, have taken over Britain. They continue to unleash mayhem with little or no provocations. They are prepared to change the laws built around God's principles into their model of sharia. The issue is not really Islam; the point is that Satan has mobilized from all fronts attacks on the Kingdom of Jesus Christ. The church is the main target. The opposition may have varying strategies, they may appear in different colors and shapes: liberals, atheists, freethinkers, Marxists, communists, etc.; they have no other enemy but the cross of Jesus Christ.

Jesus is an offense to them because He is the only true God who came to the world in human form. For centuries before He came, the world waited in pain for Him. Satan knew that Jesus is the only power that he would finally bow to and he has been on the rampage against the name of Jesus Christ. But the Bible says, "Therefore God exalted him to the highest place and gave him the name that is above every name, that at the name of Jesus every knee should bow, in heaven and on earth and under the earth, and every tongue acknowledge that Jesus Christ is Lord, to the glory of God the Father" (Philippians 2:9-11). There is nothing Satan and all his soldiers can do, Jesus is the Lord. We shall all one day bow before Him. I have bowed to Him already so that I can be part of His Kingdom.

The next target of the world's jihadists is the United States of America. America is the only obstacle for Islam to conquer the world. They are working to take control. But the great disaster is that American Christians do not get it. We have been overtaken by the lukewarm spirit. The spirit of fear and timidity has entered the church. The spirit of boldness and sound mind has left us because of our unwillingness to carry the cross of Christ and follow Him as He commanded. The activities of the church are limited to mostly things that the world is comfortable with. That is why we often find our leaders and pastors messed up by the people of the world because the world has identified our weaknesses. The Bible says, "Friendship with the world is enmity with God" (James 4:4). The church, which is responsible for steering the ship of the nation to a good shore, has abandoned the ship and the ship is fast sinking. Our laxities in today's church have given the enemy the assurance that they would soon succeed in taking over the nation. While we are struggling with our differences of race and political ideologies, Bible doctrines and denominations, the opposers of our Christian faith are perfecting strategies to launch attacks on our faith.

We need to be careful not to think that the ship of the nation and of our faith sailing fast into storms are not matters for serious concern. When our nation is completely weakened spiritually and God abandons us (God forbid); the church that is free today may also go underground. Those who think this is impossible should think again.

Solutions

Our Mouths Must Speak

When the mouths of Christians stop talking, the salvation of the millions around the world is in jeopardy. Paul said: "How, then, can they call on the one they have not believed in? And how can they believe in the one of whom they have not heard? And how can they hear without someone preaching to them?" (Romans 10:14). The apostles of old in the early church demonstrated boldness in speaking to their generations because that was the only way to rescue the perishing. They were told by the ruling class not to talk or speak about the name of Jesus Christ again but they said: "Which is right in God's eyes: to listen to you, or to him? You be the judges! As for us, we cannot help speaking about what we have seen and heard." (Acts 14:20)

C. S. Lewis said, "Christianity is not merely what a man does with his solitude. It is not even what God does with His solitude. It tells of God descending into the coarse publicity of history and there enacting what can- and must-be talked about."[181]

Our mouth must speak. We are speaking but it appears we are not speaking out loud enough. The United States takes in thousands of immigrants annually. The nation is also sympathetic towards people in the oppressed countries of the world to give them opportunities to have a more comfortable life which America's land offers. This is a good and godly program, but it goes with additional responsibilities for Christians, who are the conscience of the nation. The issue is that the immigrants that are being accepted into the United States come into the country with cultures and gods that are strange to the God of America.

There are two possibilities: One is that America teaches them American culture as they enter so that they can be acquainted with the godly culture that made the nation of America attractive to other countries. Secondly, they may settle to practice their foreign cultures alongside the American culture and/or despise the American culture. But the true case so far has been that over the years, the immigrants not only practice their culture, they despise the American culture and also seek to replace American culture with theirs. The godly heritage which the nation was known for is therefore being threatened with lawsuits in the name of individual rights.

The trend requires Christians to speak out. It is what God wants us to do. God called us to be watchmen and women. The silence of Christians is not doing any good to the nation. If the trend is allowed to continue, God will hold us responsible for our sins of negligence and disobedience. God told Ezekiel what He would do when the watchmen and women refuse to speak to a fast decaying world. He said: "Son of man, speak to your people and say to them: 'When I bring the sword against a land, and the people of the land choose one of their men and make him their watchman, and he sees the sword coming against the land and blows the trumpet to warn the people, then if anyone hears the trumpet but does not heed the warning and the sword comes and takes their life, their blood will be on their own head. Since they heard the sound of the trumpet but did not heed the warning, their blood will be on their own head. If they had heeded the warning, they would have saved themselves. But if the watchman sees the sword coming and does not blow the trumpet to warn the people and the sword comes and takes someone's life, that person's life will be taken because of their sin, but I will hold the watchman accountable for their blood" (Ezekiel 33:1–6).

One of the responsibilities of Christians is to speak against iniquities in the land, but some of our Christian leaders have gone from this task of declaring righteousness in the nation, America. They have joined the world to declare that America is not a Christian nation, and some sadly on the church pulpit. This is cowardice in Christian faith. The fact that Satan has destroyed the Christian virtues of this country does not make the nation less a Christian nation. Such utterance that America is not a Christian nation shows lack of faith on the part of Christians and is altogether negative and a disservice to the memory of the Christian founders of this great society. "Faith is calling those things that are not as though they were" (Romans 4:17). Satan cannot conquer America; the Christian values in this society shall be revived.

Professor Michael Youssef, a man of God, summed up the frightening situation in our nation by saying, "I have always thanked God that America has been a bastion of Gospel hope for the world for the past 250 years. I never thought I would see the day when the Gospel would be so desperately needed here. I have pleaded with the Lord and asked, "What would you have me do?" After much prayer, I sensed Him saying to me, "I brought you to this country to wake-up sleeping Christians, to challenge the apostate church, and to call out the sin of indifference among believers. I want you to warn believers before it is too late."[182]

The call is not only on Youssef but on thousands of Americans and Christian immigrants who probably have forgotten the covenant they made with God when entering into America that they would do the will of God. American born-Christians should be equally grieved.

Our Lives Must Speak

The other obstacle to revival in the world is the life of the Christians. Our life should speak to the world and cause them to repent. But rather, the aching coming out of our lives is terrible and devastating to the world. If the church had shown purposeful leadership in the nation with our lives, the enemy of Christianity would have taken flight to the jungles. But our lives are often opposite of what we preach. This is why iniquities are being vaunted on the streets of the nation by those who identified with Satan and are out to mock the name of our Lord Jesus Christ. Our hypocritical life is doing serious damage to the gospel of Jesus Christ. C. S Lewis said, "If the divine call does not make us better, it will make us very much worse. Of all bad men religious bad men are the worst.

Of all the created beings the wickedest is the one who originally stood in the immediate presence of God."[183]

The sophisticated world of today does not get convicted with the gospel according to St. Luke, Matthew, Mark or John; not even the gospel according to Paul, but they are attentive to the gospel according to our Christian living. Satan knows the effect of the distortions our lives are making on the gospel, the reason why he keeps messing with our lives daily. We have come to the point when we should see clearly the appearances of evil everywhere. Once divorce enters into the church, the world celebrates it as if it is the normal life. Once the church begin to struggle with the sins of homosexuality, the world celebrates it as if it is the normal life. The situation of the world is the indication that all is not well in the church.

But God is in the church doing His works through His obedient children. For example, a brother, Larry Powell, made the church proud in the midst of public service that had been ravaged with corruption. The man of God, a Baptist minister, stood out for God as a witness that some soldiers of Christ are still out there. Larry Powell, the Fresno County school superintendent gave up monetary gain to shine for God. "Fresno County School Superintendent Larry Powell, who's really giving back. As in $800,000 – what would have been his compensation for the next three years. Until his term expires in 2015, Powell will run 325 schools and 35 school districts with 195,000 students, all for less than a starting California teacher earns."[184]

If nothing gladdens my heart about this story, Larry's words did. "How much do we need to keep accumulating? … There is no reason for me to keep stockpiling money."[185] Powell is living out the gospel which says: "But godliness with contentment is great gain. For we brought nothing into the world, and we can take nothing out of it" (1 Timothy 6: 6-7). We cannot change the society until we are prepared to change and speak change with our lifestyle. Powell is only living to make a difference.

The only people known to build and rebuild the society are in the church; but as Nehemiah did, we have to purge ourselves of the iniquities in us. We need God to forgive us. And He is always willing and ready to forgive if we come to Him.

Speaking With Our Steps

God gave His people the spirit of boldness. American Christians have become timid. We are concerned about our liberty. The opponents of Christian faith have therefore taken the forefront, the rightful place of Christians. The first instrument of the devil that the church needs to deal with is fear. David in the Bible said, "The Lord is my light and my salvation, whom shall I fear? The Lord is the stronghold of my life, of whom shall I be afraid?" (Psalm 27:1). "The Lord is with me, I will not be afraid. What can man do to me?" (Psalm 118:6). When the Philistine giant came against Israel; David said to Saul the king, "Let no one lose heart on account of this Philistine, your servant will go and fight him" (1 Samuel 17:32). Therefore we must make up our minds to fight and win; because our God has never lost a battle.

The truth is that the world came into existence by the word of God. It will continue to exist only by the word of God. When the end of the world comes, it will only be by the word of God. The church needs to be assertive within the society to make a positive impact. Those who are against God today will one day come to bow before Him. Those who think God is not relevant today will look for Him possibly when it is too late.

The government and the school managers lack the moral right to take away Bibles and deny our children the right to pray in schools, while these noble godly practices have been replaced with ungodly practices, such as dressing up as witches, ghosts, and monsters in the Halloween season. It is an assault on the church and what the church stands for. The church will continue to witness failure when children in schools are not allowed to have access to the Bible, the source of growth for the kids, but are continuously exposed to things that depict evil. Halloween has found its worship in the White House, the same territory where godly national prayers for the nation have been banned and later reduced to a joke; a joke because it is all kinds of prayers and not the prayers to the God of Israel that Americans used to worship.

Make Hay While the Sun Shines

The time to act is now. As Nehemiah refused to procrastinate, men and women of God must act and move to:

- The school: The only way to reverse the consequences of bad leadership in tomorrow's generation is to catch our youth now while they are still in their tender minds that we can easily mold with the word of God. We must do all we can do now to return the awareness of God back into our schools. We are breeding executives, law makers, and judges of tomorrow who are not just far removed from God but have been brainwashed with anti-God knowledge. We need to act without delay to reverse the trend. We should lay aside our differences in denominations, doctrine, race, and conventions and pay all attention to the dissemination of the word of God among our young people. We need to build an army that would be able to resist the satanic forces as they come into our nation.

- Change our political understanding from that of race to that of faith. Let our faith dictate our leaders. God has given human beings, whom He created, the power to make their choices. Often, the choice is between God and Satan. Whatever we freely choose is ours. The lack of unity among the Christian believers today has given the enemy an advantage over us. When they unite against the Christian faith to promote and elect liberals (and I do not mean just political party but ungodly individuals) who often see themselves as opposed to Christianity, they legislate against our faith and they stand against the works of God in our nation. The liberals and their sponsors promote unrighteousness in our land claiming the defense of human rights. We do not need to agree on every point of doctrine, but we can agree on the essentials, the righteous living of the Lord Jesus Christ. We should be wary of being induced by their economic blue print. No economic theory will work in the land unless the heart of the people is changed.

- Rise to take the challenge of changing the leadership of the nation to those who fear God, those who would not shy away from the responsibility of the call of God upon their lives. Like Nehemiah, they are required to leave their comfort zone to help bring our nation back to God. Executive, legislative, and judicial arms of our nation's government should be deliberately dominated by men and women of proven convictions about their faith in the Lord Jesus Christ. The point here is that it is not all those who are claiming to be conservatives that really are. Church leaders need to emphasize to their congregations the importance of voting for righteousness in political elections. Our ministers, reverends, pastors, apostles, and bishops are responsible for training and encouraging believers with political talents to participate in the government. The ministers of the word of God must counsel the church people so that they can have good directions in their war against ungodly leadership in our nation. Our teachings should center on the qualities of a Christian who would be reliable in a position of leadership. The choice will then be made by informed members of the church. Our church leaders should stay away from racial and any form of divisions in the body of Christ. The call on the church to exercise her right to choose godly leadership in the nation is not a call for a religious state, but God counts on his people to go for righteousness.

- Support Christians who venture into politics through our prayers. This will ensure that they succeed. We must also keep in touch with them throughout their terms in office. Prayer gives the church a united voice on the will of God. When we pray, members of the church gain understanding and discernment in their choice of leaders.

- We should engage the Creator of heaven and earth as consultant in intercessory prayers for our nation, for leaders, and for sinners. Prayer is the key to change in any society. We must pray to elect good government. Prayers do not stop with election of leaders but in continuing support for the government in power. It is in the interest of society to do so. Paul said it is good and acceptable in the sight of God. "I exhort therefore, that, first of all, supplications, prayers, intercessions, and giving of thanks, be made for all men; for kings, and for all that are in authority; that we may lead a quiet and peaceable life in all godliness and honesty" (1 Timothy 2:1-3).

It does not matter whether we vote for the government in power or not. It does not matter if the sitting President is not our candidate. As soon as a government is sworn into power, the responsibility falls on the church to be a guide in prayers to ensure no decision against the gospel of God, and good governance will be taken. Damages are being done daily in the nation because Christians refuse to unite in prayers.

So far the point in this book is for you and me to decide which side of history we would like to be. It is not late to decide. Those who have played or are playing the spoiler against God have the chance to repent and do what is right. Those who are doing what is right have the opportunity to continue, and to do more. Those who are indifferent also have the chance to change and be on the positive side of history. We are making history.

Our time on earth, no matter how long, is short compared to eternity that awaits us when we leave this world. We shall be measured by how much we have contributed to our world when we meet our maker.

Jesus said, "Look, I am coming soon! My reward is with me, and I will give to each person according to what they have done. I am the Alpha and the Omega, the First and the Last, the Beginning and the End" (Revelation 22:12).

"But you, dear friends, by building yourselves up in your most holy faith and praying in the Holy Spirit, keep yourselves in God's love as you wait for the mercy of our Lord Jesus Christ to bring you to eternal life" (Jude 21).

The changes that we need today are a change of heart, that God may rule in our hearts, and that righteousness may return to our land. There lies the truth of the American Dream.

My prayer is that the tender mercy of our God, by which the rising sun will come to us from heaven to shine on those living in darkness and in the shadow of death, to guide our feet into the path of peace and progress.

The Star Spangled Banner

September 20, 1814

By Francis Scott Key

Oh, say can you see, by the dawn's early light,
What so proudly we hailed at the twilight's last gleaming?
Whose broad stripes and bright stars, through the perilous fight,
O'er the ramparts we watched, were so gallantly streaming?
And the rockets' red glare, the bombs bursting in air,
Gave proof through the night that our flag was still there.
O say, does that star-spangled banner yet wave
O'er the land of the free and the home of the brave?

On the shore, dimly seen through the mists of the deep,
Where the foe's haughty host in dread silence reposes,
What is that which the breeze, o'er the towering steep,
As it fitfully blows, now conceals, now discloses?
Now it catches the gleam of the morning's first beam,
In full glory reflected now shines on the stream:
'Tis the star-spangled banner! O long may it wave
O'er the land of the free and the home of the brave.

And where is that band who so vauntingly swore
That the havoc of war and the battle's confusion
A home and a country should leave us no more?
Their blood has wiped out their foul footstep's pollution.
No refuge could save the hireling and slave
From the terror of flight, or the gloom of the grave:
And the star-spangled banner in triumph doth wave
O'er the land of the free and the home of the brave.

Oh! Thus be it ever, when freemen shall stand
between their loved homes and the war's desolation!
Blest with victory and peace, may the heaven-rescued land
Praise the Power that hath made and preserved us a nation.
Then conquer we must, for our cause it is just,
And this be our motto: "In God is our trust."
And the star-spangled banner forever shall wave
O'er the land of the free and the home of the brave![186]

AMEN!

ENDNOTES

1. U.S. Department of Homeland Security, U.S. Citizenship and Immigration Services, Office of Citizenship, *The Citizen's Almanac,* Washington, DC 2007. Pg. 15
2. Ibid, page 23.
3. Arthur Simon, *Christian Faith and Public Policy* (Michigan: Eerdmans Publishing Co., 1987).
4. Roy Herron, *How Can a Christian Be in Politics? A Guide to Faithful Politics* (Ill.: Tyndale House Publishers, Inc., 2005).
5. *Quotable Quotations,* compiled by Lloyd Cory (IL: Victor Books, SP Publications, Inc., 1985).
6. Dr. Gregory Tucker, "Life in the Dream: Why People Fight," July 2, 2006 (http://www.lifeinthedream.com/why-people-fight/).
7. Joseph R Holmes, ed., *The Common Sense and Straight Talk of Former California Governor Ronald Reagan* (San Diego, CA: JRH & Associates, Inc., 1975), 185.
8. Dwight D. Eisenhower, *Pictures I've Kept: A Concise Pictorial Autobiography* (New York: Doubleday and Company, Inc., 1969), 210.
9. Robin Prior and Trevor Wilson, *The First World War* (London: Cassel, Wellington House, 1999).
10. Ibid.

11. Ibid.
12. Fergal Keane, *Season of Blood: A Rwandan Journey* (England: Penguin Books Ltd., 1995).
13. Ibid.
14. Francis B. Carpenter, *The Inner Life of Abraham Lincoln: Six Months at the White House* (Lincoln: University of Nebraska Press, 1995), 258–259.
15. Joan Comay, *Who's Who in the Bible* (New York: Bonanza Books, 1971).
16. Clyborne Carson, *The Autobiography of Martin Luther King, Jr.* (New York: Brown and Company, 1999).
17. Ibid.
18. Ibid, 366.
19. Ibid, 281.
20. Ibid.
21. Tom Lodge, *Mandela: A Critical Life* (New York: Oxford University Press, 2006).
22. Joseph R. Holmes, ed., *The Common Sense and Straight Talk of Former California Governor Ronald Reagan* (San Diego: JRH & Associates, Inc., 1975).
23. Ibid., 16.
24. Ibid., 229.
25. Ibid., 238.
26. Ibid., 240.
27. Paul Kengor, *God and Ronald Reagan: A Spiritual Life* (New York: HarperCollins Publishers Inc., 2004).
28. Ibid., 275.
29. Ibid., 275.
30. Reagan Inaugural Address, Capitol, 1/20/81. Ronald Reagan Presidential Library Archives (reagan.utexas.edu).
31. *Memorial Tributes Delivered in Congress* (Washington, DC: United States Government Printing Office, 2005), xix.
32. Paul Kengor, *God and Ronald Reagan: A Spiritual Life* (New York: HarperCollins Publishers Inc., 2004), 115.
33. President George W. Bush's Address to Congress and the Nation on Terrorism, Courtesy of the White House online, September 21, 2001 (www.whitehouse.gov).

34. President George W. Bush, Landon Lecture, January 23, 2006. Courtesy Kansas State University Media Relations (www.k-state. edu/media/newsrelease).

35. Ibid.

36. President George W. Bush, Landon Lecture, January 23, 2006. Courtesy Kansas State University Media Relations (www.k-state. edu/media/newsrelease).

37. CBC News Online, November 19, 2004 (cbc.ca/news/background/ bush).

38. Zaryab Iqbal, *War and the Health of Nations* (Stanford: Stanford University Press, 2010).

39. Ibid., 1.

40. Andre Dumoulin, *The Historical Encyclopedia of World War II* (New York: Facts on File Inc., 1980).

41. US Census Bureau, *Statistical Abstract of the United States*, 130th edition (Washington, DC: PUBLISHER?, 2011).

42. J.M. Winter, *The Experience of World War I* (New York: Oxford University Press, 1989).

43. Tori Richards, "Laid-Off California Worker Leaps to Death Off City Hall," AOL News Online. California, March 18 2011 (http:// www.aolnews.com/2011/03/18 laid-off-california-worker-leaps-to- death-off-city-hall/).

44. Dave Grossman, *On Killing: The Psychological Cost of Learning to Kill in War and Society* (New York: Back Bay Books/Little, Brown & Company, (Hachette Book Group, 1995), 88.

45. Ibid., 87.

46. www.liberiandevelopmentfoundation.org/pages/en history_of_ liberia.

47. Zaryab Iqbal, *War and the Health of Nations* (Stanford: Stanford University Press, 2010), 3.

48. UN Security Council Resolutions (www.un.org/en/). [there's nothing at this particular URL that backs up what you say here. You need a specific URL to the page that discusses this, with at least a title of an article, preferably also an author's name and/or date]

49. Susan T. Jackson, summary of "Chapter 5, Arms Production," Stockholm International Peace Research Institute, Year Book 2011 (www.sipri.org/yearbook/2011/05).

50. Ibid.
51. Tracy Jan, Globe Staff: Boston and Beyond Now Metro Desk. July 29, 2009 (www.boston.com/news/local/breaking_news/2009/07/harvard.html).
52. Ibid.
53. Anahad O'Connor and Eric Schmitt, "Terror Attempt Seen as Man Tries to Ignite Device on Jet." New York Times, 12/25/2009 (http://www.nytimes.com/2009/12/26/us/26plane.html).
54. Kimberly Dozier, "Truck Bomb Destroys Marriott in Pakistan," *CBS News*, September 20, 2008.
55. Stephanie Chen, CNN Justice, April 20, 2009. (http://articles.cnn.com/keyword/columbine-high-school).
56. Christine Hauser, "Virginia Gunman Identified as a Student," *New York Times*, April 17, 2007.
57. Centers for Disease Control and Prevention, 2010 (www.cdc.gov/tobacco/data_statistics/fact_sheets/health_effects).
58. Ibid.
59. Missouri Department of Mental Health (www.well.com/user/woa/fspot).
60. Marcus Wohlsen, "California Conflicted over Legalizing Marijuana," *Daily Breeze*, September 27, 2010.
61. Joseph E. Stiglitz and Linda J. Bilmes, *The Three Trillion Dollar War* (New York: W. W. Norton & Company, 2008).
62. US National Debt Clock, (www.usdebtclock.org) Source –Federal Reserve.
63. Laura Rozen, "Obama, ordering drawdown of surged US forces in Afghanistan, urges nation building at home." Yahoo News, 06/22/11
64. War Resisters League (www.resisters.org/pages/piechart.htm).
65. Bureau of Labor Statistics, United States Department of Labor 2011 (www.bls.gov).
66. Kathleen M. Howley, "Record 19 Million U.S. Homes Stood Vacant in 2008," *Bloomberg Magazine On-Line*, February 3, 2009 (www.Bloomberg.com).
67. David Barrett, *World Christian Encyclopedia* (New York: Oxford University Press, Inc., 2001).
68. Joan Comay, *Who's Who in the Bible* (New York: Wings Book, 1980).

69. Robert Goldston, *The Sword of the Prophet: A History of the Arab World from the Time of Mohammed to the Present Day* (New York: The Dial Press, 1979), 26.

70. Tanya Gulevich, *Understanding Islam and Muslim Traditions* (Detroit: Ominigraphics, Inc., 2004).

71. Fred James Hill and Nicholas Awde, *A History of the Islamic World* (New York: Hippocrene Books Inc., 2003).

72. Robert Goldston, *The Sword of the Prophet: A History of the Arab World from the Time of Mohammed to the Present Day* (New York: The Dial Press, 1979).

73. Frances Gumleyand Brian Redhead, *The Pillars of Islam: An Introduction to the Islamic Faith* (London: BBC Books, 1990).

74. Reuven Firestone, *Jihad: The Original Holy War in Islam* (New York: Oxford University Press, 1999).

75. Amnesty International: Public Statement, Index: MDE 13/077/2011, August 31, 2011.

76. Mervyn Thomas: Christian Solidarity Worldwide. Press Release, 2011. www.csw.org.uk.

77. Elizabeth Williams, "Times Square Bomber Gets Life and Warns of More Attacks," *Daily Breeze*, October 6, 2010.

78. Bernard Lewis, *The Crisis of Islam: Holy War and Unholy Terror* (New York: Modern Library, a division of Random House, Inc., 2003).

79. Adam Robinson: *Bin Laden, Behind the Mask of the Terrorist* (New York: Arcade Publishing, Inc, 2001), 88.

80. Adam Robinson, *Bin Laden: Behind the Mask of the Terrorist* (New York: Arcade Publishing, Inc, 2001), 88, 90.

81. Dean Schabner and Karen Travers, "Osama bin Laden Killed: 'Justice Is Done,'" ABC News Online 5/1/2011

82. Jimmy Carter, *We Can Have Peace in the Holy Land: A Plan that Will Work* (New York: Simon and Schuster, 2009).

83. Manu Goel, "The Importance of Education," July 6, 2007, www.SearchWarp.com/swa230219.htm.

84. Stephen E. Ambrose, *Eisenhower: Soldier and President* (New York: Simon & Schuster, 1990), 242.

85. (www.christianity.com/pastors/11557891)

86. Paul Kengor, *God and Ronald Reagan: A Spiritual Life* (New York: HarperCollins Publishers Inc., 2004), 90.

87. Edmund S. Morgan, *The Puritan Family* (New York: Harper & Row, Publishers, Inc., 1966).

88. Kieran Doherty, *Puritans, Pilgrims, and Merchants* (MN: The Oliver Press, Inc., 1999).

89. Gordon S. Wood, *We Americans* (Washington, DC: The National Geographic Society, 1975).

90. Ibid., 119.

91. Ibid., 120.

92. Amy L. Matzat, "Massachusetts Education Laws of 1642 and 1647" (www.nd.edu/rbarger).

93. Kay Kizer, "Puritans," University of Notre Dame (www.nd.edu).

94. Ibid.

95. "Darrell Scott Testifies before the House Judiciary Sub-Committee" (www.free2pray.inf/darrellscott, 1999).

96. David Frum, *The Right Man: The Surprise Presidency of George W. Bush* (New York: Random House, Inc., 2003), 283.

97. Ronald Brownrigg, *Who's Who in the Bible* (New York: Bonanza Books, a division of Crown Publishers, Inc., 1971).

98. Ibid., 285.

99. David Barton, *The Myth of Separation* (TX: WallBuilder Press, 1992), 36.

100. Ibid., 23–39.

101. Yale Law School, Lillian Goldman Law Library, Avalon Project (http://Avalon.law.yale.edu). [that quote is not on THIS web page. Include the full URL for the page where you found this. If available, include the name of the article and its author]

102. *The Massachusetts Centinel*, October 14, 1789.

103. D. James Kennedy, *The Faith of Washington, Jefferson and Lincoln* (FL: Coral Ridge Ministries, 2003), 58.

104. HomeOfHeroes.com, Alexandria, VA (www.homeofheroes.com/presidents/inaugural/index.html).

105. Gerhard Peters and John T. Woolley, *The American Presidency Project* (http://www.presidency.ucsb.edu/ws/index.php?pid=9920&st=&st1=#axzz1Y2tuHJKq).

106. Knights of Columbus (Kofc.org/un/en/resources/communication/pledgeofallegiance.pdf).

107. David Barton, *The Myth of Separation* (TX: WallBuilder Press, 1992), 119.

108. Ibid., 55.

109. Ibid., 53.

110. Ibid., 54.

111. Eric Landstrom, "In God We Trust!" (http://www.ovrlnd.com/Evangelism/InGodWeTrust.html).

112. Paul Kengor, *God and Ronald Reagan: A Spiritual Life* (New York, HarperCollins Publishers Inc., 2004), 198.

113. *The Myth of Separation*, 11–12.

114. Ibid., 11.

115. (http://www.youtube.com/watch?v=ANBMgYxZfH8&feature=related)

116. David R. Spinger, James L. Regens and David Edger, *Islamic Radicalism and Global Jihad,* 218.

117. Karl Barth, *Church Dogmatics Vol. 2.* (New York: Haper Touch Book, 1962) 317.

118. Wayne Martindale and Jerry Root, editors, *The Quotable Lewis* (Illinois: Tyndale House Publishers, Inc., 1963).

119. Judith Wallerstein, Julia Lewis, and Sandra Blakeslee, *The Unexpected Legacy of Divorce: The 25 Year Landmark Study* (New York: Hyperion, 2000), xxvii.

120. Governor Edmund G. Brown's Charge to Family Commission, May 11, 1966 (www.liberary.ca.gov).

121. Wayne Martindale and Jerry Root, *The Quotable Lewis* (Ill.: Tyndale House Publishers, Inc., 1989).

122. Ibid., 97.

123. Rene Noorbergen and Ralph W. Hood, *The Death Cry of an Eagle* (Ill.: Zondervan Publishing House, 1980), 165.

124. Paul Kengor, *God and Ronald Reagan: A Spiritual Life* (New York: HarperCollins Publishers, 2004), 239.

125. Aaron Klein: Election 2008 Obama: America is 'no longer Christian'. WorldNet Daily, June 22, 2008 (http://www.wnd.com/?pageId=67735#ixzz1Rl449dlq).

126. OABITAR (www.teachingaboutreligion.org/Demographics/map_demographics).

127. John MacArthur, Jr., *Alone with God* (Wheaton Victor Books, division of Scripture Publications Inc., 1995), 69.

128. "Corruption Perceptions Index 2010 Results," Transparency International (http://www.transparency.org/policy_research/surveys_indices/cpi/2010/results).

129. 2008 ACFE Report to the Nation (www.acfe.com/resources/publications).

130. Matthew Jaffe and Karen Travers: ABC World News with Diane Sawyer, April 22, 2010.

131. *Webster's New Riverside University Dictionary*, 11th edition (Boston, Houghton Mifflin Company, 1994).

132. Bruce Bickel and Stan Jantz, *Creation & Evolution 101* (Ill: Tyndale House Publishers, 1996).

133. Paul Kengor, *God and Ronald Reagan: A Spiritual Life,* 302.

134. Ronald Reagan Presidential Library: Public Papers of Ronald Reagan February 1988 (reagan.utexas.edu/archives/speeches).

135. Barbara A. Lewis: What do you stand for. Free Spirit Publishing, Minneapolis, MN 1988.

136. David Herbert Donald and Harold Holzer, editors, *Lincoln in the Times* (The New York Times Company, New York, 2005), 226.

137. Richard O. Boyer, *The Legend of John Brown: A Biography and a History* (New York: Alfred A. Knopf, Inc., 1973), 14.

138. James Robert Kessler, "A Presidential Handshake (http://inchristvictorious.com/index.php?option=com_content&view=article&id=121:a-presidential-handshake&catid=1:articles&Itemid=4).

139. Art Marroquin, Staff Writer: Daily Breeze (Media News Group Newspaper) October 18, 2011, Page A1.

140. C. S. Lewis: A grief Observed. HarperCollins Publishers, Inc., New York. 1961.

141. Paul Johnson: The Quest for God, A Personal Pilgrimage. HarperCollins Publishers, Inc., New York. 1996.

142. Mitchel Stokes: Isaac Newton, (Thomas Nelson, Nashville, Tennessee, USA.) 2010 pg 65.

143. Albert Einstein: The World As I See It, (Citadel Press, NJ USA,1949) Pg. 5.
144. Michael McCabe, "The Role of the Church in Civil Society: Some Theological Orientations" (www.africamission-mafr.org/mccabe_gb.doc).
145. Bruce Bickel and Stan Jantz, *I'm Fine with God...It's Christians I Can't Stand: Getting Past the Religious Garbage in the Search for Spiritual Truth* (Oregon: Harvest House Publishers, 2008), 13.
146. Ibid., 18.
147. C.S. Lewis: Mere Christianity. HarperCollins Publishers, New York, 1952. Pg. 83.
148. Janet and Geoff Benge, *Christian Heroes Then and Now: Rowland Bingham into Africa's Interior* (Seattle, WA: YWAM Publishing, 2003), 56.
149. Ronald Reagan Presidential Library, National Archives and Records (www.Reagan.utexas.edu).
150. Fredrick S. Lane: The Court and the Cross. Beacon Press, Boston Massachusetts, 2008.
151. David Gardner, "McCain Severs Ties with Preacher," Mail News, May 23, 2008 (http://www.dailymail.co.uk/news/article-1021398/McCain-severs-ties-preacher-claims-God-sent-Adolf-Hitler-help-Jews-reach-promised-land.html).
152. Roy Herron, *How Can a Christian Be in Politics?* (IL: Tyndale House Publishers, Inc.,1996), 19.
153. Jeffrey Goldberg: August 15, 2008 (Theatlantic.com/international/achive/2008/08/the-rick-warren-interview-no-c).
154. Ibid.
155. Paul Kengor, *God and Ronald Reagan's Spiritual Life* (New York: HarperCollins Publishers Inc., 2004).
156. David Halton: Faith and Politics, Larkin-Stuart Lectures Toronto, March 2007. (http://www.trinity.utoronto.ca/News_Events/News/halton.htm).
157. Brian Ross and Rehab El-Buri: ABC News March 13, 2008 (http://abcnews.go.com/Blotter/DemocraticDebate/story?id=4443788&page=1).

158. Dr. John Townsend: Beyond Boundaries. Zondervan Publisher, Grand Rapids, Michigan, 2011.

159. Ibid,

160. Andrew Malcolm, "Obama Ends Bush-era National Prayer Day Service at White House," *Los Angeles Times*, May 7, 2009.

161. Ibid.

162. Ibid.

163. C. S. Lewis (edited by Walter Hooper): God in the Dock. William B. Eerdmans Publishing Company, Grand Rapids, Michigan. 1970.

164. David McCasland: Our Daily Bread, September 29, 2011. RBC Ministries Grand Rapids MI.

165. Ibid.

166. Harold Myra Marshall Shelley: The leadership Secret of Billy Graham. Zondervan, Grand Rapids, Michigan, 2005.

167. Rebuilding Together New Orleans. 923 Tchoupitoulas St. New Orleans, (http://www.rtno.org/get-educated/hurricane-katrina/).

168. S. K. Eleton, "Christian Values," *Theocracy Watch*, March 18, 2009 (www.FaulkingTruth.com/cgi-bin/Printable.cgi?commentary&1093).

169. Ibid.

170. C.S. Lewis (Edited by Walter Hooper): God in the Dock. William B. Eerdmans Publishing Company, Grand Rapids, Michigan. 1970

171. Douglas Wilson: For Kirk and Covenant, The Stalwart Courage of John Knox (George Grant – General Editor). Cumberland House Publishing, Inc., Nashville TN, 2000.

172.

173. Billy Graham, National Day of Prayer and Remembrance Address in Washington, DC, September 14, 2001 (www.nationalcathedral.org/worship/sermontexts).

174. Wayne Martindale and Jerry Root, *The Quotable Lewis* (Illinois: Tyndale House Publishers Inc., 1963), 192.

175. Jimmy Orr, "Miss California Sparks Outrage over Gay Marriage Remarks," *The Christian Science Monitor*, April 20, 2009.

176. Lisa Leff, "Bill Would Require State Schools to Teach Gay History," *Daily Breeze*, April 15, 2011.

177. John MacArthur, Jr.: Alone with God. Victor Books, Wheaton, Ill, 1995.

178. Jonathan L Graf: The power of Personal Prayer. NavPress Publishing Group, Colorado USA, 2002.

179. Wayne Martindale and Jerry Root, Editors: The Quotable Lewis. Tyndale House Publishers, Inc. Wheaton, Ill. 1988.

180. Paul Kengor, *God and Ronald Reagan* (NY: HarperCollins Publishers Inc., 2004), 86.

181. C. S. Lewis: God in the Dock, the founding of the Oxford Socratic Club.

182. Michael Youssef: Restore Sanity to a World Gone Mad (A Letter to Believers). Leading the Way, Atlanta GA 2011.

183. Wayne Martindale and Jerry Root: The Quotable Lewis. Tyndale House Publishers, Inc. Wheaton, Ill. 1989.

184. Tracie Cone: The Associated Press, Daily Breeze. August 29, 2011.

185. Ibid.

186. http://www.ushistory.org/documents/creed.htm.

CONTACT INFORMATION

To order additional copies of this book, please visit
www.redemption-press.com.
Also available on Amazon.com and BarnesandNoble.com.
Or by calling toll free 1 (888) 305-2967.